Stellar Transformations

STAR ★★★★★★★★★★★ DECADES AMERICAN CULTURE / AMERICAN CINEMA

Each volume in the series Star Decades: American Culture/American Cinema presents original essays analyzing the movie star against the background of contemporary American cultural history. As icon, as mediated personality, and as object of audience fascination and desire, the Hollywood star remains the model for celebrity in modern culture and represents a paradoxical combination of achievement, talent, ability, luck, authenticity, superficiality, and ordinariness. In all of the volumes, stardom is studied as an effect of, and influence on, the particular historical and industrial contexts that enabled a star to be "discovered," to be featured in films, to be promoted and publicized, and ultimately to become a recognizable and admired—even sometimes notorious—feature of the cultural landscape. Understanding when, how, and why a star "makes it," dazzling for a brief moment or enduring across decades, is especially relevant given the ongoing importance of mediated celebrity in an increasingly visualized world. We hope that our approach produces at least some of the surprises and delight for our readers that stars themselves do.

ADRIENNE L. McLEAN AND MURRAY POMERANCE
SERIES EDITORS

Jennifer M. Bean, ed., *Flickers of Desire: Movie Stars of the 1910s*

Patrice Petro, ed., *Idols of Modernity: Movie Stars of the 1920s*

Adrienne L. McLean, ed., *Glamour in a Golden Age: Movie Stars of the 1930s*

Sean Griffin, ed., *What Dreams Were Made Of: Movie Stars of the 1940s*

R. Barton Palmer, ed., *Larger Than Life: Movie Stars of the 1950s*

Pamela R. Wojcik, ed., *New Constellations: Movie Stars of the 1960s*

James Morrison, ed., *Hollywood Reborn: Movie Stars of the 1970s*

Robert Eberwein, ed., *Acting for America: Movie Stars of the 1980s*

Anna Everett, ed., *Pretty People: Movie Stars of the 1990s*

Murray Pomerance, ed., *Shining in Shadows: Movie Stars of the 2000s*

Steven Rybin, ed., *Stellar Transformations: Movie Stars of the 2010s*

Stellar Transformations

☆☆☆☆☆☆☆☆☆☆

Movie Stars of the 2010s

EDITED BY

STEVEN RYBIN

RUTGERS UNIVERSITY PRESS

NEW BRUNSWICK, CAMDEN, AND NEWARK,

NEW JERSEY, AND LONDON

LIBRARY OF CONGRESS CATALOGING-IN-PUBLICATION DATA

Names: Rybin, Steven, 1979– editor.
Title: Stellar transformations : movie stars of the 2010s / edited by Steven Rybin.
Description: New Brunswick : Rutgers University Press, [2022] |
Includes bibliographical references and index.
Identifiers: LCCN 2021011643 | ISBN 9781978818323 (cloth) |
ISBN 9781978818316 (paperback) | ISBN 9781978818330 (epub) |
ISBN 9781978818347 (mobi) | ISBN 9781978818354 (pdf)
Subjects: LCSH: Motion picture actors and actresses—United States—
Biography. | Celebrities—United States. | Fame.
Classification: LCC PN1998.2 S7165 2022 | DDC 791.4302/80922 [B]—dc23
LC record available at https://lccn.loc.gov/2021011643

A British Cataloging-in-Publication record for this book is available from the British Library.

∞ The paper used in this publication meets the requirements of the American National Standard for Information Sciences—Permanence of Paper for Printed Library Materials, ANSI Z39.48-1992.

www.rutgersuniversitypress.org

Manufactured in the United States of America

Being real in showbiz gets you nowhere, kid.

—Parker Posey

CONTENTS

Stellar Transformations

INTRODUCTION

Stardom in the 2010s

STEVEN RYBIN

Hollywood stardom, in at least some of its facets, was much the same during the 2010s as it was throughout most of the twentieth century and the first decade of the new millennium. Star-driven blockbusters from the U.S. film industry circulated across the globe, fans flocked to see the films of their favorite performers on opening weekend, and Oscars were awarded to stars reaching the peak of achievement in an industry still dependent on their commercial viability, performative talents, and glamorous allure. This surface continuity, however, belies the ways this decade reshaped how stars and their performances touched the lives of moviegoers. The growing ubiquity of outlets such as Facebook and Twitter (to mention just two) has intensified the ways in which the celebrities of cinema, already brought down to earth in previous decades, are now a familiar part of an everyday flow. And these celebrity performers continue to populate numerous series premiering on platforms such as Amazon, Hulu, and Netflix (to mention just three), a form which may reduce the grand scale of the cinema star's image but in doing so provides, as a kind of compensation, an extended engagement with the actor across a continuing narrative, not unlike the earliest cinema serials. Formerly the citizens of a detached and celestial world of gods and goddesses, stars now frequently glow on the smaller screens of a socially mediated reality.

Such ubiquity can threaten banality. For that reason, an observation Murray Pomerance makes in the concluding pages of the 2000s Star Decades volume still holds true for experiences of stardom and celebrity as the 2010s turned into the 2020s: "Movie stars after 2010 will have to 'work' for us when their images are quite tiny, just as well as they do when the images are huge, since there will no longer be any way to predict which kind of venue fans will use for seeing them" ("In the Wings" 241). These various and contingent venues increasingly enabled stars to become involved—either directly, or indirectly, through the discourse of both fans and a plethora of self-anointed social commentators—in the fraught cultural terrain of the 2010s, their presence encompassing both the hopes and disappointments of the Obama years and the subsequent and severe cultural and economic fractures separating Americans during and after the 2016 election. While keeping one eye on the way stars reflect and become enmeshed in larger cultural and social transformations, this collection of essays also attempts, at times, to step back from this offscreen fray, thinking further about the valuable work these stars do in the movies themselves, as performers who vividly express a range of screen characterizations. In looking at both the screen work of the stars and the larger cultural contexts in which their work is in turn refracted, the authors in this book work to illuminate what stars and their screen performances meant to the United States, and to the global film culture in which Hollywood products circulate, during the decade of the 2010s.

★★★★★★★★★★ A Broken Decade

It is difficult to frame such a discussion without mentioning the devastating experience accompanying the writing of many of the words in this book: the COVID-19 pandemic, in which a deadly coronavirus spread around the globe in the waning days of the 2010s, starting in December 2019. The seeds of this catastrophe provided an especially cruel punctuation mark to the end of the preceding ten years—even if this was a mark that did not become experientially visible to most citizens of the world until the first months of 2020—and in a way that is terribly appropriate for a decade that had more than its share of upheavals and anxieties. The moniker of this collection is *Stellar Transformations*, and there will be more to say on the cautious optimism implicit in that phrase. But I first want to consider the central American political event of the last decade that preceded and largely determined the U.S. leadership's response (or, more accurately, nonresponse) to the emergence of the global pandemic, and to speculate upon some of the ways in which stardom and celebrity were unavoidably caught up in it.

The 2010s were irrevocably marked by the election of the staggeringly unqualified and disturbingly unhinged mass media personality Donald J. Trump, puppet master of an increasingly and collectively sycophantic Republican Party, to the presidency of the United States of America in November of 2016. It is not insignificant to the topic under consideration here that Trump is a star (of sorts), a television personality who has also appeared in a number of films, frequently figured as some variation of "himself" (whatever kind of "self" or subjectivity this figure of discord might be publicly understood to possess). These appearances range from the mundane—incarnations of vapid "billionaire" personae in dreck like *Home Alone 2: Lost in New York* (1992) and *Eddie* (1996)—to films that are stamped with the imprimatur of an auteur (Paul Mazursky's 1993 *The Pickle* and Woody Allen's 1998 *Celebrity*). His actual appearances in these movies are of no performative interest; they are cited here mainly as a reminder that whatever else Trump is, and whatever cultural, social, and economic diseases his election to the presidency enables scholars to diagnose, he is and was a media star, and so is unavoidably also now a salient and determining part of the history of stardom and a contemporary signpost for navigating celebrity and its relationships to politics. Trump, who is by all publicly available evidence bereft of complexity or interiority (in other words, entirely absent those qualities brilliant performers yearn to make visible), has not strategically used the film medium in the intentionally monstrous way that Adolf Hitler did via Leni Riefenstahl's epic *Triumph of the Will* (1935). Although it can perhaps be argued that he has used Twitter and television in something like that way, his tyrannical, thoughtless ravings have spaced themselves out, over the years, across many different outlets. Trump's ascendance in pop culture and media as a television star on fourteen seasons of the NBC reality show *The Apprentice* (2004–2016), for example, marks the work of a small-minded, if dangerously lethal, opportunist who seeks to stoke flames of fear in the economically disenfranchised class he has successfully duped through the circulation of his blustery star image. His particular brand of stardom—and it is nothing more than a brand—offers not a new understanding of, or escape from, reality so often promised by the performances of viewers' favorite stars but rather the vulgar and ugly degrading of our existing one.

In reflecting upon star actors, the above mention of Trump leads to a discussion of the cultural movement he (unwittingly, of course) helped generate in the second half of the 2010s, one that centrally involved stars in the movie industry: the #MeToo movement, a series of protests, online and in the form of marches in the streets of cities, against sexual harassment and violence perpetuated against women. That Trump was elected to office despite an *Access Hollywood* video documenting him gleefully sharing strategies for assaulting women (a particularly pessimistic individual might suggest it was partially because of it) played no small role in sparking a series of pointed outrages over the treatment of women in U.S. culture generally, and in the American film and media industries in particular. The most publicly notorious perpetrator exposed by #MeToo, in the media industry at least, was not Trump, whose subsequent "work" in the White House seemed largely unaffected by it, but rather former Miramax studio head Harvey

Weinstein, whose decades-long reputation as a violent and habitual abuser of women (a reputation apparently well known within Hollywood and by its stars during these years, if not by the larger public of viewers) culminated in his being sentenced, in February 2020, to a term in prison of twenty-three years (Jan Ransom, "Harvey Weinstein's Stunning Downfall: 23 Years in Prison," *The New York Times,* 11 March 2020, accessed via nytimes.com). In terms of stardom and the larger film culture, #MeToo has had at least two overarching and interrelated consequences: it brought attention to the cases of particular female stars who had been abused (by Weinstein or by others) in the industry (such figures outed as abusers included news anchor and interviewer Charlie Rose and Roy Price, former head of Amazon Studios); and it also served as a touchstone motivating, once more, the demand from female movie stars (and from female performers of all ranks) for equal treatment in the industry. #MeToo, as well as Hillary Clinton's preceding presidential campaign in the 2016 election, can also be seen in relation to gendered shifts in star-driven content in big-budget film production, including a cycle of genre films late in the decade which performed gendered inversions on familiar material, positioning female stars in roles occupied in earlier film versions of the same narrative by men: Taraji P. Henson in *What Men Want* (2019) (preceded by Mel Gibson in the 2000 Nancy Meyers comedy *What Women Want*); Cate Blanchett, Sandra Bullock, and Anne Hathaway, among other leading actresses, in *Ocean's Eight* (2018) (taking over from a range of male stars, including George Clooney, Brad Pitt, Frank Sinatra, Dean Martin, and Sammy Davis Jr., in two earlier generations' worth of *Ocean's* films); and *Ghostbusters* (2016), starring Melissa McCarthy, Kristin Wiig, Kate McKinnon, and Leslie Jones (taking over from the earlier team of Bill Murray, Harold Ramis, Dan Aykroyd, and Ernie Hudson), to name just three such films.

The four devastating years of the Trump administration may have defined the latter half of the decade, forming a particularly grotesque closure to a tumultuous ten years and an unsettling beginning to the 2020s, but the early stretch of the 2010s was marked by its own share of global and domestic anxieties and crises, as well as more positive political and cultural shifts. The final years of Barack Obama's presidency, from 2010 to early 2017, paralleled encouraging signs in the U.S. film industry in the 2010s, a decade which marked significant (if nevertheless incremental) gains for the representation of African Americans in major screen roles. It was possible to go to the movies during these years and be encouraged not only by the presence but also the stirring performative work of the charismatic Mahershala Ali (a two-time Academy Award winner, first for the

The ensemble cast of *Ocean's Eight* (Gary Ross, 2018). Production photo.

independent 2016 film *Moonlight* and then for 2018's *Green Book*) and the Kenyan Mexican performer Lupita Nyong'o (an Academy Award winner earlier in the decade for a supporting turn in the 2013 film *12 Years a Slave*, and on the cusp of major stardom in her own right at the end of it via her leading part in Jordan Peele's 2019 blockbuster *Us*), among other stars mentioned later in these pages. One could very well enjoy these and other movies and celebrate the gains they represented for performers of various ethnicities even if the Black Lives Matter movement, founded in 2013 after the acquittal of George Zimmerman for responsibility of the death of seventeen-year-old Trayvon Martin in Sanford, Florida, continued to remind the United States and the world of ongoing racial injustice in America's law enforcement and judicial systems. Major celebrity performers became actively involved in the Black Lives Matter movement at various points in the last ten years—including figures such as Idris Elba, Michael B. Jordan, Queen Latifah, John Cusack, Sarah Paulson, and Emma Watson—but this indicates not so much the centrality or importance of these particular stars to the cause (it is not difficult to imagine the movement continuing with force and fervor without them) as the way in which many stars are now seemingly already immediately immersed in everyday political discourse in American life.

The cultural conversation generated by #MeToo, Black Lives Matter, and other movements involving questions of cultural representation signals the ongoing way in which stars in the 2010s continued to be interpreted through larger frameworks of identity. But even as stars continued as part

Lupita Nyong'o battling doppelgängers in *Us* (Jordan Peele, 2019). Production photo.

of this conversation in the 2010s, there were stark reminders that their work was performed in relatively rarefied air. The protest movement Occupy Wall Street, which began in September 2011 and continues into the 2020s, targeted the inherently unjust economic structuring of American social reality, and its relevance as a movement demands some thought about what aspects of social experience Hollywood celebrity, particularly today, cannot meaningfully represent. Billions of dollars circulate around the creation and marketing of movies, a reminder that stars, regardless of the cultural shifts they signal, are themselves generated by the same economic system that perpetuates material inequality. A way of putting this in terms of star reception is to ask, for example, if economically disenfranchised Americans of any demographic collectively care about the representation of a young, impoverished woman by Jennifer Lawrence in her 2010 breakthrough performance, *Winter's Bone*, or if they have time, energy, or inclination to be outraged by Steven Soderbergh's *Logan Lucky* (2016), which featured wealthy stars Channing Tatum, Adam Driver, and Daniel Craig mucking about in working-class drag. Marcel Proust wrote, nearly a century ago:

> And as for subject, the working classes are as bored by novels of popular life as children are as bored by the books which are written specially for them. When one reads, one likes to be transported into a new world, and working men have as much curiosity about princes as princes about working men. (280)

While sexuality, gender, race, and ethnicity remain salient in discussions of celebrity, it is questionable whether or not discourses of representation centered on movie stars have much of substance to teach us about what the Occupy Wall Street movement—and the ensuing, economically centered presidential campaigns of Bernie Sanders in 2015–2016 and 2019–2020—confronted head-on: the ongoing strife and ever-widening gulf between capital and labor, a conflict that is necessarily and substantively invisible in the majority of the cultural products circulated by the industry. Even as the performers who are now becoming celebrities slowly become more diverse, and even as star actors, occasionally, give us performances that grapple thoughtfully and empathetically with the psychological damage inequality can generate, the fact that star celebrity remains ineluctably in a position of vast wealth is an important consideration when reflecting upon the limits of the transformative potential of stars.

☆☆☆☆☆☆☆☆☆★ Heroes or Stars?

To focus only—or, I should say, squarely—on politics, economics, or questions of morality is to repress the reason why many moviegoers flock to see cinema stars in the first place: pleasure and desire. Notably, though, star personae and celebrity presence are largely effaced in the very films that, overwhelmingly, were the most profitable and popular products the Hollywood industry produced during the 2010s: the seemingly endless cycle of superhero fantasy movies and other big-budget, effects-driven franchises (many of them animated, with star voice-over turns, and often based on recognizable, pre-existing properties), all of which blend the attraction of movie stars with the consumerist lure of pre-established, already-popular characters—Batman, Thor, Wonder Woman—who are themselves, and largely autonomously of any actors who might play them, objects of desire and figures of fascination. It is only anecdotal, but I marvel (bad joke) at how often my film studies students, most of whom are agog at the release of every new superhero movie, recognize the name and image of Robert Downey, Jr. from the three *Iron Man* films (2008, 2010, 2013) but have no experience of his earlier films, such as *Pretty in Pink* (1986), or as Charlie Chaplin in *Chaplin* (1992), or *Home for the Holidays* (1995), *Wonder Boys* (2000), or even a contemporaneous, if not widely seen, star turn in a nonsuperhero film such as *The Judge* (opposite Robert Duvall, 2014), or indeed any other nonsuperhero movie. This is probably not a matter of increasing cultural amnesia, since it is doubtful that most American viewers today have any substantially greater or lesser grasp of the film history that preceded them than any previous generation, but a sign that these fantasy franchise movies, which dominate discussions of cinema in American culture presently, have found ways to incorporate movie stars even though they seem, at least on the surface, not to need them very much. The superheroes would seem to be the stars, or at least the primary ones. Celebrity actors nevertheless remain an important presence in the cultural circulation of these films, and for many of the fans who flock to them, undoubtedly they function, in relation to the hero they play, as complex and significant objects of desire: Scarlett Johansson in *The Avengers* (2012, 2015, 2018) and *Black Widow* (2021), Natalie Portman and Chris Hemsworth in a string of *Thor*s (2011, 2013, 2017, 2022), and Michael B. Jordan, Lupita Nyong'o, and Chadwick Boseman in *Black Panther* (2018), to name only a handful of A-list stars and only a few such films. These films also generate new or more widespread stardom, of course, as in the case of Gal Gadot in *Wonder Woman* (2017), although whether or not Gadot's new fans will be interested in following her into other kinds of movies remains an open question. One of the interesting future problems, in terms of this popular genre's relationship to star studies, will be to further explore the meaning of stars and their larger personae to these films: Will the stars most visible in this genre continue to develop careers that transcend, even as they include, these movies, or will their star images be themselves consumed by franchise "universes" that depend on a ceaseless remaking and remodeling of superhero, and not necessarily star, presence?

But as has been true for as long as movie stars have existed, we do not find our pleasures in stars only through the movies themselves. Extrafilmic trends during the decade continued to shape how movie stars communicated with their public, ensuring that star actors could retain a cultural presence even when the characters they played onscreen threatened at times to overwhelm their own iconicity. At least some stars in the 2010s did seem to earnestly seek grounded and everyday connections with the viewers who saw their movies and thereby enabled their careers, as was evident in the increasing use by stars of various social media platforms. Returning to a discussion of the still raging (at the time of this collection's writing) COVID-19 pandemic provides some evidence of this ongoing trend. Some (in the United States, at least) may remember that their first very salient awareness of the human toll of the coronavirus came with the news that the married celebrity couple Tom Hanks and Rita Wilson had contracted the virus in Australia during the production of a movie. The charmingly affable Hanks, in particular, became an outspoken advocate of COVID-19 awareness as the year slogged on, as did other stars such as Antonio Banderas, Idris Elba, Olga Kurylenko, and Rachel Matthews, who shared their encounters with the virus on various social media outlets (Nicole Sperling, "Tom Hanks Says He

Has Coronavirus," *The New York Times,* 11 March 2020). This phenomenon of stars reporting their experiences with the illness and offering suggestions to their fans about how to deal with its repercussions was a practice largely in keeping with the presence of star actors on such social media platforms as it had developed throughout the 2010s, enabling forms of discourse that mixed publicity and marketing with, insofar as it is possible through this detached and highly atomistic medium, grounded, human connection. Such online content produced by star celebrities, in a medium in which it is impossible to imagine earlier, reclusive figures such as Greta Garbo or Marlon Brando having any interest, bears contradictory signs of how contemporary star engagement with everyday people functions in our age: on the one hand, the use of such technology by movie stars confirms that they are "just like us," that they seek connection and commiseration in a collective, common experience just as the viewers of their films do; on the other, through the very plethora of attention their social media posts and appearances receive, viewers are reminded in fact that stars are not very much like us at all, occupying more salient and efficiently monetized presences in the ceaseless scroll of online currency and capital.

☆☆☆☆☆☆☆☆☆★ The Stars of the 2010s

This introduction's overview of a few of the major trends, questions, problems, and anxieties pertaining to Hollywood stardom in the American culture of the 2010s will now give way to the more fine-grained case studies in the pages to follow. The authors in these pages intriguingly explore, in a range of methods and voices that approach stars from different and revealing angles, the work of one, two, or a trio of stars during the last decade, and in doing so offer brilliant examples of the complex and significant questions movie stars and their various enchantments continue to pose for us.

Brenda Austin-Smith's "Joaquin Phoenix: Ascendant," the first chapter, studies the star persona and performances of an actor who has become increasingly known for playing psychologically tortured individuals. And yet, as Austin-Smith's chapter vividly demonstrates, there is variety in the types of men Phoenix plays. The chapter uses Phoenix's performance-art version of himself in the mockumentary *I'm Still Here* (2010) as a touchstone for his work in the ensuing decade. Phoenix was so adept at "playing himself" in this film that many critics assumed his performance style to be largely the product of an intuitive naturalism. Yet Phoenix himself reminds us that the emotional state of an actor is not always the cause for the performance we see onscreen, and this chapter's study of Phoenix's major roles in the 2010s shows us how this actor's work is a product of both sharp intuition and careful and intelligent preparation. Phoenix received numerous accolades early in the decade for his remarkable performances in two films by Paul Thomas Anderson, *The Master* (2012) and *Inherent Vice* (2014), among other films; the former found his performance style thrown into relief against that of Philip Seymour Hoffman, while the latter projected the actor into the convolutions of a Thomas Pynchon plot. But as Austin-Smith shows through close analysis, Phoenix's most important performances arrived in the late 2010s, as deeply troubled men in *You Were Never Really Here* (2017) and the blockbuster supervillain film *Joker* (2019), the latter of which functions as a kind of self-reflection upon Phoenix's own penchant for celebrity performance art in the earlier *I'm Still Here*.

The second chapter, "Amy Adams and Emma Stone: Escaping the Ingénue," finds Karen Hollinger exploring the remarkable parallels as well as the striking differences between the acting careers of Amy Adams and Emma Stone. Both actresses, at the outset of their careers, found themselves confined to the image of the female movie star as "star ingénue," a type that could potentially limit the trajectory of any actor's career. While neither Stone nor Adams was classically trained, both performers successfully navigated their way out of these perceived limitations of their early career roles. As Hollinger's chapter shows, unlike earlier Hollywood actresses, both Adams and Stone have relied almost entirely on their onscreen work rather than glamorous offscreen personae; both keep their private lives private (or as private as any celebrity can). The chapter explores the ways in which both Adams and Stone have established reputations through their acting talent rather than their public image, a talent which substantively avoids the gendered stereotypes of extrafilmic glamour, as each has crafted a brilliant career based on performative skills, careful choice of roles, and distinctive personalities. At the same time, both performers have carefully navigated waters that flow back and forth between relatively conventional roles in popular big-budget features and riskier, and perhaps more rewarding, performances in less commercial films. Stone and Adams can in this way be understood as female performers who eschew glamour and the trappings of the "starlet," establishing careers through talent, diligent work, and often surprising, unconventional characterizations.

Rick Warner's "Oscar Isaac: Brooding by Degrees," the third chapter, looks at the Guatemala-born actor's striking emergence as a major star in the 2010s, a career that has so far developed in both independent films and major Hollywood blockbusters. During this decade, Isaac appeared in an astonishing number of features (thirty), his prolific body of work including blockbuster franchises such as *Star Wars, X-Men*, and the Jason Bourne series. But like Adams and Stone, these roles do not overshadow his performances in smaller, more eccentric films. Isaac shuttled between both supporting and lead roles during the decade, sharing the screen with many of the decade's other most distinguished performers (including Viggo Mortensen, Jessica Chastain, Ryan Gosling, Natalie Portman, Alicia Vikander, Jennifer Lawrence, and Willem Dafoe). Warner's chapter offers a survey of Isaac's professional and cultural background and a broad look at the highlights of this young actor's already stellar career before focusing primarily on what Warner characterizes as Isaac's "multidimensional mastery of melancholic tones" in three films: *Inside Llewyn Davis* (2013), *Ex Machina* (2014), and *A Most Violent Year* (2014). Each of these films frames Isaac's performance style in the context of different genre conventions and different formal and stylistic constraints. In all three, Isaac's performances serve as a seductive, beguiling conduit of mood and atmosphere organically tied to each film's tonalities, sensibilities, and themes.

In the fourth chapter, "Armie Hammer: The Elusive Appeal of an Ever-Emergent Star," David Greven takes as his object of study the unusual and seemingly perpetual emergence of Hammer as a major movie star. Hammer's career and the development of his perhaps surprisingly complex star personality, as Greven's essay shows, has been quite strikingly protracted. After his breakout dual role as Cameron and Tyler Winklevoss in David Fincher's *The Social Network* (2010), Hammer made several high-profile movies which seemed poised as opportunities for the young actor to break out into the mainstream of conventional Hollywood stardom. But intriguingly, Hammer's appeal remained elusive, and his career took further unexpected turns as the decade continued. This chapter argues that Hammer's appeal as a movie star lies precisely in his distinctive elusiveness, and a kind of unattainability shaped not only by his privileged background but also by the still ongoing development of his screen persona. Exploring both the serious and comic sides of Hammer's presence and performance style, the chapter shows how the actor develops an intriguing tension between the self-parodying and more stolid modes of his personality across multifaceted characterizations. The chapter explores several of the major films in which Hammer appeared during the decade, including *The Social Network, Mine* (2016), *Final Portrait* (2017), and *Sorry to Bother You* (2018), a discussion which culminates in a close analysis of Hammer's star-making performance in *Call Me by Your Name* (2017).

As the mention of that last film might suggest, many of the stars in this book have appeared in transnational films in the last decade, and many of them, regardless of where their films are made, carry a global appeal. The fifth chapter, Celestino Deleyto's "The Multiple Trajectories of Transnational Hollywood Stars: Marion Cotillard, Kristen Stewart, Diane Kruger," offers a trio of such case studies. The transnational careers of Cotillard, Stewart, and Kruger constitute three different variations upon the centrality of the Hollywood industry in the global circulation of stardom. As Deleyto shows, of the three actors discussed here, Cotillard embodies the most typical of transnational trajectories, beginning her career in Europe before moving to Hollywood. Yet Cotillard is still unique in that she was the first French star since Charles Boyer and Maurice Chevalier to equal in Hollywood her high profile in France. Inversely, Kristen Stewart, who began as a child actor from a Hollywood family, has become a transnational performer relatively recently, moving from the blockbuster *Twilight* films (2008–2012) to two fascinating turns for French director Olivier Assayas in *Clouds of Sils Maria* (2014) and *Personal Shopper* (2016), among other interesting recent films. As this essay explores, the recent developments in Stewart's career offer a fascinating example of a less trodden trajectory across the Atlantic. The essay ends with a close look at the career of Diane Kruger, who is arguably the most distinctively transnational celebrity of these three performers. As Deleyto shows, Kruger's background as a star in Germany, the United Kingdom, France, and Hollywood positions her as that rare star who works to deconstruct national identities, speaking to a varied and global constituency.

Jennifer O'Meara's "Tilda Swinton: From Avant-Garde Androgyne to *The Avengers*," the sixth chapter, offers a look at another unconventional star who has appeared in films by directors from different parts of the world. Swinton's long and prolific career, which involved over fifty screen productions prior to the 2010s, has found her developing a star presence that has only gained in visibility and public exposure in the last decade. Even as Swinton has increasingly appeared in mainstream Hollywood productions during the last ten years, the British performer has also brought her distinctive qualities as both actor and performative presence to a range of films by both American and European auteurs (including Wes Anderson, Luca Guadagnino, Jim Jarmusch, and Lynne Ramsay). As O'Meara's chapter argues, roles in quirky independent movies made in America have enabled Swinton to dabble in relatively mainstream comedies such as *Trainwreck* (2015) and the *Avengers* superhero franchise. While other writers have underscored Swinton's mutable and eccentric qualities as a screen performer, O'Meara shows that during this last decade, Swinton's edgier elements were stabilized in some of these more mainstream films (even if her appearances in some of these films remained memorable), even as public and promotional discourse about the more unusual aspects of Swinton's personal life (such as her open marriage and long-term boyfriend) continued to draw attention to the less normative, and more distinctive, aspects of her public persona.

The seventh chapter returns to America with a close look at one of the country's major actor-director celebrity performers of the 2010s. In "Tyler Perry: The Multihyphenate Lane Changer," Danielle E. Williams reminds us that not only is Perry one of the most bankable actors and directors of the last ten years—the eleven films in his *Madea* franchise, in which he appears as the title role and also serves as director behind the camera, have collectively grossed over $500 million at the box office—but also one of the industry's major players as a studio head. Tyler Perry Studios, established by Perry in 2015 in Atlanta, Georgia, is itself an important intervention not only in the representation of actors of color onscreen but also behind the scenes, in roles as executives and producers. This role also allowed Perry to extend his sphere of influence beyond the *Madea* franchise, and developed along with his appearance in a range of films by other directors. Even as his role as Madea ended with the final film in the franchise in 2019, Williams shows that Perry's acting career expanded beyond this series into a motley collection of other kinds of films, including *Gone Girl* (2014), *Teenage Mutant Ninja Turtles: Out of the Shadows* (2016), *Brain on Fire* (2016), and *Vice* (2018). Williams's essay explores how Perry's roles in these films from other directors nevertheless still contain important aspects of his earlier onscreen personae as well as his offscreen, public persona as a major studio head and director.

A philosophical approach is taken in a discussion of the artistic and cultural significance of two of the major actors of the 2010s in the eighth chapter, Daniel Varndell's "Jessica Chastain and Michelle Williams: Open Windows." As Varndell notes, where Hollywood stars both past and present tend to call attention to themselves through virtuosic performances that distinguish them from the surrounding cast as stars, Chastain and Williams have preferred a more self-effacing account of their own careers. And as Varndell shows, this ostensibly self-effacing sensibility finds its way into the performances of the two actresses: although both have been celebrated for playing strong, complex characters, both Chastain and Williams depend more on the subtle effects of gesture, movement, and expression rather than ostentatious methods or approaches. Although both actors made several notable films in the 2010s, this chapter makes a convincing argument that some of their most striking work can be found in two films: for Chastain, her turn as the FBI agent Maya in Kathryn Bigelow's *Zero Dark Thirty* (2013), and for Williams, as Gail Harris, mother of John Paul Getty III, in Ridley Scott's *All the Money in the World* (2017). Varndell's chapter, which pays close attention to the work Chastain and Williams do in specific moments in these films, shows how their onscreen work is not only relevant to the narratives of the films but also the empowerment of women in the film industry.

The ninth chapter, "The Predicaments of Queer Stardom: Ben Whishaw, Zachary Quinto, Ezra Miller," by Kyle Stevens, studies the first openly queer male Hollywood stars. Even if they are familiar from mostly supporting roles, Wishaw, Quinto, and Miller have nevertheless become household names, especially due to their presence in the blockbuster franchises of James Bond, *Star Trek*, and *Fantastic Beasts*, respectively. Unlike earlier stars such as Rock Hudson or Ian McKellen, who were outed or came out well after establishing a successful career, these actors have continued to find success while being publicly identified as queer. This essay considers such aspects of their personae and bodies as their whiteness, thinness, youthful appearance, and epicene gestures. Stevens also explores the idea that although these three stars were often erotic object choices for fans, they were not always presented as such in their films, which allows—perhaps for the first time—the sundering of the impulse to both desire the star and desire to be the star that has long been endemic to queer spectatorship. Stevens also argues that while these three stars challenge traditional depictions of masculinity both onscreen and off, they are, at the same time, something of a reboot of the original visible homosexual type in Anglophone culture (what Richard Dyer formulates as "the sad young man").

In the tenth chapter, "Timothée Chalamet: Refashioning Hollywood Masculinity," Matt Connolly shows how the rise of Chalamet's celebrity and his well-received performance in Luca Guadagnino's *Call Me by Your Name* intersected with two types of critical and cultural discourse. Reviewers uniformly praised Chalamet for his acting abilities, particularly a kind of hyperspecific physicality noted for its emotional nuance, intensity, and naturalism. Many fans, as well as cultural commentators, also publicly lauded Chalamet for the seeming comfort he presented as a heterosexual actor embodying intimate, onscreen details of his character's queer desire. This chapter connects these two conversations about Chalamet, with conceptions of the actor's neo–James Dean intensity on the one hand and openness to queer experience on the other feeding off one another within the actor's performances and persona, as well as the larger cultural reception of these dimensions of his celebrity. Through an examination of the films Chalamet made during the decade as well as these discourses that surrounded the emergence of his stardom, Connolly's chapter shows how the intertwined understanding of Chalamet's relationship to queerness in

Call Me by Your Name—fierce onscreen embodiment coupled with relaxed offscreen appreciation—allowed the actor to position himself adjacently to queer experience in ways largely eluding questions of appropriation. This chapter not only studies the interplay between performance skill and star image at this early stage in Chalamet's career but also offers an illustrative case study of the shifting mores surrounding male stardom's expressions of masculinity and sexuality in contemporary Hollywood.

The eleventh chapter, "Chadwick Boseman and Michael B. Jordan: Twenty-First-Century Stars," also looks at new types of masculinity embodied by a younger generation of Hollywood performers. Both Boseman (who tragically passed away at the young age of forty-three while this publication was in preparation) and Jordan won wide acclaim in the early part of the 2010s, with Boseman praised for his performance as Jackie Robinson in *42* (2013) and Jordan recognized for his characterization of Oscar Grant in *Fruitvale Station* (2013). The superhero fantasy *Black Panther* then ensured their wide appeal and mainstream success, cementing certain aspects of their star images: Boseman's characterization builds upon his portrayal of characters with quiet inner strength (as in *Marshall*, 2017) while Jordan's portrayal amplifies his characterizations of tough individuals who experience inner turmoil (*Creed*, 2015). Although Boseman was a decade older than Jordan at the time of his breakthrough as a star, both actors established their careers in the 2000s in television and independent films before moving on to more visible film careers in the ensuing decade. Baron's chapter contextualizes the stardom of these major new Hollywood stars by analyzing selected moments in their careers and performances in relation to pertinent industrial and cultural developments, particularly in connection to Black talents' visibility in music, sports, television, and theater in the 2010s, in light of the fraught Obama-era dilemma of celebrating the success of exceptional individuals and grappling with the ongoing effects of systemic racism.

In the twelfth chapter, "Natalie Portman: Smart Star," I take Portman as a case study for examining the way in which intelligence becomes legible in both discourse about stars and in their performative work onscreen. Portman made her mark in the 1990s as a child actor, appearing in films alongside established adult performers with a command and maturity that belied her age. Portman's early performances can be seen as a precocious representation of childhood as the foundation for intelligent adult life, complementing her emerging public persona as a Harvard-educated individual. As an adult in the new century and particularly in the last ten years, one of the salient traits of discourses about Portman's persona—her perceived intelligence—informed receptions of her characterizations of a range of brilliant, if often very troubled, adults. In *Black Swan* (2010), for example, Portman's character tests the very limits of the mind against the demands made upon the bodies of ballet dancers; and in *Jackie* (2016), Portman's Jacqueline Kennedy must reconcile her public image with her tumultuous inner life after the assassination of her husband. And as I also discuss, her own directorial debut, *A Time of Love and Darkness* (2015), afforded Portman a means to portray onscreen aspects of her own identity as a Jewish woman, an aspect of her background usually effaced in her high-profile Hollywood roles.

No one book could ever account for the full range of performative vitality generated by the Hollywood film industry during any given decade. But through these twelve chapters and nineteen stars, our authors nevertheless shine brilliant lights on many of the decade's most memorable performers, while bringing thoughtful inquiries to questions and problems their celebrity poses for us.

Chapter 1

Joaquin Phoenix

Ascendant

BRENDA AUSTIN-SMITH

Joaquin Phoenix crossed the threshold of the second decade of the new millennium in the guise of a hot mess. Having won a Golden Globe Award and a Grammy for his portrayal of singer Johnny Cash in *Walk the Line* (2005), Phoenix suddenly announced in 2008 that he was retiring from the movie business. *Two Lovers* (2009), it seemed, was to be his final film. In the last two years of the century's first decade, Phoenix had apparently abandoned the certified star status heralded by his role in *To Die For* (1995) and consolidated by his turn in *Gladiator* (2000).

In one way, the move made no sense at all given his achievement and profile in the industry at the time. From another perspective though, Phoenix's declaration that he was no longer an actor but, from that moment on, a singer—a rapper, even—provided an oddly credible conclusion to a career begun in childhood, shadowed by tragedy, and affected in several ways by addiction and instability. It was entirely possible that walking away from Hollywood was a delayed reaction to the death of his older brother, River, and the various pressures of living up to the legacy of his unorthodox and famously peripatetic family. Phoenix's personal experience of alcohol dependence and his time in rehab after the release of *Walk the Line* offered another gloss on the announcement, as did the Grammy itself, bestowed in recognition of Phoenix's genuine talent in singing all of Cash's songs himself for the film. Maybe the actor really was quitting the Tinseltown life in order to pursue a more artistically felt calling.

The release of *I'm Still Here* in 2010 at first neither confirmed nor denied these possibilities. Offered as a documentary of Phoenix's determination to refashion himself as a former film star turned rap artist, the film followed the shambolic actor through impulsive press appearances and disheveled interviews, capturing a two-year breakdown characterized by cocaine use, delusions of musical talent, and verbal abuse of the assistants in his entourage.

Joaquin Phoenix

The most infamous of the film's moments was a guest spot on the *Late Show with David Letterman* in early 2009, during which an aggressively unkempt Phoenix kept looking down at his hands before responding a few beats late to softball questions by the host. After some seconds of silent mugging at the camera, Letterman turned to Phoenix and asked, "What can you tell us about your days with the Unabomber?" The studio audience laughed, both uncertain and tickled. After a few more verbal gambits were launched and blocked, Letterman concluded the interview with, "Sorry you couldn't be here tonight."

The *Letterman* appearance was disastrous or hilarious or both, depending on how one received *I'm Still Here*. Initially touted as a documentary tracing the toll taken on Phoenix by the stress of fame and professional disillusionment, the project was eventually revealed as a spoof, a mockumentary conceived by Phoenix and his then brother-in-law Casey Affleck, who held the camera that followed "JP" (the actor's rapper name) through his tirade and drug-fueled breakdown. Vomiting on camera, being quite literally shat upon by an aggrieved personal assistant, and put off by Sean Combs when he asked for help in producing a recording, Phoenix comes across as an addled has-been, a fried pudge ball of residual white privilege without a smidgeon of the talent he imagines himself to possess. His rapping is tuneless and his beats flabby; the title of the film is plucked from his inane rhymes. Watching him perform in front of a nightclub crowd, we don't know whether amusement, embarrassment, or pity is called for. For those who watched carefully, hints that the film was actually an extended performance art prank appeared not just in faux celebrity news reports comparing Phoenix to Britney Spears but, more tellingly, in the final credits. These listed Tim Affleck, cameraman Casey Affleck's father, as Phoenix's "Dad," who shows up in the ultralyrical concluding scenes of Phoenix seeming to find refuge at a family compound in Panama.

In September 2010, Phoenix returned to the *Late Show with David Letterman* to apologize for his previous appearance there in character as himself in professional free fall. Slim, clean-shaven, and neatly dressed, Phoenix sat down to engage in a conversation that both was and wasn't a typical publicity push for an actor's latest film. At one point in the interview Phoenix described his study of reality television as a generative impulse for the project and explained his willingness to appear on Letterman's show because he felt confident that Letterman's experience with the industry meant that he could tell the difference between a character and a person. As a paratextual text in itself, this postfilm interview fascinates because of the paradox it incarnates of an actor insisting to an audience that because the film he appeared in is an inauthentic instantiation of its purported genre (an unscripted documentary), his appearance in that film is not just a performance but, as Philip Drake puts it, "a dramatic mode of performance that highlights the presence of character" (Drake 2) and is therefore authentic as an intentional act.

The revelation that *I'm Still Here* was a mockumentary rather than a cinema verité portrait of a film star's public disintegration brings documentary into neat juxtaposition with the perplexities of performance, and in Phoenix's case, star acting. Discussions of both documentary and film acting provoke debates about authenticity and contrivance, effort and ease, as well as the recognition that any aesthetic achievement relies on the manipulation that we call art. Nonprofessional social actors who appear on camera in documentaries are not often credited as performers because, as Elizabeth Marquis observes, "doubts about their performance competence might be especially rife" (Marquis 46). This does not or should not obtain in the case of a seasoned Hollywood actor like Joaquin Phoenix. And yet in the wake of *I'm Still Here*, it did, which required the actor to argue for the film's definitive falsity in order to secure recognition of his artistry in it. Phoenix's portrayal of himself was also complicated by his stardom. Drake notes that stars are often regarded as not very good actors because "they can never fully obliterate all signs of their celebrity from the characters they play," becoming iconic performers for viewers convinced that stars always play versions of themselves onscreen (Drake 2). *I'm Still Here* occasionally surfaces in discussions of Phoenix's rehabilitation of his image and his career, suggesting not just how effective so-called reality productions can be in shaping the public reception of celebrities (which was the purported goal of the film) but also how credible it was that Joaquin Phoenix was teetering on the edge of a professional crash. It would take a few years of appearing in more conventionally scripted roles for Phoenix to completely overcome concerns about his health and his ability to control his own efforts in performance.

The singularity of *I'm Still Here* in Phoenix's filmography acts as a palate cleanser for his achievements over the last decade, washing away the remnants of celebrity flotsam and jetsam from his star image, and putting to rest any doubts about his talent and skill as an actor. The range of roles and genres in which he has appeared since then confirms his ability to stretch and his willingness to take chances. He is not an iconic star actor who looks and sounds the same no matter the part, though there are commonalities to many of the characters he plays. For whatever reason, he often selects or agrees to the portrayal of troubled characters who do not handle their vulnerability very well, responding to emotional pressure with eruptions of violence that deny or distract from their need and uncertainty. But this tendency is leavened by his portrayal of softer men subdued by affective circumstances that leave them swamped by the complexities they find themselves facing. Responses to the variety of Phoenix's performances, though, are often seeded with plaudits that downplay his actual labor as a performer, focusing instead on qualities of immediacy or impressions of the unstudied in his work. An example of this is an interview in the *New York Times* in 2017 following his Best Actor Award at Cannes for *You Were Never Really Here* (2017). In the piece, Bret Easton Ellis describes Phoenix as the "most soulful screen actor of his generation . . . inquisitive and improvisatory," who dislikes rehearsing and works "in an intuitive, untrained way" in auteur-directed movies that match this essentially independent and rebellious spirit. Phoenix himself agrees with this assessment of his style, claiming that, "It's just instinct," that being self-conscious is bad acting, and that he is content to let directors shape his performance and thus the character's arc. Phoenix elaborates on the time it takes on set for him to "find something" to work with, and adds that the best directors he has collaborated with were those who "adjusted to what was happening with the actor" ("The Weird Brilliance of Joaquin Phoenix, *The New York Times,* 6 September 2012).

The exchange is in keeping with Erving Goffman's "doctrine of natural expression," discussed in detail by Murray Pomerance in relation to our culture's assumption that acting is produced in the first instance by a performer's emotional rather than intellectual resources. More than just encouraging our belief that the emotions we witness in a character originate with the performer, writes Pomerance, the doctrine of natural expression often satisfies a viewer's or interlocutor's curiosity for discovering more about the fashioning of the performance, short-circuiting further inquiry (Pomerance 141–142). Cynthia Baron and Sharon Carnicke write that viewers can "elide the training, experience, and creativity that actors bring to filmmaking," often overlooking "the bank of knowledge and experience that actors draw on to produce the gestures, expressions, and intonations that collaborate and combine with other cinematic elements to create meaning in film" (Baron and Carnicke 17). A contrast to the Easton Ellis interview is a much earlier one with Conan O'Brien in 2005 about Phoenix's turn as Johnny Cash in *Walk the Line.* In their conversation, the actor describes the vocal training he had had to approximate Cash's accent and baritone singing voice. When asked by O'Brien to demonstrate, Phoenix apologized that he could no longer do Cash's voice, having lost the practiced control over vowels that made Cash's delivery distinct. Pomerance refers to another example, an interview with Terry Gross in which Phoenix recalls asking his dentist to fix metal brackets to his teeth to assist in mechanically keeping one side of his mouth tense and tight (Pomerance 125). Despite Easton Ellis's emphasis on what he sees as Phoenix's channeling of mysterious acting mojo, Phoenix himself gives evidence of being steeped in his craft, open to training and coaching, and fully aware of the interdependence of actor, director, and crew in creating memorable film performances. His actorly intuition is the product of preparation, experience, and thought as well as of inspiration or genius. He is someone James Naremore would call a pragmatic rather than doctrinaire actor, "Willing to use whatever technique works in particular circumstances," whether drawn from "the school of psychological naturalism or the school of classical imitation" (Naremore 2). As often as Phoenix has stressed his preference for not overthinking his performances by rehearsing scenes, and his interest in keeping choices open and unpredictable rather than nailed down by a script, he also speaks about the impossibility of guaranteeing that a great scene can always be tied to the emotional state of the actor: "Probably some of the greatest moments in movies the actor was just thinking what was for lunch" ("'Movies Are Strange, Man': Joaquin Phoenix Talks about Not Knowing What's Next," *The Village Voice,* 27 March 2018).

★★★★★★★★★★ Tormented Sad Sacks

Phoenix's return to film acting in *The Master* (2012) was also his first partnership with Paul Thomas Anderson. Phoenix plays Freddie Quell, a psychologically damaged and alcoholic soldier returned from WWII. Freddie is an aimless vet fueled by an addiction to homemade booze and the fantasy of reuniting with a former love interest. At the end of a bender that takes him to the San Francisco waterfront, Quell climbs onto a yacht belonging to Lancaster Dodd (Philip Seymour Hoffman), the leader of a spiritual community called The Cause. After sharing a mug of Quell's firewater below deck, Dodd takes Quell onboard as a personal supplier of hooch (made, we see, from ingredients like turpentine and aviation fuel), telling Quell that he will be Dodd's "guinea pig." The two play out a complicated and obscure struggle for dominance and recognition shot through with erotic and familial dynamics. In Dodd, Quell seems to have found someone to follow and protect, while in Quell, Dodd meets the kind of would-be disciple he cannot control. The challenge posed by Quell to the charismatic Dodd is Quell's strange imperviousness to the teachings of The Cause, even though he is willing to act in the service of Dodd himself as a combination of mascot and enforcer. Quell is a follower but not a believer, something Dodd cannot accept or leave alone. He both admires and is maddened by Quell's resistance to him as a teacher-prophet. *The Master* earned both Phoenix and Hoffman Oscar nominations and a bushel of accolades. One of the most interesting of these was Bilge Ebiri's consideration of the film as a contention between two styles of acting. Phoenix stands in for "the tormented, physical acting styles of the latter half of the twentieth century," while Hoffman represents the "controlled, elusive manner of the previous half" and draws on Orson Welles for his portrayal of Dodd ("What Is *The Master* Really About?: Five Interpretations," *Vulture*, 25 September 2012).

The physical as well as psychological intensity associated with Phoenix's performance style in this decade is fully apparent in Freddie Quell. Even when Freddie is fully dressed, Phoenix's interpretation of the character creates the impression that he is always in rags, his bones insistently cutting through the cloth. Phoenix lost considerable weight for the role, his knifelike cheekbones and scarecrow physique embodying a man whose obsessions consume his body as well as his mind. And for a character so focused on sex that he sees genitalia in every Rorschach image he is shown, Phoenix gives Quell's body remarkable stiffness. In shot after shot we see Quell stand with hands on hips, his upper body not bending but rather leaning forward, as if creakily hinged at the waist. In contrast to the balloon-shaped body Phoenix conjured for *I'm Still Here*, arms slightly bowed and hanging, here he concentrates Quell's pathology and anxiety in his shoulder blades and neck, his head thrust forward as if to peck at the world like an agitated bird.

Viewers and critics single out the scene in which Dodd subjects Quell to "processing," firing questions at Quell that he must answer without blinking his eyes. The shot–reverse shot close-ups between the two characters show us how Dodd uses this tactic to break his would-be follower and at the same time highlights the dynamic between these two actors, one whose face and voice is firm and commanding, the other both indicating and controlling his character's agitation. Quell's grimace as Dodd begins the processing questions is his best approximation of a smile, his mouth stretching partway across his face as his eyes narrow, both leaking and containing his anguish. At least as interesting, though, is a later scene in which we see Dodd direct Quell to move back and forth across a living room between the wall and a window, touching each extremity, commanded by Dodd to describe it each time in new ways. The order and its execution echo the repetitive elements of the processing scene but this time as form. We see Quell's readiness to perform meaningless movement at the behest of another even as the enlightenment or revelation that might result from such a studied practice eludes him; repetition without understanding is his fate, one Dodd is powerless to affect. In the end Quell refuses Dodd's offer of either friendship or permanent enmity. Quell's obduracy frustrates Dodd's need for progression, quietly cementing the reversal of their hierarchy.

Though Phoenix became well known in this decade for playing characters with coiled-spring personalities always on the edge of explosion (from Freddie Quell in *The Master* to Charlie Sisters in *The Sisters Brothers* [2018] to Arthur Fleck in *Joker* [2019]), he has been equally able to portray nebbish men who act out, if and when they do, in deflected gestures of unwitnessed or passive aggression. Theodore Twombly in *Her* (2013) and Doc Sportello in the stoner noir *Inherent Vice* (2014) are two examples of these gentler, bewildered figures facing software upgrades and drug gangs that threaten their hold on reality and happiness.

In the character of Theodore Twombly (whose name recalls the experimental sculptor and painter Cy Twombly), we find Phoenix slightly rounder in the face. He sports a moustache that hides the distinctive scar on his upper lip, the one that makes him look like someone familiar with fistfights. We first see Theodore in close-up at his desk, dictating letters for his job at BeautifulHandWrittenLetters.com. As he speaks the phrases that appear in script onscreen, Phoenix shakes his head slightly, and then rolls his eyes up and around in wonder at the sentiments he delivers in someone else's stead: "Fifty years since you married me!" The work done and sent to print, he looks up and touches his glasses briefly, signaling the end of his immersion in another's perspective and bringing the task to conclusion. The gesture brings to mind one of Harry Caul's recurring tics in Coppola's *The Conversation* (1974). This opening sequence demonstrates Theodore's capacity for deep emotion as well as his habit of compartmentalizing, keeping himself removed and protected from the swells of feeling he can perform but backing away from them in his private life and relationships. His job requires a multitude of compelling daily performances of short-form sincerity reminiscent of acting itself. As the camera pans from Theodore's cubicle to range across the workspace, we hear the voices of his co-workers composing similar scripts out loud that convey an array of feelings, from sorrowful respect to gratitude to loneliness. Something about voicing these sentiments, it seems, gives them their particular force and quality.

As sad sacks go, Theodore is an interesting one, retaining his fashion sense from what we assume is a happier time (he has a marked preference for orange shirts and jackets) and sporting highlighted hair, even as he walks from his office to the subway, head down with his man bag slung over his shoulder. Animating this dispirited character, Phoenix walks with his center of gravity somewhere near his knees, not shuffling or shambling but moving as a man whose heart is in his shoes. Until the final scene, Theodore's failure to be cool comes through in his habit of pushing his poorly fitting glasses up his nose and his fondness for tea. He might once have been certain and graceful, but his divorce from Catherine (Rooney Mara) has floored him, drained him of the confidence that would have let him pull off wearing a deerstalker hat in the woods and not look like a striving goof. His relationship with Samantha, his new OS (Scarlett Johansson), flatters and comforts him, restoring the physical exuberance that sends him dashing through the LA subway, veering nimbly around commuters, filming his antics to share with his virtual mate. By the film's end, after Samantha and the other operating systems have left for an AI equivalent of enlightenment, Theodore dictates an email to his ex-wife apologizing for his failings and wishing her well, wherever she may be. In that moment, Samantha and Catherine intersect as evanescent women equally unavailable to Theodore, a revelation that provokes from him an expression of emotional presence we are to take as more genuine than any letter he has composed on the job. In the final scene with his friend Amy (Amy Adams) on the roof of their apartment building, Theodore is no longer despondent but calmly accepting of both Catherine's and Samantha's departure. Phoenix's familiar handsomeness is now suddenly resurgent. Theodore's glasses are gone, his back is straight, and his emotional baby fat has melted, exposing Joaquin's resolute jawline and cheekbones which announce Theodore's delayed achievement of maturity.

Muttonchops straight from the 1970s all but bury Phoenix's features in *Inherent Vice*, making him look like a seedy Pete Cochran from *The Mod Squad*. An adaptation of Thomas Pynchon's novel of the same name, the plot has the meandering charm of *The Big Lebowski* (1998), the incoherence of *The Big Sleep* (1946), and a central character out of *The Long Goodbye* (1973). Doc Sportello is a private eye engaged by his ex-lover to foil a plan to have her current lover committed to a psychiatric hospital. His face wreathed in dope smoke for much of the film, Sportello is a good-natured and observant detective. Everyone around Sportello treats him as dope addled, but he actually follows and puts together most of the clues scattered throughout the ridiculously convoluted plot. That this effort doesn't result in much of a resolution doesn't take away from the earnestness of Phoenix's interpretation of the character. Sportello's chill persona is shattered only by a scene of intimate sexualized violence with Shasta Fay Hepworth late in the film. Sportello's doofus-savant figure is a witness and confidant for most of the other characters in the film, even as his weed habit dulls his ability to respond to their horrors and secrets with the energy we'd expect.

Phoenix is often filmed in close-up, his face impassive and nodding as his character is regaled with details of layered conspiracies. Once in a while we are reminded that Sportello has actually not missed a trick, as when he negotiates the safety of Coy Harlingen (Owen Wilson), though the entropic nature of the plot eludes not his understanding of what is going on but certainly his effect on much of it.

Though his profile as a lead actor continued to rise in the 2010s, Phoenix has also been a part of strong ensemble casts, and in notable cases such as in *Don't Worry, He Won't Get Far on Foot* (2018) and *The Sisters Brothers* works generously with the gently excellent Jonah Hill as Donnie Green in the first film and John C. Reilly as the protective and reluctantly violent Eli Sisters in the second. Phoenix has also made on average a feature film each year since 2010, in addition to voice-over work in documentaries and occasional short films. The actor's ability to project a variety of complex psychological states—from depressed lassitude to anxiety, or from soulful menace to wiry psychosis—through body work is aided by his voice. This isn't as simple as the actor relying on low registers for characters like Joe in *You Were Never Really Here* or higher ones for Arthur Fleck in *Joker*. Phoenix's vocal delivery as John Callahan in *Don't Worry* makes the character's self-pitying justifications for his drinking intensely irritating to the ear as well as logically unconvincing. It is really hard to stomach a voice that seems to come straight out of *Beavis and Butthead*. For the voice of Charlie Sisters, Phoenix ensures that we hear a strain of high-strung hysteria, the sound of a man who cannot control his tone of voice any more than he is able to control the direction in which he fires a gun or his impulse to pour acid into a river.

☆☆☆☆☆☆★★★★ Depth and Anguish

Of his performances in the last five years, though, two especially show Phoenix's depth of engagement. The first is his portrayal of Joe, a suicidal Gulf War vet and former FBI agent working on contracts to rescue trafficked young girls from their captors in *You Were Never Really Here*. The second, of course, is his incarnation of Arthur Fleck in Todd Phillips's *Joker*. Both films are thrillers that focus on the personal conditions that contribute to the pathologies of their main characters. Joe's childhood was marked by domestic abuse, and his military service has left him in the grip of PTSD. Arthur displays symptoms of something like Tourette syndrome early in the film but later blossoms into full-blown sociopathy. Both characters are, or become, horrifically violent, but Joe is always on the verge of

Joaquin Phoenix as the tortured Joe in *You Were Never Really Here* (Lynne Ramsay, Amazon Studios, 2017). Digital frame enlargement.

turning that violence on himself. Inflicting bloody retribution on the (apparently numerous) pedophiles who populate the New York political elite seems equivalent to turning a gun or knife away from his own body at the last minute. If it were not for these contracts, we gather, which allow him to direct his self-destructive energy at morally—though not legally—acceptable targets, Joe could not survive his own anguish.

You Were Never Really Here opens with a visual and audio montage: the sounds of a train, an underwater shot, a girl's whispery voice counting down from eleven, a man's voice muttering and then counting down from the number forty. We see the terrible image of a man trying to breathe, his head in a plastic bag, his mouth open and sucking the plastic into his face. A cut takes us to the aftermath of what we later realize was one of Joe's hit jobs in a hotel reminiscent of the murder scene in *The Conversation*, right down to bloody evidence flushed down a toilet. Joe is dressed in a nondescript gray hoodie, and we see him drop a plastic bag (containing a hammer, his weapon of choice) into the trash before walking down a sketchy corridor and out into an alley, where he is suddenly attacked. Repelling the attack with an efficient head butt, Joe pauses for a moment and then retreats, choosing another exit from the scene, one we do not see. What we realize later is that Joe is scrupulous when it comes to leaving a job site. He makes sure that no one—even a random dude who saw a chance to roll someone in an alley—can confirm his movements. He takes a cab to an unnamed airport and uses a pay phone to report that "it's done" to an unknown person. We see a young girl stretched along an airport seat, sleeping. The mystery of her presence there, and the impression we have of her vulnerability, becomes resonant in retrospect, once we learn the nature of Joe's work.

While the plot of *You Were Never Really Here,* adapted from a novel by Jonathan Ames, is compact, intense, and rather incredible—how many pedophile rings are there in New York City, and how likely is it that there would be an office from which a hit man like Joe receives orders to obliterate them?—once inside the film's hothouse world, the actions of the characters make sense. Joe is a tortured man one moment ahead of his self-annihilating impulses, playing with a knife or toying with asphyxiation. And yet in the midst of offing what we assume are an endless array of slimy sexual predators, Joe lives with and takes care of his mother. We see him in one scene knock on the door of the bathroom, insisting that his mom open the door and let him in. She refuses, and in frustration, Joe imitates the shrieking sounds and stabbing motions of Norman Bates in *Psycho* (1960). The moment is genius, as Phoenix combines the exasperated affection of a son (whose work involves serial killing) with the cultural afterlife of a Freudian tale of murderous repression. We guffaw in shock as we take in that, off the clock as he is in this scene, Joe feels the same kind of maddening love for a parent we all might; it's just that most of us do not wield ball-peen hammers against other people's skulls in our day jobs. Phoenix convinces us that the bond between Joe and his mother (forged in part because of their survival of past abuse) helps keep him from giving in to his suicidal despair. It is in her presence that he can sing, be silly, and relax. We know that she has died later in the film when we see Phoenix lower his head and hide his face from us, having climbed up the side of the house to her window. The privacy the actor lends to the character at that moment is more affecting in its quietness than the later discovery of her body in bed.

Phoenix's physical presence is bulky in this film, much as it was in *I'm Still Here,* but he is deliberate and unobtrusive rather than pitiful in his carriage. He walks carefully but not swiftly, his upper body swaying slightly back and forth, often moving out of visual range before the camera has a chance to track him. A water fountain at the airport continues to run on its own after he has disappeared; a pay phone stays in frame for several seconds after he has used it. Cuts replace transitions in this film, allowing Joe to keep a low profile and maintain his professional invisibility, even where the camera is concerned. Unless Joe is attacking someone, Phoenix keeps his movements deliberately restrained. The turns of Joe's head are slow and considered rather than darting. There is a trace of Forest Whitaker's samurai figure in *Ghost Dog: The Way of the Samurai* (1999) in Joe, who shares Ghost Dog's occupational rigor and physical precision, but none of his spiritual calm.

In two notable scenes, Phoenix balances Joe's physical stoicism with rage, canniness, grief, and compassion. Having shot both agents responsible for killing his mother (the image of her cracked and bloody glasses takes us back to *Battleship Potemkin* [1925]), the injured and coldly furious Joe watches one of them crawl from the dining room to the kitchen gasping and moaning in pain. After putting his foot on the dying man's back and pushing him into the floor as he cries out in agony, Joe relents. He rolls the man on his back and jams a pill down his throat, easing his pain enough to ask about his mother's death and what has happened to Nina. The man lies on his back on the flowered vinyl tiles, staring at the ceiling while he slowly bleeds out, and begins to sing along with the radio. Joe slumps down on the floor beside him. The dying man reaches for Joe, and the two men lie there holding hands, softly singing along to the jarringly cheesy 1970s song "I've Never Been to Me." The scene is macabre and moving, the agent standing in for Joe's mother, his hand for hers.

As Joe drives away from the house, the black garbage bag around his mother's body flaps and rattles in the breeze from the car window, echoing the many plastic bags we have seen Joe torment himself with. He drives to a lake, a patch of blue appearing in a stand of trees, and, dressed in a suit and tie, weighs his mother's body with rocks before walking into the water with her in his arms. It is a dreadful and beautiful scene of burial and baptism that Phoenix plays with grace and awkwardness. Having filled his own jacket pockets with rocks, Joe's intention is to formally attend his mother, travel with her through the water, and see her safely to the bottom. It is less certain that he plans to return. He holds her in a reverse Pietà, drifting downward in a shaft of sunlight, and then lets her go. Phoenix's arms hang down in the water, his hands partly open in a release that may also be a surrender, and we hear his voice counting down once again in voice-over in anticipation of his breath finally running out.

☆☆☆☆☆☆☆☆☆★ The Impression of a New Body

Joker follows Arthur Fleck's metamorphosis from woebegone clown and failed stand-up comedian to conscienceless villain. Fleck's very name announces his insignificance, a state confirmed as we see him tormented by kids who steal his sign, blamed and fined for its destruction, and eventually fired from his job as a party clown. Arthur is a nobody,

Joaquin Phoenix as the supervillain *Joker* (Todd Phillips, Warner Bros., 2019). Digital frame enlargement.

living with his mother in an apartment building in which almost everything is brown and set dressed to convey hopelessness. *Joker* has been rebuked for its suggestion that the intersecting mental illnesses and neurological conditions Arthur exhibits (he is on seven different medications) lead him to sociopathy and a future as the leader of a mass movement of chaos. On the other hand, the film has also been praised for its depiction of austerity's effects on the already vulnerable. When his social worker tells him that funding cuts mean that he will no longer receive his medication, she adds that the Gotham authorities in charge of things like social services do not care about people like him, or people like her either. In the landscape created by the underfunding of services ranging from garbage collection (the film is set during a 1981 garbage strike) to the provision of mental health care across the city, it is not a surprise that desperation and anger are on the rise. "It is certainly tense," says his social worker at one point. "People are upset, they're struggling, looking for work. These are tough times."

The role of Arthur/Joker is the one for which Joaquin Phoenix won an Academy Award for Best Actor in 2020. Even reviews of the film that criticized it as empty and uninteresting—A. O. Scott accused it of being "besotted with the notion of its own audacity—as if willful unpleasantness were a form of artistic courage"—gave Phoenix's performance in this supervillain origin story its due ("Are You Kidding Me?" *The New York Times*, 3 October 2019). It is a physical and intellectual extravaganza of acting; over the course of the two hours of running time, Phoenix shows us all that Arthur imagines himself to be, something nevertheless superseded by the greater capacity of the actor's range of power. Though this is true of all of Phoenix's offerings in the 2010s, in his role as Arthur/Joker we can see how he creates the impression of different bodies on the screen. While we are used to watching actors create expressive characters, and use their physical selves to animate and communicate the being of other personalities, Phoenix does something other than lend his body and voice to the inner life of another. The first element of his performance we come into contact with in *Joker*, as in his other films of this decade, is the impression of a new body.

As in *The Master*, Phoenix lost a considerable amount of weight for *Joker*, something audiences always take as a sign of genuine commitment to a role, perhaps because messing with the looks that had a part in making you a star is seen as a major sacrifice. More than a scrawny clown, though, what Phoenix conjures for us is the belief that this is a different physical self from the one we saw in *You Were Never Really Here*, *Don't Worry*, or *Her*. Part of his work is endowing the characters he plays with psychic presence from which their choices and gestures flow. Phoenix seems to treat his body as a living prop available for fashioning, something thrown up in front of us to block us from accessing the working actor, who is indicated only by the trace of his choices in the moment. The effect is not the same as someone channeling or being possessed in some way by the spirit of a scripted character, as if the body were a pre-existing vessel or conduit; it is more akin to an actor invoking or rendering a new carnal framework—bulky, thin, intimidating, or fast—as the first step in infusing that frame with generative energy.

That invocation creates a number of remarkable screen moments that radiate quite different facets of Arthur on his way to becoming the homicidal Joker, some of which suggest Arthur's sexual and gender fluidity. An early exchange in the clown locker room, for example, gives his relationship with Randall an exploitative undertone. Looking up at Randall, who has just handed him a gun for protection, Arthur's demeanor and voice are mannered as he half-whispers that Randall knows Arthur can't have a gun. "You can pay me back some other time," says Randall. "You know you're my boy." Soon after this we see Arthur in his living room, imagining being hit on at a club—whether gay or straight isn't clear—for being a good dancer. Phoenix's skinny arms are raised above his head, which elongates his torso and emphasizes his ribs as he moves his hips to imaginary club beats. Lost in the fantasy, he accidentally fires the gun out the window and then crumples to the floor in a surprised and awkward heap. Later of course, Arthur will indeed pay Randall back.

Phoenix often makes Arthur's physicality pitiful to us, as when he turns away from the detectives who suspect him of the subway murders and walks forcefully but unknowingly into the glass door of the hospital where his mother is recovering from a stroke. It is physical comedy manqué, an unintentional pratfall of a move too shocking and ill-timed to be funny in any way. In that sense, it is in keeping with the rest of Arthur's stand-up routines. Phoenix mixes embarrassing physical failures like this (an earlier example is Arthur's clumping along the sidewalk in oversized clown shoes, chasing the kids who took his sign) with the creepy grace of Arthur's body in other scenes. One of these takes place in the public bathroom after Arthur has shot his subway harassers. Arthur runs away from the carnage in a panic, his arms away from his body, his elbows bent, and his shoes clopping on the pavement. He is breathless as he enters the bathroom and pushes the door closed. Then his arms straighten and the camera pans down to his feet. One foot is pointed out from his body and the other slowly crosses in front of it. We pan up again to Arthur's arms and hands, his wrists circling as he begins to dance, turning and bending to imaginary music. His body is serpentine, flexible, repellent and magnetic all at once. He is captivated, fascinated by the start of his own transformation. Right after this we see Arthur stride confidently and purposefully down the hallway of the apartment building to knock on the door of his neighbor, Sophie, push his way in, and begin to kiss her, a delusion born of the erotic rush of murder.

It is movement and dance that announces the emergence of Joker in Arthur's psyche. Even as Arthur stumbles pursuing the street kids who stole his sign, he skid-slides into a fall, catches himself before fully touching the ground, and launches himself back up into a run; the move is pure slapstick. After he is fired and walks downstairs to the street, we see him raise his arm and begin a syncopated skip down the steps, the move an overture for the full-blown debut of Joker as maniacal song-and-dance man making his way down an outdoor staircase to the strains of pedophile Gary Glitter's "Rock and Roll, Parts 1 and 2." *New York Times* dance critic Gia Kourlas sees in Phoenix's dancing the influence not just of vaudeville but also of performers like Fred Astaire and Ray Bolger (whom Phoenix himself has credited, along with Buster Keaton) and traces of Gaga movement technique ("A Dance Critic Reviews Joaquin Phoenix's Moves," *The New York Times*, 31 October 2019). The delicacy of Gaga is gone by the time Arthur/Joker strut-dances down those stairs, kicking and pumping. He jumps, then lands on the wet steps; water sprays up like sparks. When the detectives call out to him from the top of the stairs, the music stops, and we hear Arthur gasp in panic, his reverie shattered.

Securing a guest spot on Murray Franklin's show is Arthur Fleck's stand-up dream come true, though all his tasteless attempts at jokes fall flat. Phoenix gives Arthur/Joker the strangled, almost coquettish voice we recall from Arthur's work at Ha-Ha's Talent Booking. Arthur sits with his legs crossed and lower body still, but his shoulders, arms, and head move constantly, twisting slightly, squirming as he becomes more agitated and furious, finally shooting Murray for being "awful."

An appearance as a performer on a fictional evening talk show couldn't be a more perfect bookend for Joaquin Phoenix's achievements over the last ten years. Entering the decade as an actor playing himself coming apart on camera, Phoenix ended it as an actor playing a character coming apart on camera. In an interview with *Vanity Fair* writer Joe Hagan, Phoenix observed that he has always thought that acting "should be like a documentary, that you should just feel whatever it is that you're feeling, what you think the character is going through at that moment" ("'I Fucking Love My Life': Joaquin Phoenix on *Joker*, Why River Is His Rosebud, His Rooney Research, and His 'Prenatal' Gift for Dark Characters," *Vanity Fair*, November 2019). The infamously evasive and deeply private Phoenix may share Arthur's fury at insincere fame peddlers like Murray Franklin, and may have used that disdain to ground and propel the performance, but by the end of the 2010s Phoenix's work makes clear the difference between a character and a person.

Chapter 2

Amy Adams and Emma Stone

Escaping the Ingénue

KAREN HOLLINGER

Emma Stone

Amy Adams

In a 2003 essay, Christine Geraghty categorizes Hollywood female stars as "glamour actresses" who perform in the style feminist critic Laura Mulvey, in her essay "Visual Pleasure and Narrative Cinema," famously labeled "to-be-looked-at-ness" (Geraghty, "Performing," 105–106, Mulvey 837). According to Geraghty, the Hollywood actress emphasizes her perfect good looks, sex appeal, and physical presence rather than her acting talents. She is constructed not as a skilled artist but as spectacle, the object of male desire kept in what Geraghty designates as the category of "star-as-celebrity" and prevented from becoming a "star-as-performer" ("Reexamining" 187). The star-as-celebrity always functions as a spectacle both in her onscreen performances and her offscreen publicity and promotion. Her status as a glamorous celebrity affords her the aura of stardom even if her movies fail to afford her box-office clout, but she is also prevented from attaining the more prestigious status of the star-as-performer who is noted for her acting skill and artistic accomplishments. For Geraghty, the Hollywood actress is typed into certain roles and genres and forced to maintain a consistent persona throughout her film career or risk losing her fan base. In order to please her loyal fans, she must display the same stable star identity from film to film and even in her offscreen publicity, and she can never attempt the range and "deeply intelligent acting" associated with the star-as-performer ("Performing" 116).

The glamour actress must use the acting mode of personification and play herself in every role, as opposed to the more critically respected technique of impersonation and creating a distinctly unique character in each film. Clearly, as James Naremore has pointed out, personification is not unskilled acting (Naremore 134). Creating a consistent star persona that seems to represent oneself is a feat of acting skill in itself, but it does not have the cultural cachet associated with impersonation. Of course, there have always been actresses who attain the status of the star-as-performer by rising above the level of to-be-looked-at-ness to become known for their craft and technique. Meryl Streep immediately comes to mind, but she is seen as the exception to the rule, the great lady of the contemporary silver screen who stands in contrast to the plethora of glamour actresses who are known for their spectacular appearance, their consistent star persona, and their tabloid-worthy personal life.

Does this characterization of the star actress really hold up? It might be worthwhile to look at two contemporary actresses who seem to be fashioning their careers as exceptions to the glamour actress model. Amy Adams and Emma Stone are not actresses who began their careers like Streep in the drama school of a prestigious Ivy League university or who quickly established themselves by demonstrating impressive acting skills and remarkable range. On the contrary, Adams and Stone started out inauspiciously in supporting roles in teen pics. Beginning as untrained actresses attempting to hone their skills on the job, they moved to establish themselves by the 2010s as stars-as-performers who sought in every film to broaden their range of performance and perfect their acting skills. They simply refused to remain in the ranks of the star-as-celebrity. If we look at their acting careers, their ideas on acting, and their attitude toward publicity about their personal lives, we see a rather different picture than Geraghty describes.

Neither Adams nor Stone was classically trained. Neither went to college, and their actor training was haphazard. Adams began in dinner theater in Minnesota and Stone in community theater in Arizona. Both came to Hollywood as unknowns and initiated their careers in teen comedies: *Drop Dead Gorgeous* (1999) for Adams and *Superbad* (2007) for Stone. They could have gotten stuck there, but they quickly moved to extricate themselves from single-genre typecasting and to establish their ability to master a wide range of roles. Adams describes this early phase of her career as her "innocent period," playing supporting roles as childlike, but sexy ingénues in films like *Psycho Beach Party* (2000). She said her performance in this film was a tribute to the 1960s breathy sex symbol Ann-Margaret (O'Neil). She didn't stay there, though; she crafted breakthrough performances that established her as more than a wide-eyed innocent, most notably in the small independent film *Junebug* (2005) and the bigger-budget studio releases *Enchanted* (2007) and *Doubt* (2008).

In *Junebug,* Adams plays Ashley, a pregnant rural teenager in what appears to be a shotgun marriage to her angry, depressed high school sweetheart. The character could easily have been played as capable only of naive incomprehension, but Adams refused to portray Ashley as lacking intellectual or emotional depth; instead, she shows her developing from giddy girlhood to profound grief in response to the tragic stillbirth of her child. Two memorable scenes in the film capture the emotional range of Adams's performance. In the first, her character is trying desperately to forge a connection with her new sister-in-law by asking her what she liked to do as a girl. Her sister-in-law says she liked to read and go horseback riding. Adams, in a completely persuasive rendition of naivete, asks, "At the same time?" In discussing her early portrayals of innocents, Adams stated that she wanted to forge a connection with these characters and portray their inherent goodness without condescending to or ridiculing the simplicity of their natures ("*Times* Talks"). Adams certainly establishes that connection in *Junebug,* and her identification with Ashley makes the scene in which Ashley tries to console herself after the loss of her baby all the more poignant. Adams's ability to move seamlessly from comedy to pathos is clearly displayed in *Junebug,* and it won her a special jury prize at the Sundance Film Festival and her first Academy Award nomination for Best Supporting Actress.

If *Junebug* was Adams's breakthrough film, the much higher budget Disney release *Enchanted* was her star-confirming vehicle. In it she plays

Giselle, a fairy-tale princess who is dispatched by an evil witch to contemporary New York City in order to prevent her from marrying the witch's son. Although the studio wanted a bigger star for the role, director Kevin Lima insisted on Adams because he felt she would approach the character of the princess without judging her (Jennifer Wood, "Amy Adams Enchants Kevin Lima," *Movie Maker*, 28 November 2007). Adams said,

> When I first read the script, I felt like I knew who she was, and I felt that it was something I understood, oddly enough. . . . I think I've always been attracted to characters who are positive and who come from a very innocent place. I think there is a lot of room for discovery in these characters, and that's something I always have fun playing. . . . And I didn't treat it like it was a joke. I treated it like I was playing Chekhov, and maybe they [the filmmakers] sensed my sincerity. (Quoted in Rick Bentley, "This Is One Serious Princess: 'Enchanted' Star Played the Role with Royal Earnestness," *McClatchy-Tribune Business News*, 23 November 2007.)

For Adams, the greatest challenge of the part was to move from the fairy-tale world to modern-day New York and make an animated character come alive without losing her sense of "goodness and kindness, and a loving spirit" (Adams quoted in Joey Berlin, "Adams Nails Down an 'Enchanted' Role, *Standard-Freeholder*, 3 December 2007). Adams said her work in musical theater helped her make Giselle believable. The film was a major box-office success, her performance was nominated for a Golden Globe, and her character was immortalized in a toy Giselle doll (Brandon Voss, "Amy Adams," *The Advocate* 998, 4 December 2007, 26). Next, Adams moved back into serious drama with her role in *Doubt* (2007), which was the first film that lifted her out of her innocent phase. Based on John Patrick Shanley's stage play, it centered on two nuns, one of whom comes to believe a priest in the parish associated with their school is sexually abusing a male student. The film was a big leap for Adams, who was part of an impressive ensemble cast with Meryl Streep and Philip Seymour Hoffman.

Emma Stone's career parallels Adams's in interesting ways. Like Adams, Stone also began acting in local theater, but on a much more amateur level. Her professional training was limited to working with an acting coach who "had been with William Morris or something in the 1970s" and who tapped some old connections to get her an agent (Stone quoted in Jonah Weiner, "The Interview: Emma Stone, Favorite to Win Best Actress at Tonight's Oscars," *The Sunday Times*, London, 26 February, 2017). She dropped out of high school at the age of fifteen after persuading her parents to allow her to go to Hollywood, accompanied by her mother, to audition for film and television roles. She finished high school by getting her GED between auditions for acting jobs. She originally began acting for its therapeutic benefits; youth theater and especially improvisational comedy helped her get over panic attacks (Josh Eells, "Emma Stone Talks 'Irrational Man,' Sony Hack and Keeping Her Personal Life Private," *WSJ Magazine*, 17 June 2015). Like Adams, Stone began in teen pics, not as an innocent but as a fast-talking teenager, the tough girl with an underlying warmth and intelligence. After a number of teen comedies came two breakout roles: the young con woman who is the love interest of Jesse Eisenberg's character in *Zombieland* (2009) and the high school girl who gets branded as sexually promiscuous unfairly in *Easy A* (2010). Stone describes *Easy A* as her "launching pad" ("D/P 30 2010: The Oral History of Hollywood: *Easy A* Actress Emma Stone, Director Will Gluck," YouTube, June 2012"). Her performance, which director Will Gluck describes in the aforementioned interview as holding the film together, won her a Golden Globe nomination and BAFTA Rising Star Award. Even in this early film, Stone, like Adams, was concerned about her technique. She said she wanted to be sure she did not overact, while "playing her [character] accurately and making sure she stayed how she was on the page" (Stone quoted in Jamie Portman, "Rock-Solid Unswayed by Hollywood Machine," *Edmonton Journal*, 17 September 2010, D3).

Also like Adams, Stone quickly set out to expand her range by moving from comedy into dramatic roles. Stone, who has said repeatedly that her first love is comedy, refused to remain stranded there. She pursued a role in the racial drama *The Help* (2011). She found the film a challenge not only because it was her first dramatic role but because of the extensive dialect training she had to undergo in order to perfect a Southern accent (Bryce). Like Adams, whose first dramatic role in *Doubt* placed her within the security of a distinguished ensemble cast, Stone worked in *The Help* with an ensemble of impressive stars like Viola Davis, Octavia Spencer, and Jessica Chastain. After breaking into dramatic roles, both Adams and Stone ventured into superhero blockbusters. Stone played the female love interest in the two *Amazing Spider-Man* films (2012, 2014), and Adams played Lois Lane in the Superman trilogy *Man of Steel* (2013), *Batman and Superman: Dawn of Justice* (2016), and *Justice League* (2017). Many critics see performances in blockbusters as involving a deskilling process in terms of acting technique, but both actresses expressed an enthusiasm for the challenges of working in the blockbuster format. Adams said she felt the format didn't offer enough opportunities for her to develop the character of Lois Lane, who she believed was just there in service to the plot (Lauren Waterman, "Amy Adams and Andrew Garfield," *Teen Vogue*, 19 June 2012), yet she still worked to portray Lois as a sort of everywoman figure (as she attests in

Scott Simon, "Amy Adams: A Steely Wife Stands behind 'The Master,' *NPR*, 15 September 2012). Similarly, Stone talked about how much she learned from working with her co-star Andrew Garfield in *The Amazing Spider-Man*, acting in front of a green screen, and being part of such a big-budget production ("D/P 30: The Oral History of Hollywood: *Birdman*, Emma Stone," YouTube, 8 December 2018). Both actresses seem to have treated the blockbuster experience as an instructive, not to mention lucrative, detour on their path to star-as-performer status.

As their careers entered the 2010s, both actresses sought major directors to help them transition into more challenging roles. Beginning with the role of a tough barmaid who becomes the girlfriend of a would-be boxing champion in David O. Russell's *The Fighter* (2010), Adams embarked on a series of intense performances very much at odds with her earlier ingénue roles. Russell, who was initially skeptical that Adams could shed her Disney princess image, said, "I just really wanted to challenge her. I wanted her to do a role that was as strong as the guy parts, and more cunning, in certain respects" (Russell quoted in Robert Ito, "A Princess Finds Her Dark Side," *New York Times*, 8 December 2013). He went on to say that once shooting began, he realized that "there are very few things that a director can have at his disposal better than an actress who's dying to break type. Amy was extremely motivated to play a sexy bitch and that's who the character is" (Russell quoted in Stuart McGurk, "Amy Adams: David O. Russell Made Me Cry Every Day on *American Hustle*," *GQ*, 7 October 2016). Adams's character Charlene not only has to support her boyfriend Micky (Mark Wahlberg) as he prepares for a championship bout but also must deal with his recovering drug addict brother-trainer (Christian Bale) and his domineering mother-manager (Melissa Leo in an Academy Award–winning performance). As she would in succeeding roles, Adams distinguished herself in set pieces that showcase her talent. *The Fighter* features two bravura scenes involving arguments that Charlene has with Micky's brother and later with his mother and sisters on the front porch of the house she shares with Micky. Christian Bale, who was nominated for an Academy Award for his performance as Micky's brother, would go on to be a frequent co-star in Adams's films. This strategy of seeking out actors with whom they have an established chemistry is another hallmark of both Adams's and Stone's careers.

The Fighter resulted in more award nominations for Adams, as did *The Master* (2012), another film with a major director, Paul Thomas Anderson. In a supporting role as part of an impressive ensemble cast including Philip Seymour Hoffman and Joaquin Phoenix, Adams's talents as a dramatic actress are again showcased as she plays a cult leader's (Hoffman) manipulative wife who hides her ruthless ambition under the facade of wifely devotion. As critic Donald Clarke described her, Adams conveyed a perfect blend of "discreet menace" and malevolent "pertness" in creating this Lady Macbeth figure (Simon, "Amy Adams," quoting Clarke). In another set piece scene, this time in a bathroom, she berates her husband while all the while fiercely masturbating him, suggesting the underlying sadomasochistic nature of their relationship and her real power behind his cult leadership. With *The Master*, Adams, nominated for another Academy Award, unquestionably established herself as a star-as-performer, not merely a glamour actress.

Stone took a similar route to star-as-performer status in the 2010s, although her road was somewhat bumpier than Adams's. She took an underwritten role in *Gangster Squad* (2013) in order to work again with Ruben Fleischer, who had directed her in *Zombieland*, and Ryan Gosling, with whom critics felt she had established a strong romantic chemistry in *Crazy, Stupid, Love* (2011). The film was a box-office failure, and Stone was given little opportunity to fill out her role as a femme fatale. Leaving behind this strategy of sticking with directors and male stars with whom she had already worked, Stone followed Adams in seeking out big-name directors who she believed would furnish her with room to demonstrate her acting ability. Her first choice was Woody Allen, with whom she worked in *Magic in the Moonlight* (1914) and *Irrational Man* (2015), co-staring with formidable actors Colin Firth in *Magic* and Joaquin Phoenix in *Irrational Man*.

Magic in the Moonlight offered Stone the opportunity to create a character based on silent film star Clara Bow (Rose), but she found that Allen was not a director interested in working with his actors to develop their characters. He has said, "I never talk to any of the actors in any of my movies about anything if I can avoid it" (Eells, "Emma Stone," quoting Allen). Allen's approach to direction did not seem to be a good fit for an actress like Stone, who regards every movie as a new learning experience. *Irrational Man* was even less rewarding than *Magic*. It starred Joaquin Phoenix, the intensity of whose performance seems to have made Stone uneasy. She said that with Phoenix she had to be "the most present I've ever been" because "he changes direction constantly. He makes different choices every time for a scene, and you don't know which way he is going to go. You have to be so on, following him" (Weiner, "7 Things"). The film was a box-office failure and one of a series of films, like *Magic in the Moonlight* and the earlier *Paper Man* (2010), in which Stone was typecast in older man–younger woman plots.

Birdman (2014) offered her the opportunity not only to break out of the younger-woman rut but to establish herself as an actress who could rise to the challenges offered by a technically complex film. She played the recovering drug addict daughter of Michael Keaton's lead character, an ex-star of superhero films trying to make a comeback in the theater. Director Alejandro Iñárritu shot the film in a series of long takes that Stone said demanded a combination of "technical exactitude" and "emotional rawness" (Stone quoted in Jonah Weiner, "The Interview: Emma Stone, Favorite to Win Best Actress at Tonight's Oscars," *The Sunday Times* [London], 26 February 2017"). Iñárritu used a Steadicam to follow his actors, creating a tight structure that Stone actually felt was liberating, although it required extensive rehearsal, multiple takes, and close collaboration among the ensemble cast. This cast was composed of experienced actors like Michael Keaton, Edward Norton, and Naomi Watts, from all of whom Stone could learn. She said the use of the Steadicam was "exhilarating," making her feel the camera was a participant in the action and she just had to relax and "dance" with it (Stone quoted in Annette Insdorf, "Conversations with Michael Keaton, Edward Norton, and Emma Stone of *Birdman,*" *Backstage,* 6 January 2015).

Like Adams, Stone is also a master of the bravura set piece scene that showcases her acting skills. In *Birdman,* that scene is one in which her character breaks down and verbally attacks her father for being emotionally absent in her life. With the camera right in her face, Stone launches into a spectacular outpouring of anger and pain. Finally, after her harangue is over, she looks at Keaton, who wordlessly expresses how deeply injured his character is. Also without words, Stone perfectly shows that her character may have finally expressed her deep anger with her father, but that she now is beginning to regret the viciousness of her attack on him. The scene is perfectly executed in an extended single take. Seeking out films that contain scenes that demonstrate their acting prowess is only one of the ways both Adams and Stone set out to use their performances to hone their acting skills.

Both women decided in midcareer to tackle the New York stage, something many film stars are reluctant to do. In 2014, Stone took the part of Sally Bowles in the Broadway revival of *Cabaret,* and Adams played the baker's wife in the 2012 Shakespeare in the Park revival of Steven Sondheim's musical *Into the Woods*. They got mixed reviews: Stone was criticized for her singing and Adams for her failure to capture the restless discontent of the character (Brantley, "Saucy Sally"; Brantley, "A Witch"). But both actresses discussed their forays into theater positively as learning experiences that helped them prepare for watershed roles in future films.

Following her theater performance, Adams embarked on what was unquestionably her most bravura acting performance to date, playing Sydney Prosser in David O. Russell's *American Hustle* (2013). The production was a troubled one. Adams and her female co-star Jennifer Lawrence were paid less than the film's male stars, Christian Bale and Bradley Cooper. When the hack of the Sony computer system revealed this, Lawrence protested. Adams was asked how she felt about the situation, and she equivocated. She said she did not disapprove of Lawrence's protest, but stipulated that she knew she was being paid less but took the role anyway because "the option came down to do it or don't do it. So you just have to decide if it is worth it for you. It doesn't mean I liked it" (quoted in McGurk). Adams also had trouble with Russell during shooting. Known to have a volatile temper that he expresses by screaming at his actors during filming, Russell apparently verbally abused Adams on the set so viciously that she was reduced to tears and Christian Bale "got in his face and told him to stop acting like an asshole" (Hadley Freeman, "Amy Adams: 'I Thought, If I Can't Figure This Out, I Can't Work Any More," *The Guardian*, 5 November 2019). Adams admitted that Russell brought her to tears, but always diplomatic, she minimized the situation: "He was hard on me, that's for sure, I was really just devastated on set. . . . It really taught me how to separate work and home. Because I was like, I cannot bring this home with me to my daughter" (McGurk, "Amy Adams").

It wasn't just Russell's abusive behavior that bothered Adams but the character she played. Adams describes Sydney as "the most miserable human being I've ever played" (Ito, "A Princess"). She says she was deeply affected by the experience of playing her because she saw Sydney as using her sexuality as a tool to gain power, but underneath she was desperately unhappy and empty ("*Times* Talks: Amy Adams," *Times Talks*, 10 November 2016). At the same time, Adams saw the role as an opportunity to build this character of a hardened, highly intelligent seductress and con woman in "complex layers" so that "everything felt justified and it didn't feel like she was just a sexy sociopath" (Hermione Hoby, "*American Hustle* Star Amy Adams Interview: There Are People I'd Love to Eviscerate," *Telegraph* [London], 20 December 2013). Adams talked extensively in interviews about how she created Sydney's character and how the role led her to take a new approach to acting. She said she had to separate herself from the character in order not to bring Sydney's troubled personality home with her. Adams disliked Sydney so much that she says when shooting was completed, she "went into the trailer and cut my hair to get rid of her. I wanted her gone" (Julie Hinds, "Accolades, Artistry, and Amy Adams," *Detroit Free Press*, 21 December 2014).

Adams may have wanted Sydney gone, but after *American Hustle*, she went on to play more deeply troubled characters in a succession of progressively

Amy Adams in close-up in *American Hustle* (David O. Russell, 2013). Digital frame enlargement.

darker films, all of which brought her more recognition and award nominations. She did her first biopic, *Big Eyes* (2014), with Tim Burton, a director with whom she said she wanted to work ever since she became an actress (Hinds). She even contacted him when she heard about the project and expressed her interest in the role (Rob Lowman, "Amy Adams and Tim Burton Discuss *Big Eyes*, and Adams' Feminist Ways," *Daily News* [Los Angeles], 18 December 2014). The film recounts the story of the artist Margaret Keane, whose paintings of children distinguished by their huge brooding eyes were a popular sensation in the 1960s. Keane's abusive husband took credit for her work until she finally broke from his control. In *Arrival* (2016), Adams plays a linguist who is hired by the government to talk to aliens who seem to threaten the earth, and in *Nocturnal Animals* (2016) she plays her most villainous character in a portrayal that a number of reviewers saw as misogynist. Significantly, all of these were starring roles, and each was darker than the last.

The most popular of this group of films with both critics and audiences was *Arrival*, most likely for its science fiction subject matter rather than Adams's performance. Adams no doubt took the role because it again expanded her range, this time into a male-dominated genre, and offered her the chance to play a professional woman who combined intelligence, dedication, and courage. Adams was also clearly the film's star. Director Denis Villeneuve said Adams "carried" the film, and her performance was particularly impressive because she was able to show emotion without words ("Times Talks"). The film's progressive elements, however, are combined with a very depressing trick ending that has Adams's character deciding to give birth to a child who she knows will suffer and die at an early age. This ending, which could easily be read as an antiabortion allegory (as

Emma Stone alongside Ryan Gosling in *La La Land* (Damien Chazelle, 2016). Digital frame enlargement.

can *Nocturnal Animals)*, moderates the film's progressivity through a retreat into the pathos of the maternal melodrama.

Unlike Adams, who moved into decidedly deeper and darker dramatic roles, Stone swerved a bit from comedy into the musical arena. Stone's watershed film was *La La Land* (2016), a work that, like *Birdman*, allowed her to demonstrate her technical mastery. Paired for the third time with Ryan Gosling, she sings and dances in big musical production numbers that might have defeated another actress, but Stone says she was fascinated by the challenge that director Damien Chazelle offered to his two stars, neither of whom was known for musical talent. The production required extensive rehearsals for three to four months before shooting even began ("Academy Conversations: *La La Land*," YouTube, 1 February 2017). Stone says she was inspired by watching Fred Astaire and Ginger Rogers movies and Jacques Demy's *The Umbrellas of Cherbourg* (1964) (Jane Pauley and Lee Cowan, "Emma Stone Has Earned an Oscar for Her Role in *La La Land*," *CBS News Sunday Morning*, 12 February 2017). She and Gosling sang their own songs and danced in long shots of long duration in order to capture their full bodily movements. As in other films, Stone has her bravura acting moment. In *La La Land*, it is when her character Mia sings for her big audition. This scene and the dance duet with Gosling in Griffith Park are twin showstoppers, and Stone's performance won her a clean sweep of major awards, including the Academy Award, Golden Globe, BAFTA, and Screen Actors Guild Award.

As follow-ups to their great success in *American Hustle* and *La La Land*, Adams and Stone both made surprise moves in turning to limited series on television for what they clearly saw as challenging acting opportunities. Television has traditionally been seen as risky for movie stars because it is said to reduce a star's aura, but more recently TV has been regarded as offering especially female stars not only more interesting roles but more control over their performances. Adams executive produced and starred in *Sharp Objects* (HBO, 2018), an adaptation of Gillian Flynn's novel dealing with a self-harming reporter who returns to her hometown to face the intergenerational violence that shaped her life. Flynn's novel was so dark that she had trouble getting it published and even more trouble getting it adapted to the screen. The television production was a female-initiated project spearheaded by Flynn, screenwriter Marti Noxon, and Jessica Rhoades, then an executive at Blumhouse Television (Alex Bhattachirji, "Gillian Flynn, Amy Adams, and Patricia Clarkson Aren't Afraid to Tackle Big Topics," *WSJ Magazine*, 21 May 2018). It focuses on three female characters played by prominent female stars Adams and Patricia Clarkson and the up-and-coming young actress Eliza Scanlen. Adams says she was attracted to the project because she saw it as a female-focused character study. She said of playing Camille Preaker: "She just has such deep pain . . . that's what I'm always interested in exploring . . . this private experience of life" (Yvonne Villarreal, "Amy Adams, Director Jean-Marc Vallée Discuss Gillian Flynn HBO Adaptation," *Chicago Tribune*, 1 July 2018). Gillian Flynn proposed that one of the attractions of the role for a female star like Adams was the opportunity to play an antihero, a role usually reserved for men (Bhattachirji). Camille is not only an antihero but a complicated one placed in a narrative that director Jean-Marc Vallée described as "character-driven stuff" (Villarreal). Flynn said she wrote the book as a character study disguised as a murder mystery (Rose 65). Adams particularly liked that the series tried to "defy expectations" (Adams quoted in Bhattachirji). Adams recruited Vallée to direct after working with him on a Janice Joplin biopic that was canceled. She said she enjoyed "the way Jean-Marc works . . . you just stop telling a story and start living the story" (Adams quoted in Villarreal).

Adams threw herself into the role, gaining weight, setting her voice a tone lower, and undergoing hours of prosthetic work every day to have scars put on her body (Villarreal, Rose 66). Once again, she said she found it difficult to separate herself from her character as well as from the series's message about the psychological violence women can inflict on one another within the dynamics of the family (Allison de Souza, "Actress Amy Adams on Courage to Turn Down Parts," *The Times*, 5 July 2018). As Flynn described Adams's performance, Adams "completely immersed herself physically, bodily, mentally into Camille" (Reggie Ugwu, "The Amy Adams Method," *New York Times*, 29 June 2018, quoting Flynn). While the series was considered a success, when asked if there would be a second season, HBO president Casey Bloys said Adams had such "a hard time" with the role that he didn't think she would want to repeat it (Zack Sharf, "*Sharp Objects* Season 2 Unlikely, Says HBO Boss: 'Feels Like One Was the Right Thing,'" *Indiewire*, 15 August 2019, quoting Bloys). Watching the series, one can imagine that the experience of portraying a woman so consumed by her inner demons would be a harrowing experience, especially for an actress like Adams who prides herself in going so deeply into character.

Like Adams, and in the same year, Stone turned to television to take on a challenging role in the absurdist dramedy *Maniac* (2018). In the ten-episode Netflix limited series based on a Norwegian television program, Stone plays multiple roles. Her character experiences drug-induced fantasies in which she takes on totally different personas ranging from a housewife to a femme fatale and even a warrior elf. Stone was again attracted by the difficulty of the role. She said, "I love that kind of technical challenge of playing all of those different people and moving in and out of these different realities and trying to find what's real and grounded within it" (Stone quoted in Liz Shannon Miller, "'Maniac': Emma Stone Loved Not Being a Love Interest in Cary Fukunaga's Surreal Netflix Series," *Indiewire*, 24 September 2018). She also found the role interesting because she got to portray a female character whose "story would be her own story and she wouldn't be a foil for the male character" (Stone quoted in Miller). She apparently agreed to take the role based on director Cary Fukunaga's verbal pitch even before there was a script. She not only agreed to star but also recommended Jonah Hill, with whom she had worked in *Superbad*, to play the male lead. It was another attraction of the series that although their relationship is the central plot point, it never develops into a romance. They are emotionally troubled people who enter an experimental treatment program that includes the consumption of drugs that cause them to hallucinate. Although they sometimes become romantically involved in their hallucinations, Stone said she liked that the series tried to "subvert expectations" by making the central story about platonic friendship, not love (Stone quoted in Miller).

The turn to television by both actresses seems to have been the result of a desire to find, as Stone has said, "a really great opportunity to dig into a character in a way you don't get in movies" (Stone quoted in Bill Gordykoontz, "Emma Stone Talks Sequels, Reputation, 'Spiderman II,'" *Times Herald* [Portland, Michigan], 8 May 2014). Neither actress remained in television, however. Both returned to film with roles that took them yet again in challenging new directions. Adams returned to a supporting role as Lynn Cheney in *Vice* (2018), a political biopic of Dick Cheney. In many ways, this was hardly a departure for Adams. She was again part of a male-dominated ensemble cast with director Adam McKay and stars Christian Bale and Steve Carell. Not only had she worked with these men before, but she played a part similar to her role in *The Master*, a Lady Macbeth figure standing behind a powerful man. This was a biographical portrait of a famous living person, however, and Adams felt an obligation to do Cheney justice and not judge her, even though she said she disagreed with Cheney's politics. As always, Adams wanted to "get into" her character, and she did so by associating Cheney with the "pioneer spirit" she had seen in her own grandmother (quoted in Neumaier).

Similarly, in the same year as *Maniac*, Stone took a role in *The Favourite* (2018) directed by Yorgos Lanthimos, the Greek director known for the outlandishness and nastiness of his unorthodox films like *The Lobster* (2015) and *Dogtooth* (2009). *The Favourite* is a dark, antimonarchical period comedy in the tradition of *The Madness of King George* (1994). It chronicles the reign of the obscure eighteenth-century British Queen Anne (Olivia Coleman) and her feuding female court favorites, Lady Sarah Churchill (Rachel Weisz) and Abigail Hill (Stone). Stone was attracted to the role by three things: First, she liked that the film centered on an ensemble cast of female characters. Second, she saw her character as someone who wasn't a clear-cut villain or hero but could be "viewed through several prisms" (Stone quoted in David Crow, "Emma Stone on the Dark Love and War of *The Favourite*," *Den of Geek* [London], 24 February 2019). Finally, as she has done with so many of her other film roles, she approached the film as a challenge. She had to work with a dialect coach to perfect her accent, overcome the physical demands of the role which included wearing a corset and heavy, oversized costumes, horseback riding, clay pigeon shooting, and being pushed out of carriages and into muddy ditches. Lanthimos also had an elaborate, extended rehearsal regimen that involved game playing, "finger-snapping, making funny noises, and holding hands as they weaved a human pretzel," all to help the actors know the script by reciting it as words "without any intention behind them" (Anne Thompson, "'The Favourite' Could Win Big at the Oscars Because Its Actors Lost Their Inhibitions," *Indiewire*, 26 November 2018, quoting Lanthimos). As the only American cast in a major role, Stone had to work hard to develop a British accent that meshed with those of her fellow actors. Her co-star Olivia Coleman described Stone's accent as flawless, and not from "flowery florid period drama but normal swearing and speech" (Thompson, quoting Coleman).

Stone confessed that she and her co-stars were completely unaware of Queen Anne when they began the film, which Stone saw as a bit of a history lesson, a view both she and Weisz maintained repeatedly in interviews but with which numerous critics have taken exception. Reviewers pointed out that the lesbian sexual triangle the film concocts is largely based on rumors and ribald ballads circulated during Anne's reign. These rumors were a product of the ongoing political struggle between the Whigs and Tories as well as suspicions about Queen Anne's close friendship with Lady Sarah Churchill and Churchill's power over the emotionally unstable queen. Although Stone commented in interviews that she was surprised how historically accurate the film was, it actually isn't very accurate at all. Not only is the sexual nature of the relationships between the queen and her two female favorites questionable, but Abigail never poisoned Lady Sarah, the queen did not keep rabbits as substitutes for her multiple failed pregnancies, and she had a husband who is never even mentioned in the film (Nate James, "Everything You Need to Know about the 18_{th} Century World of *The Favourite*," *New York Vulture*, 27 November 2018).

This sketch of the trajectory of Adams's and Stone's careers provides ample evidence of their rejection of the role of the glamour actress. They may at first glance seem quite different, with Stone remaining largely a comedy actress and Adams moving from early comedy roles into heavier dramatic turns. Stone's breakthrough to stardom also came in her early twenties, whereas Adams didn't find real success until her thirties. They both, however, came to Hollywood without formal training and have said they learned their craft from working with other actors. Both began in teen films, Adams as a wide-eyed innocent and Stone as a smart-talking tough girl, but their early careers were primarily based on their ability to convey a sense of likability and inner warmth. Both initially found their niche in comedy, but refused to be typed there, with Adams moving into serious dramatic films and Stone tackling technically challenging roles.

Neither actress comfortably identifies as glamorous, although they both have been recognized for their beauty. They also refuse to publicize their personal lives, and no scandals are attached to them. Adams has been married to artist Darren Le Gallo since 2001, and they have one young daughter. She has described her everyday life as "very boring. I do the same thing all the time. I hike, I exercise, I go to the grocery store, and I work, a lot, and I take my kid to school" (Adams quoted in Hoby). Stone was involved for several years with Andrew Garfield, her co-star in the *Spider-Man* films, but she refused to talk in interviews about their relationship, and when they broke up, internet celebrity gossip columnists weren't even sure that they had.

As this essay has shown, both actresses' careers developed in stages, and they have aimed at range rather than creating consistent personae. Adams has moved from portraying innocents to layered performances that penetrate deeply into characters who vary widely: from a tough, working-class bartender in *The Fighter*; Lady Macbeth figures in *The Master* and *Vice*; an intelligent, determined professional woman in *Arrival*; a sexy, scheming con artist in *American Hustle*; to an emotionally damaged reporter in *Sharp Objects*. Her determination to go deeply into her characters has even led some to see her as a Method actress (see Ugwu, for example). Stone's range does not seem to be quite as wide as she has largely stayed within the genre of comedy, but within that genre she has gravitated to challenging roles that mix comedy with drama and are technically complex, as in *Birdman, La La Land, Maniac,* and *The Favourite*. Both have continued to build their careers on their acting rather than their looks in the decade of the 2010s. Their comments on acting demonstrate clearly that they have prioritized developing their craft over establishing a glamorous image. Both talk about their determination to find challenging roles, penetrate deeply into character, work with noted directors, and learn from performing with other actors, often in ensemble casts. Adams has sought out film roles with such notable directors as John Patrick Shanley, David O. Russell (twice), Paul Thomas Anderson, Tim Burton, and Denis Villeneuve. Stone has worked with Woody Allen, Alejandro Iñárritu, Damien Chazelle, and Yorgos Lanthimos, all directors known for their innovative approaches.

The hallmark of both of their acting styles is not glamour. In fact, both have discussed how uncomfortable they are with celebrity. If there is a dominant characteristic of their work, it is range. Although both began as comedic actresses and Stone says she doesn't see herself leaving comic roles behind, she has ventured far from the teen pics of her early career. Adams decisively left comedy for dark, introspective, dramatic roles, but she still signed up to return for the sequel to her early comedic success *Enchanted*. Both actresses are shapeshifters in the mold of Meryl Streep, with whom Adams worked in *Doubt* and *Julie and Julia* (2009) and from whom she seems to have learned much about acting. Like Streep, Adams and Stone are very character-centered actresses who say their selection of roles always involves a connection to the characters they will play. Adams said she felt an affinity with her early roles as innocents because "there was a lot of room for discovery in the characters" (Adams quoted in Bentley). Stone, too, proposes that in order to play a character she must "identify so completely with her" (Stone quoted in Philip Galanes, "Eddie Redmayne and Emma Stone on Acting, Fame, and Protecting Their Privacy," *New York Times*, 24 January 2015).

Adams has talked much more about her process than Stone. She says that she looks for scripts in which the character she plays is not just "a tool of the story" but is fully developed ("*Times* Talks"). Since her early days in Hollywood, she has worked with acting coach Warner Loughlin, who advocates a technique whereby the actor creates a backstory for the character extending all the way back to the age of three to understand what drives her psychologically. Adams says her process involves using this backstory to build her character before shooting so she is free to be reactive on the set (Nell Scovell, "The Adams Chronicle," *Vanity Fair* 56, no. 1, January 2014, 53). She also explains that she bases her characters on people she knows, which helps her understand even those like Lynn Cheney, with whom she disagrees about politics ("*Times* Talks"). This process creates problems for her in disconnecting from characters when she goes home after shooting for the day is completed. When she had her daughter, she realized she couldn't bring her characters home, so she had to learn to come out of character and not use her own emotions to develop a role. Instead, she learned to separate herself by building the character's "existential and emotional biography" (Adams quoted in Ugwu).

Stone, however, seems to be a less disciplined actress. She describes her approach as using "substitutes" and "imagination" to "completely identify with" a character and "tell the truth about who that person is and what they are feeling" ("Emma Stone: Personal Quotes," IMdB). She doesn't talk about having the control that Adams does; instead, she portrays acting as a liberating experience: "Once you lock into a role or improvise, it's like flying . . . acting threw me into situations where you just have to go with it" (Stone quoted in Galanes). She describes acting as therapeutic, helping her get over anxiety attacks (Stone quoted in Waterman). Andrew Garfield said he was bored when doing auditions for *The Amazing Spider-Man*, "and then she [Stone] came in, and it was wild and exciting. I couldn't help but try to stay with her, keep pace with her and not let her get away (laughs). Like an animal preying on a smaller animal, but a wily smaller animal" (Waterman, quoting Garfield). Stone also constantly hunts for challenging roles. She has chosen to work with innovative directors who push her to stretch her abilities to meet technical challenges. She has also repeatedly sought out technically challenging projects because they "allow you to be free with the structure" (Stone quoted in Thompson). She says, "I'm interested in things that are really scary and ambitious lately. Obviously, *Birdman* was like that. And then doing the play [*Cabaret*], I was like, 'This feels like it could go wrong every single day.' And something about that feels vital" (Stone quoted in Eells).

Both Adams and Stone have received a remarkable number of award nominations for their work. Adams has been nominated for six Academy

Awards, nine Golden Globes (winning two), seven BAFTAs, and nine SAG awards. Stone has been nominated for three Oscars (winning one), five Golden Globes (winning one), four BAFTAs (winning one), and five SAGs. It seems clear that these stars are not glamour actresses but dedicated professionals who shaped their careers to hone their skills and pursue challenging, demanding roles that require technical mastery.

Chapter 3

Oscar Isaac

Brooding by Degrees

RICK WARNER

Oscar Isaac

As one of the most protean actors of the 2010s, Oscar Isaac (born Óscar Isaac Hernández Estrada in Guatemala City) rose to cinematic stardom in both independent and mainstream productions. He appeared in nearly thirty feature films that ranged widely from small, low-budget eccentricities to tentpole blockbusters. Distinguishing himself in both starring and supporting roles, he collaborated with many other standouts of the 2010s, including Viggo Mortenson, Jessica Chastain, Ryan Gosling, Natalie Portman, Alicia Vikander, Jennifer Lawrence, Willem Dafoe, Charlize Theron, Laura Dern, John Boyega, and Adam Driver. Critics have made much of Isaac's adaptability where race and ethnicity are concerned. In addition to Latino characters who match his actual ancestry, which also includes Jewish and French origins, he has played characters of Egyptian, Indonesian, Armenian, Greek, Welsh, East Timorese, English, Polish, and vaguely European heritage. Isaac's mutable qualities factor into my discussion, but I want to focus on his dexterity at the level of mood. He has skillfully embodied several different affective dispositions—sensitive, flippant, romantically charming, hyperintelligent, neurotic, cynical, sinister, and menacingly violent—but his most accomplished work manifests a gift for brooding and melancholic tones with fine gradations. In the films that most crucially ushered him into stardom—*Inside Llewyn Davis* (2013), *A Most Violent Year* (2014), and *Ex Machina* (2014)—his performances display a forceful command of mood and atmosphere that is not simply the result of technical devices grafted onto his body and voice. I aim to show that Isaac's screen presence is itself a conductor of atmospheric intensities that pervade and carry some of the films in which he stars. He finds ways to mesh his ruminative acting with particular film styles, while remaining a primary creative agent, and his leading-man appeal follows from this resourcefulness.

☆☆☆☆☆☆☆☆★★ From Expendability to Stardom

While a student at Miami Dade College, Isaac's talent as a performer initially surfaced in music and theater. Between local stage roles, he played guitar and sang lead for a ska/punk band that, at its zenith, opened for Green Day and The Mighty Mighty Bosstones. He soon focused on acting and enrolled in New York's esteemed Juilliard School in 2001. It was there that he honed the subtleties of his multidimensional craft. "They taught me how to sing," how to abandon the bad vocal "habits from my band days," he told *Broadway World*. "Also, verse and Shakespeare, and working on Chekhov, relaxation techniques, the voice and articulation—the words you hit. I use that for everything: how you say a phrase, what words you emphasize, what words you don't. . . . All these technical things that help paint a picture for the audience" (11 February 2006).

In his early minor film roles, Isaac makes the most of the few lines he is given, supplying emotional complexity not just verbally but also through his attractive face and piercing stare. In Steven Soderbergh's *Che: Part One* (2008), where he plays Che Guevara's (Benicio del Toro) interpreter at the United Nations in black-and-white images shot in a cinema verité manner, Isaac momentarily steals the scene. The close-up of his character absorbedly translating Che's rhetoric into English has such a magnetic pull that Soderbergh, for the good of the biopic, never lingers on his face again. We find an underused Isaac in *Drive* (2011), even as he indelibly hits notes of ferocity and desperation opposite Ryan Gosling and Carey Mulligan. *The Bourne Legacy* (2012) casts him as a nameless operative who dies quickly for the purpose of setting up a plot starring Jeremy Renner. But with impressive economy, including his signature up-from-under look of guardedness, he moves the viewer to speculate about a tragic history that may have landed him in his state of solitude. In essence, he provides the film's emotional equivalent to Clive Owen's "look what they make you give" line in *The Bourne Identity* (2002).

Across Isaac's early performances, it is primarily his dark, heavy-lidded eyes that betray unused potential. Especially in supporting turns, his eyes are instruments that outstrip the cursory dialogue he is given. As he ascended to franchise-level stardom later in the decade, he still relied on eye work for punctuation. He is never idle as Resistance pilot Poe Dameron in the *Star Wars* sequels *The Force Awakens* (2015), *The Last Jedi* (2017), and *The Rise of Skywalker* (2019). Whether brashly asserting himself, pondering his faults, or sensing the gravity of the moment, his gaze and brow operate at high voltage. Even in his role as a revived ancient Egyptian mutant in *X-Men: Apocalypse* (2016), which almost comically conceals and immobilizes him beneath latex and computer-generated cosmetics, his eyes and voice send forth a compelling, melancholic intensity that refuses to be suppressed.

Coinciding with his climb up the Hollywood ladder, Isaac, on the strength of his alluring physicality, has endeared himself to millions of admirers on the internet and social media. "Have you heard the news?" asks Sulagna Misra of *The Cut*, an offshoot of *New York* magazine. "We're all in love with Oscar Isaac now. He's filling up your Tumblr dash, blanketing your Twitter feed, and featuring in your daydreams. He is the internet's new boyfriend" ("How the Internet Picks Its Boyfriends," *The Cut*, 6 January 2016). There are, indeed, countless GIFs and memes devoted to Isaac that make their rounds from computers to smartphone screens. Add to this the viral videos of him enchanting fellow cast members, both male and female, while promoting the recent *Star Wars* sequels. From the standpoint of fandom, Isaac's celebrity in this stage of his career entails the offscreen persona of an omnisexual charmer. His star image circulates in fan-based economies of desire that delight in the possibility of his queerness. In a heavily retweeted interview clip with *Entertainment Weekly,* Isaac is asked whether he approves of how fans have "shipped" (a slang term for the longing for a romantic relationship between characters) his Poe Dameron with ex-stormtrooper Finn (John Boyega). He earnestly replies: "Oh, I'm cool with it, baby." At the same time, Isaac maintains a low profile on social media, lacking as he does personal Twitter, Facebook, and Instagram accounts (although one can catch glimpses of his unglamorous daily life away from acting on the Instagram channel of his wife and longtime partner, the Danish filmmaker Elvira Lind, with whom he has fathered two children). In a twenty-first-century media environment in which film stardom and celebrity have become interchangeable, Isaac holds his public image partially in reserve. As with his performances in his best films, he almost teasingly offers flashes of charisma while preferring a more subdued, if not altogether hushed, identity.

In the three ventures that cemented his status as a leading man—*Inside Llewyn Davis, A Most Violent Year,* and *Ex Machina*—Isaac is granted enough time and space to use his gifts in quieter registers of expression, and with greater range. While all three of these films are rigorously stylized by their directors, we will see that Isaac's presence wields an atmospheric power that is primary. Studying his star performances in these films requires us to focus not just on a voice or body captured in the frame but also on a conduction of mood that circles between his expressive figure and the milieux he inhabits.

Inside and Outside Llewyn Davis

Isaac's role as a Welsh Italian folk musician in Joel and Ethan Coen's *Inside Llewyn Davis* remains his most extraordinary work to date. The film takes place in Greenwich Village in 1961, on the eve of Bob Dylan's transformation of the folk revival. Isaac's titular character is loosely based on folk singers Dave Van Ronk and Ramblin' Jack Elliott, yet Llewyn is fated to fall well short of their accomplishments. The plot evokes *The Odyssey*—a motif initiated by a runaway cat called Ulysses—but Llewyn's nomadic journey is a nightmarish loop of failures leading him right back to where he began. Icy mise-en-scène and cinematography suggest a perpetual winter as Llewyn gracelessly deals with a host of personal conflicts and tragedies, still mourning the suicide of his friend and musical partner. The Coens fastidiously recreate the historical period, but the main purpose of the images—pallid and softly radiant, with figures and objects often marked by heavy shadows—is to put across a deathly and dreamlike atmosphere in tune with Llewyn's experience.

Isaac's melancholic work in the film sustains a complex interplay between character and environment. He isn't simply placed within settings that metaphorically comment on Llewyn's psychological state; rather, his performance conspires with a cinematic mediation of affective tones that suffuse the entire world on-screen and defy borders between exterior reality and inner life, between objective and subjective registers of expression. In other words, his acting partakes of the aesthetics of *Stimmung*, a concept best translated from German into English as "mood" or "attunement." *Stimmung* involves not just the creative constitution of a world on the basis of a governing mood that permeates each element of form and content, it also refers to the process whereby this affective atmosphere extends to and envelops the spectator, who may then become attuned accordingly to the film's world (Sinnerbrink 148–153). Various resources may conjure this feeling: camera style, editing, lighting, mise-en-scène, or sound. Offering a theory of cinematic *Stimmung* from a phenomenological perspective, Robert Sinnerbrink rightly views performance as a key component (152–163). In our example, Isaac's expressivity as Llewyn is the film's most pivotal source and conduit for the transmission of mood. As Inga Pollmann observes in her meticulous account of *Stimmung* as the cinematic mediation of life, the term's sense of attunement is closely linked to music and its potentially harmonic resonances between self and world, as well as between artwork and audience (168–171). *Inside Llewyn Davis* revolves around Isaac's musical talent: his mastery of Travis-style guitar picking and his total credibility as a musician. His performances were filmed live instead of prerecorded, resulting in a spontaneous, unbroken quality that few actors could match. Thematically, the film hinges on Llewyn's longing for connection, which goes beyond his singing and playing. Llewyn is himself a vibratory instrument who seeks the shared emotional attunement of others. He isn't just trying to succeed professionally as a solo act. His unspoken quest in the wake of his partner's death is to rediscover affective kinship, an ambition that collides with both bad luck and self-sabotage.

This despairing quest plays out through a contrast between Llewyn's manner of musical performance and that of his folk contemporaries in the plot. The film opens with Llewyn onstage in the middle of a gig at the

Gaslight, singing a ballad: "Hang me, oh hang me / I'll be dead and gone." He doesn't play to the crowd but turns inward, absorbed instead of theatrical, his eyes clenched shut, his face half-hidden by shadows. Those in attendance at the club respond with pensive nods and stares, relating to his sullen tune almost privately, as individuals. Conversely, when the sprightlier folk singers—Troy Nelson (Stark Sands), Jim Berkey (Justin Timberlake), and Jean Berkey (Carey Mulligan)—entertain at the Gaslight, they stir the crowd to sing in unison, instilling a rush of collective spirit. Llewyn, who is both derisive and envious of this power, has no such gift. This contrast between Llewyn and his fellow musicians has as its complement a running tension between how Isaac's performance dynamically attunes the film's spectator and how Llewyn fails to achieve and uphold an equivalent within the film's diegesis. Isaac's performance mediates a gripping melancholy between the inside and outside of his character, and between the screen and its audience. But the fiction repeatedly stages reduced, or failed, versions of such communication.

Llewyn's inability to connect materializes across a series of tragicomic interactions: with the intellectual Gorfeins and their dinner guests; with a grotesque jazzman (John Goodman) and his poet chauffeur (Garret Hedlund); with legendary music producer Bud Grossman (F. Murray Abraham); and, finally, with his dementia-afflicted father. These latter two encounters—both of which showcase Isaac's dexterity with the Coens' blend of tones—unfold as meditations on the ambiguities of emotional correspondence between performer and audience. These scenes align us with Llewyn in that we, much like our protagonist, struggle to decipher signs of empathy in his listener's uncertain or impervious body language. When auditioning for Grossman in an empty club, Llewyn performs "The Death of Queen Jane," a ballad that is neither the best in his repertoire nor the most advantageous for the occasion. Yet choosing a song about a woman who dies in childbirth semiconsciously riffs on multiple deaths and absences that mark Llewyn's life. It evokes his dead musical partner, of course, but also his dead mother, his nearly dead father, his child who lives in Ohio and has never met him, and the unborn child that he and Jean have decided not to have. This song choice, then, reminds us that the stakes of the moment are more than just professional. The scene cuts back and forth between Llewyn playing and Bud Grossman intently listening, as the camera's gradual push-ins on either side of the shot–reverse shot alternations imply that the song perhaps affects Grossman more than he lets on. There is also a Kuleshov effect by which we project affective qualities onto his stony face. But Grossman isn't altogether deadpan. Although he rejects Llewyn, he does so purely on monetary

Llewyn Davis (Oscar Isaac) auditions for Bud Grossman, grippingly but self-defeatingly performing "The Death of Queen Jane." *Inside Llewyn Davis* (Joel and Ethan Coen, Studio Canal, 2013). Digital frame enlargement.

grounds, with subtle notes of approval in his bearing. He advises Llewyn to give up becoming a front man and to "stay out of the sun," suggesting that his ethnic appearance isn't white enough for the commercial folk revival, as opposed to Troy, who "*connects* with people." But Isaac's nuanced interplay with Abraham hints at connectedness of a profounder register. Their acting betrays their characters' mutual, if temporary, attunement through music—a feeling that we experience more acutely as viewers.

Even when silent, Isaac conveys woundedness and regret in understated ways that mesh with the film's overall mood and cut against the unsavory tendencies of his character. He reported to *Rolling Stone* that he took inspiration from Buster Keaton when preparing for the role of Llewyn, namely the comedian's steely, unsmiling resolve in the face of absurd hardship (12 December 2013). Llewyn, however, less easily secures our sympathy and allegiance. He is closer in character to Bobby Dupea (Jack Nicholson), an antiheroic concert pianist turned oil rigger in *Five Easy Pieces* (1970). The two films share several tropes beyond an emphasis on music: disabled fathers; road trip segments; mismanaged romantic relationships resulting in pregnancy; and, most relevant of all, their arrogant, outwardly hard-to-love protagonists. Both films launch their lead actors into stardom through a tension between charismatic, multilayered performance and unattractive characterization. Bobby has already failed to make it, and Llewyn is fated to follow suit. Yet Isaac's face and eyes have a fragility to them, and a capacity for self-critique, not just self-hatred, that Nicholson lacks. Isaac's close-ups are instruments of *Stimmung* that allow for the "mutual permeation of person and milieu, the empathic relation of subject and object," while also drawing the viewer into a state of intimate identification (Steimatsky 33). One of the film's most moving scenes occurs when Llewyn, driving a borrowed car overnight back to New York after the Grossman audition in Chicago, passes the interstate exit for Akron, Ohio. At this point, he has learned that a past lover carried to term without his knowledge and moved to Akron with their child. Wordless close-ups display Llewyn's mixed response as he gazes at the city lights, appears to consider taking the exit, but continues along his path. Ever so gently, his eyes transition from wonder and curiosity to the recognition of suffering he caused, of mistakes that are likely beyond repair. We deduce from his expression the thought that he will never know his child and will never know the joys of putting down roots, which his artistic ethos regards as self-betrayal. His insinuated regret includes the acknowledgment that he has repeated his carelessness once again in his relationship with Jean.

His juggling of sentiments is accented by the nocturnal atmosphere, the hum of the car, the hissing wind. His mental turnings are fluidly caught up with the mise-en-scène, his face at once projective and absorbent. Isaac's performance is part of a mediation of melancholy into which we are also drawn. The scene conveys this dynamic by cutting to a reverse shot of the empty road from Llewyn's viewpoint, pulling us into a nearly abstract vector of unpromising motion and inhospitable sound. Isaac's acting isn't an object to study at a distance so much as a vehicle for our intimacy at the level of mood. This, indeed, is how Llewyn connects with people, over and against his serial failings in the fiction.

★★★★★★★★★★ Under Pressure

Isaac's performance for the Coens earned him a Golden Globe nomination and the National Society of Film Critics' Best Actor award. The next year, with J. C. Chandor's *A Most Violent Year* (2014), he received equal praise and won Best Actor at the National Board of Review awards, tying with Michael Keaton for *Birdman* (2014). Another period film, this time a New York gangster drama set in the winter of 1981, *A Most Violent Year* further attests to Isaac's virtuosity in the domain of austere rumination. His look and manner, however, are strikingly different. Clean-shaven and arrayed in dapper suits, his portrayal of Abel Morales, a budding entrepreneur of a heating-oil company in the midst of a crisis, is a study of poise, calculation, and ethical ambiguity that channels Al Pacino as Michael Corleone.

Javier Bardem was originally slated to play Abel, with Jessica Chastain affixed as Abel's wife, Anna. When the Spanish star withdrew over creative differences, Chastain, who had been a classmate of Isaac's at Juilliard, pushed for Isaac to be cast as the lead. And when Isaac came on board, he devised, in collaboration with Chandor, a fuller backstory for Abel, one that loosely related to Isaac's own Latin American background. As Charles Ramírez Berg reports, Isaac contributed "a vital piece of character-building, that Abel and his family" immigrated to the United States "from Colombia, fleeing the ferocious civil war called 'La Violencia' during the 1950s" (266). For Ramírez Berg, this detail, although it receives no direct mention in the finished film, is essential in that it furnishes Isaac's performance as Abel with a propensity to shun violence and maintain a calm, rational attitude in the face of extreme adversity. The plot finds Abel under immense pressure. He has just contracted to purchase a strip of land with oil silos facing Manhattan, a property that will secure his industrial and political power, but as he tries to close on the deal (which offers no refund on his deposit), one or more of his competitors hijack his oil trucks and threaten his workers as well as his family. Abel also becomes the target of an investigation by the district attorney for corrupt business practices from fraud to income tax evasion. The film hinges on Abel's painful struggle to preserve his code of nonviolence even as he finds himself in a climate where aggression and criminality are unavoidable.

Ramírez Berg points out that Isaac's role as Abel substantially revises the stereotypical ways in which Latinos have appeared in the history of the gangster film. As opposed to "the vicious and impulsive Latino male" epitomized by Tony Montana (Al Pacino) in *Scarface* (1983), Isaac portrays Abel as a "thoughtful and self-regulated businessman struggling for success," "as an ambitious but non-violent non-gangster, as an anti-*bandido*, and as the Latino Everyman" (272). That Isaac brings multilayered refinements to his character is undeniable. The film indeed deserves accolades for its ethnic representation, as Hollywood still rarely grants Latinos starring roles. A recent study found that between 2008 and 2018, only 3 percent of the top 100 highest-grossing films in the United States featured Latinos as leads (USC Annenberg Inclusion Initiative, "Latinos in Film: Erasure on Screen and behind the Camera across 1,200 Popular Movies," August 2019). That said, Ramírez Berg's account of the film overlooks important aspects of Abel's characterization as a flawed individual. While Abel wants to steer clear of criminal activity, and revels in declaring his uprightness to others, the film makes the audience aware that his heating-oil enterprise is not entirely legitimate, that Abel knows this to a degree, and that Anna and their attorney (Albert Brooks) allow him to sanctimoniously deceive himself while they engage in unlawful operations to keep the company afloat. As Anna observes in more than one of their arguments, Abel's need to present himself as honorable comes with a high capacity for self-delusion. To argue that Abel is an honest, coolheaded businessman who heroically avoids becoming a gangster is to neglect some of the most interesting ethical complications that texture the film as he is pushed to his limits.

Through an interplay of proximity and distance relative to Isaac's onscreen figure, the film explores this running tension between Abel's code and the perilous situation in which he finds himself. The film opens with rhythmic sounds of breathing as the camera tracks forward along a snowy neighborhood street. Subsequent shots reveal this first shot to have been from Abel's vantage while jogging and listening to Marvin Gaye's "Inner City Blues," a song that shifts from the tinny sound quality of Walkman headphones into fuller, nondiegetic musical accompaniment. Through both optical and aural focalization, the film thus immediately aligns the viewer with Abel, but over the next several scenes, he appears for the most part in medium-long, long, and extreme long shots, in spacious yet stark compositions that play up the physical surroundings in relation to his figure. The cinematography by Bradford Young features Abel in cold exteriors streaked with golden tones from the sun that resonate chromatically with rusted industrial facilities, yellow-orange leaves in the trees, Anna's blonde hair, and Abel's pristine camel hair coat, which he wears (self-deludingly) as a kind of shield against the gritty milieu of corruption in which he must maneuver. Across these shots, a number of which decenter Abel in the frame, the camera pushes in almost imperceptibly to suggest the encroachment of pressures around him. Abel's green-and-orange company trucks constantly move through the background, underscoring the high stakes that bear on his strained negotiations with Anna, their attorney, the company drivers, the union delegate, bank loan officers, professional rivals, and the district attorney.

A lesser actor might struggle to stand out within such a formal system and to make this gangster drama as riveting as it is despite its shortage of physical violence. But even when Abel is graphically overwhelmed by his environment, Isaac's performance exudes a brooding force that inflects each composition in which he appears, no matter how small or distant his body. In extreme long shots where Abel interacts with others, Isaac's elegant bearing, together with the reverberance of his voice as it violates sound

At his newly acquired oil terminal, Abel Morales (Oscar Isaac) stares down his fugitive truck driver with a mix of sorrow and icy contempt in *A Most Violent Year* (J. C. Chandor, FilmNation Entertainment, 2014). Digital frame enlargement.

perspective and thus registers more loudly than it should, powerfully orchestrates a feeling of tension amid the escalation of external problems that ought to be a cause for panic.

Through the film's middle and late stretches, Abel more often inhabits tighter framings that put his facial expressions on vivid display—albeit with shadowed eyes in the style of *The Godfather*. He tends to tilt his head forward and stare intensely at his interlocutor, his brow furrowed and his hair brushed up into a flawless pompadour. Performance emerges as a theme within the diegesis itself. Abel calculatingly uses his affected persona to persuade, impress, and command others. In one of the film's most gripping scenes, Abel offers new salespersons a master class on how to manipulate and assure a customer in subtle psychological ways when making a house call. Ramírez Berg observes how Abel delivers an "acting lesson" that passes down to his employees his own pose of superiority relative to the competition (267–268). Abel here models an authoritative yet seductive manner that calls to mind the actorly grace of Raul Julia, one of Isaac's childhood idols, as he has noted in many interviews. As though on a stage, Abel carefully demonstrates the craft that, we gather, he cultivated while himself a salesman working his way up to management. He instructs them to rely on dramatic pauses marked by prolonged stares with eye contact. In modeling this technique for the trainees, Abel is such an efferent force onscreen that everything else in the scene—the behavior of the other characters, the sense of mood, the logic and rhythm of the editing—orbits around him, taking cues from his orchestration. Isaac's performance as Abel dictates the grammar of the film, rather than the other way around. In a later scene,

Abel uses this laconic stare-down method when he meets with his competitors at a restaurant, exposes their dishonesty, and orders them to stop stealing from him: "Have some *pride* in what you do, and stop." Here, too, everything in the scene's makeup is commanded by the pace and affective authority of Isaac's performance choices. At the same time, the film's reflexive treatment of Abel's acting invites us to consider the degree to which he has worked his charms on us.

Abel ultimately prevails, securing his industrial and political foothold with the purchase of land, but this triumph only comes about as his code of legitimacy is revealed as false to both the viewer and himself. He only makes good on the contract because Anna has been embezzling from their company for years. Moreover, Abel only escapes his legal snares because he agrees to hand over to the police a fugitive Latino truck driver who armed himself when Abel knowingly put him in a life-threatening position. In the final scenes of the film, Isaac's performance walks a fine balance between the guilt Abel feels toward the driver (who is a kind of double for Abel, as a version of his younger self) and Abel's desperation to succeed professionally at all costs. After a botched handover to the authorities, the gun-wielding driver confronts Abel, Anna, and their attorney at the property they have bought. He turns the weapon on himself, an act that Abel nonverbally sanctions. Blood splatters on a silo and mixes with the black oil that pours from a bullet hole. Calmly, Abel walks past the driver's body and attends to the leaking oil, stopping it with a handkerchief. In these last moments of the film—which drive home anticapitalist sentiment—Isaac chillingly embodies the onset of amorality in Abel despite his pretense of honor and nonviolence. At the film's end, Abel meets with the district attorney, who now genuflects to him and insinuates a future of shared corruption. In spite of the realities Abel has had to learn about himself and his business, he boasts, in medium close-up, with head again tilted and brow creased: "You should know that I have always taken the path that is most right. The result is never in question for me. Just what path do you take to get there. And there is always one that is most right. And that is what this is." These words trigger a cut to a wide shot that stresses the environment, as Abel's trucks now dominate the scene visually and sonically. The disarming calm of Isaac's delivery takes on a tragic tone, as we have come to see his character's performance as a self-delusional form of ignoring the destructive and illicit operations to which he is bound. Isaac's Abel remains sympathetic to the end, but we are left with dismay that all his brooding hasn't led him to alter or at least acknowledge this false pose, which nourishes the very practices he believes he spurns.

☆☆☆☆☆☆☆☆☆☆ The Mad Genius

Isaac's penchant for moody rumination runs together with an expression of intellect that slips into egotism. Hints of Generation X derision in his demeanor serve him well when playing characters who are not only clever but prone to condescension and hubris (e.g., his Paul Gaugin in *At Eternity's Gate* [2018]). If Abel pontificates while neglecting his own criminal complicity, Llewyn Davis talks down to those he deems less authentic or less talented than himself. In Alex Garland's *Ex Machina*, Isaac is cast as Nathan Bateman, an exceedingly smart and narcissistic CEO of a search engine company, Blue Book. Nathan has created an AI humanoid robot named Ava (Alicia Vikander), and he recruits Caleb (Domhnall Gleeson), a young programmer who works for Blue Book, to conduct a Turing test with Ava to see whether she credibly displays human consciousness. With close-cropped hair, glasses, and full beard, Isaac appears and speaks nothing like Abel or Llewyn, but he veers more disturbingly into misanthropic arrogance.

Ex Machina finds Isaac again playing a character who performs within the diegesis. "He has to portray someone who's a very specific character in order for the experiment to go the way he wants it to go," Isaac explains in a *GQ* interview. "But he goes Method with it a little bit, and he goes so deep in that, at a certain point, where is the role he is playing, and where is he really? Because he is a nihilist. He knows that the [technological] singularity is coming, that it's going to be the end for us." Isaac also recounts that while preparing to play this hyperintelligent recluse, he listened over and over to an audio interview with Stanley Kubrick. "There was something about his voice that I really liked," he recalls. "So I started trying to play with that voice, and I used the same shape of glasses that he had" ("Oscar Isaac Breaks Down His Most Iconic Characters," *GQ*, 15 November 2018). Isaac's inclination to turn to Kubrick was rather on point, given that Garland's formalistic science fiction exercise is thoroughly Kubrick-inspired, evoking as it does *2001: A Space Odyssey* (1968): sleek surfaces, undercurrents of dread, the unsettling use of red coloration, and, of course, the theme of humanity becoming eclipsed by the technological developments it fosters. Beyond being a Kubrick-like recluse and artist figure, Nathan can be read as a grotesque male character of the type that one encounters in Kubrick's films. James Naremore has linked aspects of grotesque masculinity in Kubrick's body of work to the hypersexualization of military and scientific technology at the level of design, from the copulating jets at the start of *Dr. Strangelove or: How I Learned to Stop Worrying and Love the Bomb* (1964) to the spaceship designs in *2001*. For Naremore, this tendency, as Kubrick critically portrays it, results from sexual projections and sublimations within systems of patriarchal authority (125–126). Isaac's Nathan, as a giant of the tech world whose exploits and interests loosely resemble those of Google co-founder Larry Page, works within a male-dominated scientific and economic sphere. The more that he describes Ava to Caleb, and the more that Caleb discovers traces of Nathan's earlier experiments, the more it emerges that Nathan's research has been perversely self-serving. The previous AI prototypes and Ava herself have all been meticulously designed as slim, model-like "females" with similar physical features, except for stereotypical ethnic differences that reflect Nathan's sexual preferences. In effect, these AI beings are sex dolls under his control in a prison house, and they dream of escape.

Despite Nathan's grotesque cruelty, Isaac makes him nuanced and captivating. By contrast, Caleb heroically tries to free Ava, but Caleb is so irritatingly naive, passive-aggressive, and smug at times (all those tedious quotations!) that Isaac's Nathan remains the more absorbing figure of the two. Their running dialogues resonate uncannily with Caleb's interactions with Ava, and thus they invite the same scrutinizing attention to gesture, facial expressivity, and vocal inflection that Caleb and the film's viewer bring to the Turing tests. Not unlike the moments I have analyzed in *Inside Llewyn Davis* and *A Most Violent Year*, these scenes dramatize the study of performance. As participants at one remove from the position of Caleb, we look and wonder about the extent to which Nathan has "programmed" the whole experiment, including its dramatic shifts as Caleb becomes Ava's abettor. We watch for telling inconsistencies. When is Nathan role-playing for the sake of his test, and when is he not? Are humans—and for that matter, cinematic figures on the screen—not themselves mechanical beings with encoded characteristics? Much of the film's dread collects around these increasingly metalevel questions.

Given that the entire narrative, except for the prologue and ending, happens in and around the space of Nathan's secluded house and research facility, virtually everything we see in the mise-en-scène characterizes Nathan. Garland's ultrastylish science fiction film brings into play a Gothic, and thus a strongly atmospheric, correlation between house and inhabitant. The home's modern construction, which integrates the natural mountainside and brings to mind Frank Lloyd Wright's Fallingwater, is both stunning and eerie. The museum-like décor—Nathan seems something of a "curator" and Aby Warburg–esque art historian (Jacobsen 27)—consists of methodically placed artifacts and artworks that hold symbolic value, from African masks to a Jackson Pollock drip canvas that ties Nathan's artistic-scientific experimentation to the hypermasculinity and sexual energy associated with action painting. We learn, well before Caleb does, that the rooms of the house are under surveillance by Nathan. This practice is microcosmic of Nathan's Dr. Mabuse–like monitoring of humanity at large through Blue Book and through his ubiquitous hacking into cell phone cameras, which yields a massive database of facial expression references for Ava. In aesthetic and thematic terms, the film works harder than it needs to when emphasizing Nathan's genius. His intellect is sometimes signaled in contrived ways, from near-gratuitous nods to philosophy (Blue Book refers to a series of lectures by Ludwig Wittgenstein, which he wrote between 1933 and 1934) to the wall of a thousand sticky notes surrounding Nathan's three-screen workstation, next to which hangs Titian's *Allegory of Prudence* (c. 1550–1565), a painted composite of three male faces (past, present, and future humanity) turned in different directions, their positions echoed by three lions below. While these pieces add intertextual layers to the film, and economically distill Nathan's pomposity, they are but paraphernalia that reinforce the sense of intelligence that Isaac, with ease, already makes palpable as an actor.

In a weighty scene, Nathan expounds for Caleb the significance of Pollock's drip method. For Nathan, the technique bears out a searching, improvisational manner of creativity in and through which intuition exceeds the stifling mechanisms of deliberation. "Not deliberate, not random," he says. "Someplace in between." Relating Pollock's approach to his own creative work, Nathan asserts, "The challenge is to find an action that is *not* automatic, from painting to breathing to talking to fucking to falling in love." It is partly ironic here, at the metalevel of performance, that Isaac's gifts are nearly displaced by the drip painting, which dominates the frame, and by the script, which forces him into a bit of hectoring that borders on triteness. In this moment he is at the mercy of the film's labored show of cultural capital. The character who most takes this painting-inspired lecture to heart is Kyoko (Sonoya Mizuno), a fembot who overhears it from offscreen. Defying her programming as a mute concubine, she will set in motion Ava's getaway. But Isaac, more so than in *A Most Violent Year* or *Inside Llewyn Davis*, is hemmed in by the film's affectations. Then again, it is possible to read his tenor of performance here as part of Nathan's manipulative playacting, which, viewed in this light, fits in with the way in which he has decorated, or rather set dressed, his house.

Garland relies on Isaac's brooding less intensely in *Ex Machina* than he does in *Annihilation* (2018). Even so, in the former film, a humanizing melancholy seeps into Nathan's alcoholism and exchanges with Caleb. Isaac also cannily brings a comic touch to his character while in the midst of embodying grotesque traits. In what has become an emblematic scene (thanks to the volume of memes it has generated), Nathan performs a choreographed disco dance with Kyoko, as Caleb watches with a mix of shock and revulsion. The scene at once reduces tension and further alerts Caleb to the more disturbing elements of Nathan's research. And yet, Isaac's rhythmic movement stands out as impressive—and amusing—in its own right. If the viewer doesn't quite share Caleb's abhorrence, this is because Isaac's playfulness, charm, and skill as a dancer shine through Nathan's villainy, putting it on hold.

★★★★★★★★★★ "That Double Thing": In Defense of Versatility

By the end of the 2010s, Isaac reached a stable and balanced position within the Hollywood "talent hierarchy," as Paul McDonald calls it (19–24). He found himself divided evenly between franchise-tier renown and artistic respectability for performances in smaller, niche undertakings that allow him ample time and space. His credentials as a dramatic actor also expanded on account of his work in theater—namely his lauded turn as the melancholic Prince Hamlet in a production of Shakespeare's tragedy at the Public Theater in New York. According to David Róman, who praised Isaac's combination of "brooding masculinity" with "easily display[ed] bro-banter and male bonding," Isaac is "debatably . . . the first Latino actor to play Hamlet in a major US production. . . . Latinos are often stereotyped as unable to master the English language, so to have a Latino actor perform the most canonical text written in English makes a statement," particularly "in a climate of profound anti-immigrant sentiment" (567). These remarks also apply to Isaac's ascendance as a bankable, but still elastic, film star in a system plagued by the same limitations and pigeonholes.

In interviews, Isaac himself has expressed a nuanced attitude that recognizes the political stakes and responsibilities of representation, yet also grants the actor freedom to inhabit a variety of characters and subjectivities. He points to the example of Raul Julia, whose identity as Latino always stays intact onscreen, but who avoided being typecast. "I'm most definitely Latino. That's who I am. But at the same time . . . I want to be hired not because of what I can represent, but because of what I can create, how I can transform, and the power of what I create." What he wants to preserve, he explains, is "that double thing," the condition of being oneself while also having creative access to ways of being beyond oneself, which requires degrees of separation "between the artist and the art form, between a craftsperson and the craft" (Melissa Leon, "Oscar Isaac on the 'Pain' of Losing

Carrie Fisher and Anti-Latino Hysteria in the Age of Trump," *The Daily Beast*, 20 November 2018). So far, his choice of roles has judiciously explored this doubleness and allowance for versatility, from his Latino émigré entrepreneur in *A Most Violent Year* to his more or less deracinated tech baron in *Ex Machina*.

One expects that Isaac's acting career will continue to evolve in keeping with his ethos of flexibility. His stardom shows no signs of regression. At the time of writing, he is slated to play a crucial role in *Dune* (2021), Denis Villeneuve's much-anticipated science fiction epic. He will also star in Paul Schrader's *The Card Counter* (2021), a solemn revenge thriller that comprises a new entry in Schrader's sketches of melancholic male characters tracing back to *Taxi Driver* (1976). Extending his mainstream visibility, Isaac will star as a loner superhero with dissociative identity disorder in the Marvel miniseries *Moon Knight* (2022). In addition, he is set to appear, alongside Robert De Niro and Anne Hathaway, in James Gray's *Armageddon Time* (2022). This isn't to say that he plans to work only with eminent auteurs or star in franchise productions. He plays the lead role, a charitable corrections officer, in *The Letter Room* (2020), a low-budget short directed by Elvira Lind, his wife. Moreover, filming has wrapped on an independent dark comedy in which he stars and which he executive produced, *Big Gold Brick* (2021), from first-time director Brian Petsos. Undeterred by his experiments with smaller and riskier projects that earned him negative reviews, such as *Mojave* (2015) and *Life Itself* (2018), Isaac seems ready to continue expanding his craft between markedly different scales of production, as well as between notably different incarnations of identity.

Chapter 4

Armie Hammer

The Elusive Appeal of an Ever-Emergent Star

DAVID GREVEN

Six foot five, blond, physically and vocally imposing, the great-grandson of Occidental Petroleum's Armand Hammer, and just so damned *rich*, the actor Armie Hammer has struggled to convince audience members of his right to star status. The one time the stars aligned and Hammer garnered near universal praise for *Call Me by Your Name* (2017), he failed to get the Supporting Actor Oscar nomination he seemed all but promised. The Italian director Luca Guadagnino was a true believer before he cast him in *Call Me*. "He is a mine of gold, and I am the digger," Guadagnino declared in an interview with *Vulture*. Pressed by his interlocutor, who noted that not many filmmakers have done much digging of this mine, the director averred, "The mold of Armie is the mold of cinema, with a capital C. I do believe in that" (17 November 2017).

Has Hammer finally become a bona fide movie star with the internationally acclaimed *Call Me*? If so, the pinnacle has been reached nearly a decade after a string of films that unsuccessfully attempted to secure his stardom. As a perceptive and problematic BuzzFeed piece by Anne Helen Petersen notes polemically, *Call Me* was the culmination of "ten long years of trying to make Armie Hammer happen" (26 November 2017). Breaking out in his dual roles as Cameron and Tyler Winklevoss in David Fincher's *The Social Network* (2010), Hammer made several high-profile films in which his stardom seemed as elusive as his particular appeal. The argument of this chapter is that Hammer's appeal as a film star lies precisely in this elusiveness, an unattainability borne out in his privileged background and appearance as well as his ongoing screen persona. Qualities of blankness and humorlessness attend this persona, as Fincher made riotous use of in *The Social Network*, encouraging the audience to chortle at the "Winklevi's" humiliation. Films like the war drama *Mine* (2016) emphasize a stolidly humorless, iconic Hammer. Yet, as *Call Me* and *Sorry to Bother You* (2018)

Armie Hammer

and television interviews also demonstrate, Hammer has a comic side, the foundation of which is a penchant for laceratingly ironic self-parody. The emergence of a newly bankable (a fragile status) Hammer stages an intriguing conflict between his self-parodying and stolid modes, his ability to undermine his all-American male authenticity and ruthless determination to be its embodiment. This chapter discusses several Hammer films, from *Billy: The Early Years* (2008) to *The Social Network, J. Edgar* (2011), *The Lone Ranger* (2013), *The Man from U.N.C.L.E.* (2015), *Final Portrait* (2017), *Nocturnal Animals* (2016), and *Hotel Mumbai* (2018), building toward an analysis of

Call Me by Your Name as a critical portrait of the specific nature of Hammer's elusive appeal. (It should be noted that this chapter was written before the spate of sexual harassment claims against Hammer, dating from 2020 forward, were made public. The rape charge made against the actor is particularly alarming. As of this writing, the status of these charges and their effect on Hammer's career remains to be seen.)

☆☆☆☆☆☆☆☆☆★ The Male Uncanny: *The Social Network*'s Winklevi

Characteristic of auteur David Fincher's penchant for perversely unconventional renderings of masculinity, his movie about the creation of Facebook may very well be best known today for his inspired idea to have Cameron and Tyler Winklevoss—scions of privilege extraordinaire, identical twins, Olympic rowers, and aspirational entrepreneurs (associated post-Facebook with Bitcoin)—played by Hammer in a dual role. Of course, the genius lies not only in the decision to have Hammer play both twins but to graft Hammer's face onto the body of the actor and model Josh Pence, creating a kind of head-suturing, digital-decapitation effect. Enhancing Hammer's emergent star qualities, Fincher makes it clear that Hammer fits the first definition of Chris Holmlund's paradigm of "impossible bodies" onscreen, the "outrageous" kind (the other two being "constrained" and the "largely invisible" racial minorities) (5).[1] When the actor's performance is indistinguishable and inextricable from special effect, when one cannot watch a performance without knowing that it is impossible to know what that performance looks, sounds, and feels like without this intensive mediation, one is left wondering what the performance actually consists of, no matter how artfully presented onscreen. There have been numerous single actors who played twins in movies, ranging from classical Hollywood (*A Stolen Life* [1946] and *Dead Ringer* [1964] with Bette Davis and *The Dark Mirror* [1946] with Olivia de Havilland) to more contemporary movies (David Cronenberg's Jeremy Irons–centered *Dead Ringers* [1988], Tom Hardy playing the famously criminal Kray Brothers in 2015's *Legend*), but Fincher seized on particular possibilities and achieved an idiosyncratic effect by having Hammer not only play two different versions of himself but also subsume the presence, indeed the corporeality, of another actor. (On one of the extras for the Blu-ray edition of the film, Josh Pence looks downright abashed and wistful discussing his journey from elation at getting the part, crestfallen at the news that his head would be replaced with Hammer's, before settling on smiling resignation.) Fincher took the sentimentalizing audacity of the finale of the digitally altered rerelease of *The Return of the Jedi* and transformed it into his movie's central running joke.[2]

Even heavily mediated and therefore a phenomenon that exceeds screen performance, Hammer's dual turn contains much within it that conveys his special screen qualities, used to satisfying, witty effect here. To begin with, Hammer creates distinct personae in Cameron (more respectful and reserved, holding on to his fantasy that "we are gentlemen of Harvard") and Tyler (brasher, curter, more pugnacious). It is Tyler who utters the now legendary line of the film about the physical attributes of the twins during a heated discussion about Mark Zuckerberg's (Jesse Eisenberg) refusal to return the Winklevosses' and their business partner Divya Narendra's (Max Minghella) phone calls. Cameron, refusing to believe Zuckerberg is dishonorable, tries to keep things respectful, but Tyler and their friend do not, as Aaron Sorkin's script pinpoints:

> *Cameron:* What, do you want to hire an IP lawyer and sue him?
>
> *Divya:* No, I want to hire the Sopranos to beat the shit out of him with a hammer!
>
> *Tyler:* We don't even have to do that.
>
> *Cameron:* That's right.
>
> *Tyler:* We can do that ourselves. I'm 6′5″, 220, and there's two of me.

Indexing male narcissism and the cinema of the double as he did in *Fight Club* (1999), Fincher consolidates his recurring themes in his depiction of the Winklevoss twins and their relationship to one another. In saying "there's two of me," Tyler effectively designates his twin as an extension, reflection, and serviceable replica of himself. This rhetoric contrasts notably with Cameron's stated goals throughout this conversation, centered in his fantasy of wealth and lineage as nobility, reserve, generosity, and honor. He wants to maintain the belief, which leaves his friend and brother aghast, that the errant Zuckerberg simply needs words of strong caution. In total opposition, Tyler, echoing but amplifying Divya, wants Cameron and himself to inflict *Sopranos*-style brutality on scrawny, no-match-for-them Zuckerberg. Hammer ably conveys the brothers' opposing styles and wishes, maintaining an impregnable reserve as Cameron (saying "I love you, too" to their father over the phone at the close of their meeting about Zuckerberg's actions with the family lawyer) and inhabiting Tyler's scoffing, hot-under-the-collar edginess. Fincher keeps Cameron seated during this conversation but frames Tyler in a doorway at one point, visualizing Tyler's dissatisfaction through his full, agitated body.

This touch deftly conveys the idea that Cameron is the "seat" of reason, Tyler enflamed form.

In perhaps Hammer's most characteristic acting here, the initial meeting, engineered by the twins and their friend between Zuckerberg and the Winklevi—as Zuckerberg, in Eisenberg's peerlessly contemptuous tones, calls them—is a master class in would-be smooth seduction. The wunderkind came to the twins' and Divya's attention when a proto-Facebook site—the "FaceMash" website, which allows users to rate people's attractiveness (created by a drunken Zuckerberg after getting dumped by a female BU student played by Rooney Mara)—went viral but also garnered bad press for its misogyny (women were being compared to animals in ratings contests for attractiveness). Ambushing, in the friendliest way possible (if a moneymaking scheme at its most lavish can be considered friendly), Zuckerberg walking out from a class still in session (indifferently answering a professor's challenging questions as he abruptly exits), the twins stop him and introduce themselves. "Mark—are you Mark Zuckerberg?" Cameron asks. Hammer nestles the question to glowering, not-at-all-impressed Zuckerberg/Eisenberg in the gentlest, most inviting tones imaginable, a kind of heterosexual male wooing of another, and most unattainable, male. Of course, Zuckerberg responds with barely contained contempt ("Are you two related?" "Good one, we never heard that before," Tyler cockily responds). Fincher and Hammer and the costume designer, Jacqueline West, keep the twins differentiated nicely: Cameron wears his lustrous blonde hair in an open manner contrasting with his dark autumn jacket and scarf, whereas Tyler, more hooded in every respect, hanging behind his more glad-handing sibling and wearing a bandana around his equally blonde head, seems to blend into a tan autumn jacket with a blonde fringe around the collar. Whereas Cameron is softly inviting and gracious, embodying gentility, Tyler conveys a strategic, cocky, unimpressible recessiveness.

When the three take Zuckerberg to the exclusive Porcellian club they clearly had no trouble getting into, reminding the computer genius that he can only be taken to the bicycle room because he is most definitely not a member, the entire scene is a study in contrasting acting styles. Hammer, using his open-faced earnestness, stays seated as Cameron woos Zuckerberg to join the young entrepreneurs in "The Harvard Connection" website, powered by the most "exclusive email address in the country," whereas Tyler, standing, chimes in with blunter comments about women lusting after Harvard men especially. Eisenberg keeps his body language still, almost inert, while the brothers and Divya pitch their idea. When he is told that the Harvard Connection would also wipe the FashMash stink off his public persona, Eisenberg responds, with a monotone that conveys inexpressible contempt, "Wow—you would do that for me?"[3]

The film may treat Zuckerberg with a horrified fascination, but it shares his attitudes towards the tall, fatuous brothers. (In comparison, the movie hardly finds any interest in Divya Narendra.) Fincher and, perhaps, Hammer have great fun depicting the competitive rower Winklevosses in their various mock tournaments on the river, the camera panning across the length of the boat so that each Hammer-faced twin is seen in succession. There is also an impressive set, a cavernous enclosed space containing boats and water where the brothers, seated one behind the other, can intensively practice their rowing skills. Never shown in this space with any of their fellow rowers, it comes to suggest a symbolic realm where duplicate male titans are created and tested, conveying the coldness and artificiality—Fincher's sensibility at its height—of the spaces inhabited and lives lived by these superhuman specimens.

The Henley Regatta rowing competition (Henley-on-Thames, England), where the twins spectacularly lose after months—years—of training, serves as a fitting set piece for their shared and symbolic failure. The Henley Regatta sequence, satirically set to the tune of Edvard Grieg's "In the Hall of the Mountain King," is, as Michele Schreiber astutely writes,

> as visually exhilarating as it is deliberately excessive. Its artificiality and uncanny exaggeration is necessary in order to communicate the degree to which the loss of this ninety-second race is symbolic of the downfall of the Winklevii and much of which they stand for. In his DVD commentary, Fincher speaks of how this sequence is meant to convey how the Winklevoss twins "miss by that much." Their imposing, muscular bodies are strained and stretched to their limit but just cannot succeed. (Schreiber 16)

With their physical prowess and seemingly boundless confidence, the Winklevosses seem like masters of the universe, but they are no match for Zuckerberg, who plays a slow but inexorable game of revenge against them (which, it is strongly suggested, has its motivation in having been taken to the bike room of the Porcellian Club), or for Napster founder Sean Parker (Justin Timberlake), a smarmy, preternaturally confident young Mephistophelean figure instrumental in Zuckerberg's and Facebook's ascendance.

After the loss of the Henley Regatta, where they are patronized by dignitaries commiserating with them about how bad they must feel, the Winklevosses and Divya return to the subject of Zuckerberg and the exponentially expanding success of Facebook-in-the-making. Much to Tyler's and Divya's delight, the reticent, brooding Cameron finally agrees to full-on legal bloodletting to strike back against Zuckerberg. "Let's gut the freaking nerd," he says to their cheers. Unlike Hammer himself in certain of his roles, the Winklevi are never in on the joke; it is always on them.

☆☆☆☆☆☆☆☆☆☆ Hammer and Heroism: *Billy: The Early Years, The Lone Ranger, The Man from U.N.C.L.E., Mine*

Taken together, these movies indicate central themes in Hammer's ever-emerging star persona. In *Billy,* about the early years of the televangelist Billy Graham, Hammer's physical stature dwarfs most of the actors around him and constantly undermines the narrative's long-prevailing attitude that Billy is hapless, unable to find his calling. Which is to say, Hammer's physical stature keeps signaling to us that his Billy will succeed, marching to fame and glory as a religious guru even as the plot continues to focus on his myriad inadequacies. In *U.N.C.L.E.,* based on the 1960s television series, Hammer's physicality is lent a superhuman edge, as we see him run toward, catch up to, and lift a speeding car from behind and hold it in place. Playing a KGB agent complete with thick, pseudo-Russian accent, Hammer often comes to the rescue of the American agent Napoleon Solo (Henry Cavill), whom he pairs up with to stop international crime. As in *Billy,* he is an unlikely hero whose narrative heroism labors to catch up to his corporeal one.

But it is *The Lone Ranger* that encapsulates the difficulties Hammer faced in transitioning from *Social Network* "it boy" to star. If it is accurate to call this a revisionist Western, it is more accurate still to call it a pastiche of revisionism. Revisiting the Old West with critical eyes, *The Lone Ranger*'s combination of comic and revisionist modes, foregrounding historical genocidal violence, recalls films such as Arthur Penn's *Little Big Man* (1970) starring Dustin Hoffman. Penn's film was clearly a Vietnam War allegory as well as a revisionist Western, but it is not clear at any point what *The Lone Ranger* seeks to allegorize. Nor does its mode of revisionist critique add much to contemporary understandings of the racism, misogyny, and genocidal violence inherent in the Old West, especially in terms of relations between whites and Native Americans, given the slew of films since Penn's of wildly varying quality that have not only trod similar ground but taken similar revisionist stances.

Plopping Hammer into the midst of an incoherent comic-revisionist historical American epic that attempts to turn a popular lowbrow television series into substantive material was bound to fail on many levels, and fail it does. (*The Lone Ranger* TV series, an enormous hit for the ABC television network, aired from 1949 to 1957.) Despite love from critics such as Scout Tafoya, writer of the wonderful online film commentary series *The Unloved, Ranger* is no misunderstood masterpiece but rather a hollow and inert work.

It is, however, a prime example of the "double-protagonist film" that emerged in the 1990s and continues to thrive.[4] In such films, two male stars, one figured as narcissistic, the other as masochistic, vie for screen dominance. The film, directed by Gore Verbinski and written by Justin Haythe, Ted Elliott, and Terry Rossio, fits its material into double-protagonist mold by making Tonto, played by Johnny Depp, a fully-fledged character, in many ways the lead protagonist. We encounter Tonto as a living exhibit in a traveling carnival in 1933 San Francisco; he comes uncannily to life as a little boy wearing a mask (perhaps a future Lone Ranger) stares at the exhibit showcasing the withered form of Tonto as "The Noble Savage." The revivified Comanche, sporting a dead black bird on his head that he continuously feeds, tells the boy of his adventures in nineteenth-century Texas with lawyer John Reid, who becomes the Lone Ranger. These adventures span real-life events, such as the building of the transcontinental railroad and attempts by the U.S. Cavalry to annihilate the Comanches.

Hammer has a maliciously knowing, self-ironizing streak that comes through in films such as *Free Fire* (2016), a failed attempt at chaotic violent comedy in the *Smokin' Aces* (2006) mode, *Sorry to Bother You*, and his finest work, *Call Me by Your Name*. In *Free Fire*, he makes the role of an illegal weapons dealer oddly and remarkably funny. Looking particularly Sasquatch-like with a heavy brown beard, Hammer has a real glint of mischief in his eye as a petty criminal (Cillian Murphy) he is frisking observes, "You smell like perfume," and Hammer responds, smiling as if the two have shared a joke, "Your mother." (He later, when the observation is repeated, hollers, "It's beard oil!") But in *Ranger*, as in his portrayal of Billy Graham, Hammer opts for a genial, verging on aw-shucks innocence that seems a ploy to win over audiences with his sincerity. Though Hammer has the physical stature and carriage of an action star, his intense focus on this sincerity in a leading role has a blinding effect, making it hard to look at him for very long (an odd thing to say about someone so physically attractive, to be sure). What his committed, single-minded sincerity in roles like *Lone Ranger* and *Mine* suggests is that Hammer must *always* ironize his screen persona lest it become ponderous, a problem of personality and scale at once.

In *Mine*, which uses the second Iraq War as a backdrop, Hammer's character is trapped in the scorching Syrian desert for countless hours, unable to take his right foot off the titular killing device while he waits for an ever-delayed rescue. As the soldier drifts in and out of consciousness, we float back to scenes of his civilian life that include his courtship of a pretty, appealing waitress in a bar and flashbacks to his childhood with a horribly abusive father; when his romantic relationship goes awry, he begins acting in his father's violent manner. *Mine, Billy* (which contains several scenes of the hero and his sternly critical, religious father at odds), and *Lone Ranger* all understand masculinity as a struggle with unresolved oedipal conflict undermining the adult male's present reality (displaced in the latter on the Lone Ranger's relationship with his upstanding, unmatchable Texas Ranger brother Dan). Hammer's intense sincerity in these roles conveys the struggling oedipal son's efforts to win over the patriarch. What these lead roles have in common is the use of the sincere, unironic mode as an expression of the son's diminished, emotionally vulnerable status; one can also read this mode as a ploy for sympathy from the audience.

Set in the cool, mod '60s, *The Man from U.N.C.L.E.* aligns itself with these other films in fashioning a backstory of oedipal agony and anger for Hammer's eccentric hero. Hammer plays Moscow-born KGB agent Illya Kuryakin, still smarting over the fate of his father, once well placed in the Communist Party but then sentenced to the Siberian gulag. The American agent Napoleon Solo taunts him at one point: Was it "your father's shame that gave you such drive . . . ? Or was it your mother's reputation? I understand that she was extremely popular amongst your father's friends." Russian superman or not, Illya suffers the same oedipal woes as Hammer's American heroes. Indeed, this theme informs *Call Me by Your Name* as well, when Hammer's Oliver tells his young lover Elio how lucky he is to have such accepting parents, comfortable with the gay relationship that blossomed between their son and himself. Oliver explains, in contrast, "My father would have sent me to a correctional facility."

U.N.C.L.E. is an entertaining misfire that works even though Hammer and Henry Cavill never convince one in their roles or interaction. Indeed, the awkwardness of their casting and would-be rapport is precisely what lends the film its interest. (In contrast, Hammer's Ranger and Depp's Tonto never seem to be in the same movie together—*The Lone Ranger* is the double-protagonist film as two solo-protagonist films on parallel tracks.) Guy Ritchie's crude, obvious direction exposes the awkwardness vividly.

At one point, however, a rather interesting sequence ironizes fantasies of '60s male action hero–cool effectively. Kuryakin and Solo attempt to elude machine gun–firing baddies on boats in a nighttime action sequence set in the water. Having extricated himself from the melee, Solo watches the suspenseful action unfold from the safety of a truck he's broken into, listening to Peppino Gagliardi's swooning pop song "Che vuole questa musica stasera" as he avails himself of the Italian meal lovingly assembled in the picnic basket at his side. As he swigs red wine from the bottle and munches on a prosciutto-stuffed sandwich, Solo watches the grueling action on the water unfold. Boats spraying gunfire careen and zigzag on the water as his Russian ally attempts to elude the assassins, who defeat him by blowing up his boat. Solo's vigil strikes a masturbatory note: he calmly continues his self-pleasuring eating and imbibing and voyeuristic viewing of Kuryakin's travails. Noticing the Russian sinking into the water to his death, Solo quite arbitrarily decides to save him, plowing the truck into the assassins' high-speed boat and sinking along with them into the water. Solo escapes the now submerged and flooding truck, swims to Kuryakin's all but lifeless form, hoists him up, and rescues him, all to the tune of Gagliardi's pop ballad. What gives this sequence its humorous, knowing edge is Hammer's cartoonish display of male action heroism, exposed as a flimsy joke. Commanding "Cowboy," as the Russian calls Solo, to watch him in order to learn how the action-daredeviltry is done, Kuryakin fails spectacularly either to defeat their enemies or to save himself. The homoerotic joke that emerges from Solo's absurdly calm, indifferent viewing of Kuryakin's predicament and impending doom has its basis in the general absurdity of Hammer's chiseled, imposing, but far from invincible superman (Cavill being, of course, an actor who plays Superman).

Ritchie's film, while not the unmitigated financial disaster of *The Lone Ranger*, was nevertheless not a box-office success, though it does have a cult of followers clamoring for a sequel. Hammer's hopes of leading-man roles fizzled, but he very astutely realized that his greatest strength lay in being a counterpoint to the main action—in being, in other words, a deft supporting player. His best screen performances have all been in this capacity.

★★★★★★★★★★ The Character Actor

While there is not a great deal one can say about Hammer's performance in *Nocturnal Animals* (2016), given that the director, Tom Ford, essentially uses him as very elegant window dressing in the role of brooding artist Amy Adams's philandering husband, Hammer's roles in *The Birth of a Nation* (2016), where he plays slave rebellion–leader Nat Turner's alcoholic master Samuel Turner, *Sorry to Bother You*, and *Hotel Mumbai* (2018) all amply demonstrate Hammer's skill in a supporting capacity. As Dennis Bingham notes, a key ability of a successful male star is the ability to adapt. Citing James Stewart, Clint Eastwood, and Jack Nicholson as prime examples, Bingham observes that it was their ability "to walk the tightrope between normality and difference, between consistency and change, that made them such extremely successful, durable stars" (12). Hammer's ultimate screen-star trajectory remains to be seen, but these films indicate that his may also be able to remain "successful and durable," albeit in supporting roles. He gives very distinct and expert performances in these films that support their larger vision rather than dominate them.

His American businessman in *Hotel Mumbai* is shown to be clueless about different cultures (he orders a hamburger in the titular hotel restaurant) despite being married to a non-American woman, and largely comes across as the embodiment of American arrogance. But he demonstrates courage and unwavering devotion to his family during the horrific terrorist attack on the hotel. A surprisingly effective and nonexploitative film, *Hotel Mumbai* treats the terrorists as ordinary, callow young men manipulated into committing unspeakable acts and treats characters such as Hammer's less as types and more as ordinary and idiosyncratic themselves. Hammer does not emerge as the action-movie hero here (Dev Patel, as a Sikh waiter who helps to protect the guests, is closer to being that, but in ways that belie the crude category admirably), far from it. The survival of his wife and daughter emerges largely from sheer luck.

Sorry to Bother You provides the most interesting of these supporting roles. Hammer plays the coked-up, terrifyingly confident and gleeful CEO Steve Lift, whose company, WorryFree, turns unfortunate men to "Equisapiens," half-man, half-horse creatures designed for maximum labor efficiency. The Steve Lift plot does not develop until well into the second half of the film; the first half tracks the hero Cassius ("Cash") Green's (LaKeith Stanfield) ascent to the top of the telemarketing world through his adoption and use of "White Voice." Written and directed by rapper Boots Riley, the film offers a complex satirical take on numerous themes related to racism, corporate greed, performance art and the contemporary art scene, and the exploitation of the labor class. Hammer plays Lift as avidly committed to his own amorality. Silencing the anguished cries of the protesting equisapiens, Lift calls them, "You beautiful perversities." He's a Dr. Moreau for the Trumpian era.

★★★★★★★★★★ Three Lives: Hammer's Gay Roles

J. Edgar (2011), *Final Portrait* (2017), and especially *Call Me by Your Name* have the distinction of being gay roles and Hammer's finest work onscreen, especially the last. Hammer's comfort level not only with playing gay roles but discussing them in interviews and other publicity tours reflects his avowed liberal politics (he's a prominent critic of Trump on Twitter and of right-wing pundits like the actor James Woods) but also a great deal more. I have argued that the 1990s were the decade in which American screen masculinity became "self-aware," an awakening stemming from Hollywood cinema's explicit acknowledgment of queer sexuality and incorporation of homo-awareness into its representation of masculinity (Greven 2009, 1–11). Postmillennial filmmaking has borne this out, especially in its foregrounding of the bromance and diverse forms of male beauty (never diverse enough for some critics, admittedly). Hammer, in my view, embodies the postmillennial awareness of male sexuality as commodity and of masculinity as ironic, self-aware citation of prior masculine styles. All of which is to say that Hammer's commitment to playing gay roles reflects his indifference to the homophobia that might unfavorably cast those roles in a suspect light.

The most notable aspect of Clint Eastwood's *J. Edgar*, written by the gay screenwriter Dustin Lance Black (Eastwood and Black making for an interesting intersection of conservative and liberal views), is that Hammer, rather than Leonardo DiCaprio, is the queer center of the film. Given that DiCaprio is even more famous for being a heartthrob than Hammer, it is interesting that DiCaprio, playing the deeply closeted right-wing FBI director J. Edgar Hoover, is presented in desexualized and deglamorized terms. In contrast, Hammer's handsomeness in the role of Clyde Tolson, Hoover's protégé and highest-ranking FBI deputy, is emphasized. Hammer's Tolson conveys the ardent intensity of homosexual desire in his knowing gaze and devotion to Hoover, as in a long restaurant scene between the men. After an evening on the town involving a dance with female movie stars, Hoover tells his homophobic mother (a stern, frightening Judi Dench) that he does not enjoy dancing with women and does not intend to do so. She chastises him with a story of the sad fate of a suspected homosexual classmate of Hoover's and makes it clear that she would rather see him dead than homosexual (in her idiolect, a "daffodil"). When Hoover tells Tolson, in a hotel room, that he intends to marry the Hollywood film actress Dorothy Lamour, Tolson becomes infuriated and accuses Hoover of humiliating him. Hammer doesn't flinch from showing us the intensity of Tolson's reaction, his commitment to Hoover and his rage at being slighted.

Final Portrait tells the real-life story of the encounter between the American James Lord (Hammer) and the Italian artist Alberto Giacometti (Geoffrey Rush). In 1964 Paris, Giacometti asks the gay art lover and writer Lord to pose for him. Initially presenting these duties as very brief, Giacometti keeps asking Lord to stay for a few more days, which leads Lord, whose male lover waits for him with increasing impatience in the United States, to keep changing his departure date.

The American James Lord poses for the Italian artist Alberto Giacometti in his Paris studio in *Final Portrait* (Stanley Tucci, Sony Pictures Classics, 2017).

David Edelstein writes,

> Hammer squirms handsomely and holds himself in: You study his face along with Giacometti's. Rush is a wonder. It takes bravery to convey closure, tunnel vision, total indifference to the camera that actors always know is there, however self-effacing they might want to be appear. *Final Portrait* is, like Rush's performance, a miniature, but there's a fullness to [director Stanley] Tucci's vision transcending every surface ("Stanley Tucci's *Final Portrait* Is Quietly Brilliant," *Vulture*, 21 March 2018).

Like Edelstein, I agree that Hammer's face makes a fine prospect for study, especially when counterbalanced with the artist's expressionist rendering. Unlike Edelstein, I do not regard Rush's performance as a "wonder." Rush gives a mannered, self-involved performance playing an artist with similar qualities. In an acting turn that would probably have worked better onstage, Rush fiddles with bits of business, looks downward, speaks to himself, and explodes in small fits of exasperation. The performance is showy and fraudulent. But Hammer's performance is exquisitely well modulated, evoking the refinement of '60s-era masculine styles and connoisseurship. At one point, the older Italian artist receives bundles of cash and begins, clumsily but theatrically, to hide them in his studio, though not very well. When

Giacometti throws a bundle over the seated Lord's head and toward a corner of the studio, Lord remarks, chuckling sharply, "What a ham." Hammer's delivery of the line is perfect: Lord is charmed by the artist's flamboyance and in no way intimidated by it.

With *Call Me by Your Name,* Hammer comes through onscreen more successfully and indelibly than ever before. A great film, in my view, *Call Me* has already been discussed at length (for a rebuttal to D. A. Miller's castigation of it, see Greven 2018). In a film whose every image has become iconic, Hammer's role and acting coalesce with Guadagnino's image-making seamlessly. It is not to diminish the skill and deftness of Hammer's performance here to say that its success not inconsequentially derives from the way the director molds, shapes, and situates it, how Hammer's face and body sculpturally posed and captured create an overall effect. Given that we are so firmly placed in the mind and libido of the protagonist, the seventeen-year-old Elio Perlman (Timothée Chalamet), and see Hammer's Oliver, a young American graduate student who visits the family's summer home "somewhere in northern Italy," almost entirely through Elio's eyes, it is fitting that we experience Hammer/Oliver as a sculptural figure posed and held up to shifting perspectives intended to invite the eye and stimulate desire. Nevertheless, never without Guadagnino's (and Chalamet's) mediation but always with a distinctively keen, taut awareness, Hammer draws surprisingly dark, somber lines in his portrait of an attractive, sardonically funny, intelligent yet enigmatic and finally thwarted, or at least resigned to resignation, character.

The Perlmans—an American academic, Professor Perlman (Michael Stuhlbarg), his Italian wife Annella (the French actress Amira Casar), and Elio—receive a graduate student in their lovely, sensual, nature-garlanded home every summer to study classical archaeology with the professor. When Oliver arrives, we see him from Elio's POV, a high-angle shot looking down on Oliver emerging from the car that has brought him to the Perlman home and introducing himself to the professor, who comments that Oliver's picture did not do his height justice. "There was no way to fit all of me into the picture," Oliver says in a line reflective of his quick-witted manner, but also an evocative one for Hammer's work here and, really, throughout his career, his always seeming somehow "too much" for the screen—except for this film, where getting all of Oliver is the impossible goal. The line also sounds like a sexual pun, suggesting his sexual entry into their apparently serenely uncomplicated milieu.

Hammer benefits greatly from having his consistent status as an object of desire made explicit here; it allows him to inhabit his physicality with a freer, more controlled manner than he had previously displayed. He also benefits greatly from having, for the first time, perhaps, a co-star who really sparks off his persona with inventiveness and delight. Hammer and Chalamet speak to and engage what Steven Rybin, drawing on the work of George Toles, describes as the "challenge for writers meditating on film acting: it requires not only appreciating the to-and-fro created in the undulating rhythms of two performers, but also appreciating what happens to the totality of a film's space, and the trajectory of its story, when two separate affective and expressive ways of inhabiting the world are intimately aligned" (29). The performances of Hammer and Chalamet take up and facilitate this critical challenge and these possibilities.

During the scene where Oliver—in what is later confirmed was a signal that he likes Elio, with whom he has an initially tense interaction—massages Elio's shoulder blade while all the males on the green are shirtlessly involved in a volleyball game, Hammer's physical power palpably suffuses the screen, especially the shot, as awestruck as it is erotically charged, of Oliver leaving behind the recalcitrant Elio and flexing his backside to hit an incoming ball as he rejoins the game. Oliver's green short shorts associate him with the natural world and signify Elio's increasingly jealous desire at once. (Costume designer Giulia Piersanti, making her second film with Guadagnino, deserves her own chapter for the 1980s couture she devises here, especially Oliver's billowy Oxford shirts, Elio's multipatterned swimming trunks, and the like.)

Perhaps not yet aware that his irritation with Oliver indicates a growing sexual and romantic ardor, Elio complains to his parents that Oliver is arrogant, an attitude expressed succinctly in Oliver's habit of exiting meals and conversations with the word, "Later," Oliver's pronunciation of which Elio humorously imitates. "Later" has a resonance: time is so crucial to this film, from Oliver's sleeping through his first night with the Perlmans and missing dinner, to Elio, once the young man and his twenty-four-year-old lover have consummated their relationship, saying, "We wasted so much time."

There is an extraordinary medium close-up of Hammer staring into the distance as sunglasses-wearing Elio, seated in the background on a lawn chair, looks down (figure 4.3). Hammer conveys the sense that Oliver is looking into the future, wondering if Elio will be found there or wondering what the future might look like without him. Or, Oliver could be contemplating his own past and how it may prevent him from intimacy in the present. What makes the shot resonant is that it contains such temporal and emotional multitudes. The always elusive quality of Hammer's star presence informs this scene poignantly and pointedly. It anticipates the moment,

Oliver stares enigmatically into the future, the past, both, or neither in *Call Me by Your Name* (Luca Guadagnino, Sony Pictures Classics, 2017). Digital frame enlargement.

during the passage where Oliver and Elio have gone on an excursion well into their brief and intense relationship, when Oliver, standing naked in the dark early morning light of their hotel room, looks out the window and then sits by the sleeping Elio with a troubled look on his face. This scene foregrounds Oliver's emotional elusiveness, once again, but hints that he struggles with his feelings for Elio and the sense of what will come next (the end of their relationship, most obviously).

In the scene where Oliver and Elio finally consummate their mutual erotic interest, Hammer plays the scene—set at night in Elio's bedroom where Oliver has been staying—in the least aggressive and domineering manner possible. A slow-burning sexual encounter, the men sit side by side at first, Oliver's foot over Elio's. "Does this make you happy?" Oliver inquires, in wonderful moments where he asks for and makes sure to receive Elio's consent, not insignificant in a film mired in controversy not only for being a gay love story but for the disparity in the men's ages.

The next day, Elio, who worked so hard to secure this sexual encounter with Oliver, pulls away and acts in a distant manner, alarming and also angering Oliver, who remarks during their gambols in the countryside, "Are you going to hold what happened between us against me?" This cold awkwardness between them dissipates, however, when Elio seeks Oliver out in the marketplace and talks to him at a newsstand. Around the corner in an alley, Oliver stands daringly close to Elio, saying, "I would kiss you if I could." No other director has brought out this combined vulnerability and centered command in Hammer onscreen, playing the desirer who is himself desire's cynosure.

I want to conclude my analysis of Hammer's performance by talking about the infamous peach scene. Chalamet has wryly mentioned in interviews that fans come up to him asking him to sign peaches and predicts that when he's elderly the same will be true. One sultry summer afternoon after he and Oliver have already begun having sex, shirtless, swim trunk–clad Elio lies on his bed and, overcome by erotic lassitude, carves out the pit from peach and uses the now stoneless fruit as a masturbation device. He visibly orgasms (in close-up) and then places the semen-filled peach on a side table.

After some time has passed, Oliver, similarly shirtless and swim trunk–clad, appears and sits by Elio on the bed. Oliver immediately begins performing oral sex on Elio, but then—all with a delectably funny amusement—asks, "What did you do?" His curiosity piqued, Oliver looks around and notices the cause of Elio's unusual taste. With amused incredulity and interest, Oliver spies and takes hold of the incriminating peach. To Elio's embarrassed demurral ("It's sick"), Oliver says, "You want to see something really sick?" and proceeds to nibble at the fluid-filled fruit. What happens next condenses the myriad tensions between these ardently connected men at insuperable odds. Elio becomes truly upset, trying to prevent Oliver from eating the polluted fruit. Elio tries to wrench the fruit loose from Oliver's grasp, but he easily overpowers Elio, who then sobs, "Why are you doing this to me?" Finally, Oliver understands that what was a taunting carnal game for him, something of an erotic "I drink your milkshake" challenge, is a wounding experience for his young lover, who collapses in his arms and exclaims, "I don't want you to leave." Oliver is able to shift gears and transition from sexual provocateur to comforting, tenderness-giving lover, but the scene is revealing: Oliver has not only a kinky but a brutally selfish side—he *will* eat that fruit whether Elio wants him to or not—which serves to remind us that there is indeed a gulf between these men, age being only the first.

Chalamet, for his remarkably attuned, controlled, and openhearted performance, deserves all the praise he has received for this film. But it is telling that the real audacity in the scene—Oliver's determination to eat a fruit filled with his lover's sexual fluids, and Hammer's confidently unflummoxed attitude in performing this—receives much less attention than Chalamet's self-pleasure by fruit. It's almost as if what Hammer does is too much to be noticed, too much to be acknowledged, and must be, as it is here, narratively contained. It will no doubt be a source of ongoing fascination to see if this unusual, perhaps impossible, sometimes improbable, deeply gifted star will be able to break free of these myriad constraints in future roles.

NOTES

1. The subject of race in the representation of white star masculinity always requires careful handling. Hammer is, in my understanding, generally viewed as a Robert Redford, blonde, blue-eyed, WASP version of masculinity, though Hammer describes himself as "half-Jewish." *Call Me by Your Name* simultaneously foregrounds and muffles the theme of Jewish identity. Elio Perlman quotes his mother as saying that the multilingual, Eurocentric Perlmans are "Jews of discretion," while Oliver, Hammer's character, talks empathetically to Elio about being a lone Jew among Gentiles. Hammer's involvement in films by Black directors, such as *The Birth of a Nation* and *Sorry to Bother You*, especially his casting as someone who causes harm to the Black protagonist in both films, requires further analysis, clearly.

2. In the closing moments of the 1983 theatrical release of *Return of the Jedi*, Luke Skywalker, gifted with the Force, sees, standing with the beatific ghosts of Yoda and Obi-Wan Kenobi, the shining Force-ghost image of his father Darth Vader, now restored to Anakin Skywalker. Anakin has been redeemed after killing the emperor to save Luke's life. In the original, Sebastian Shaw plays the happy ghost Vader/Anakin, but in the 2004 DVD release of *Return of the Jedi*, the head of the actor playing the young Anakin in George Lucas's later *Star Wars* trilogy, Hayden Christensen, has been grafted on to the original actor's body. Whereas Lucas uses the new digital capabilities available to him to idealize and "correct" his earlier vision, Fincher seizes on the possibilities of this technology to mount elaborate, cutting jokes.

3. Analyzing this scene in her essay "Tiny Life: Technology and Masculinity in the Films of David Fincher," Michele Schreiber observes:

> The scene where the twins find Mark outside of his classroom and their subsequent meeting in the lobby of the Porcellian Club constitute the only sequence in which Mark shares the same physical space with them in 2003. Like the 2007 deposition scenes in which they are on opposite sides of the table and are never shown in the same shot, Mark rarely shares the frame with Narendra or the Winklevoss twins during the Porcellian scene. If they are in the same shot, it is photographed from behind Mark's head. This creates a visual demarcation between the adversaries and offers a striking contrast between Mark's body, which as Bordwell puts it, is "straightjacketed," and the Winklevosses, who are larger in stature but who also "use their arms and hands freely" (13).

4. See Greven, "Contemporary Hollywood Masculinity and the Double-Protagonist" and "The Hollywood Man Date," *Manhood in Hollywood from Bush to Bush*.

Chapter 5

The Multiple Trajectories of Transnational Hollywood Stars

Marion Cotillard, Kristen Stewart, Diane Kruger

CELESTINO DELEYTO

This chapter focuses on three transnational stars of the 2010s. In spite of its recent currency, the term "transnational" has been difficult to define and pinpoint, with scholars, according to Meeuf and Raphael, prone to overuse it and underclarify it (2). It has too often been used as a synonym of and interchangeable with the term "global." I will argue that in connection with film stars, as indeed in other fields of cultural enquiry, the value of the transnational may lie precisely in its distinction from the global. To offer an initial hypothesis, I would argue that global stars represent the culture of globalization in that they have a global reach and offer cultural meanings that may be shared by a great number of people around the planet. For this reason, they are generally associated with Hollywood, the only global film industry. Transnational stars, on the other hand, evoke more localized mobilities and are more explicitly connected with border crossings and with the interplay between two or more national identities, both at industrial and narrative levels. As such, they exclude global modes of engagement and offer, instead, more specialized, geographically concrete meanings. Thus, the term rejects, within film studies, the homogeneity associated with the global (see Durovičová ix) while often crisscrossing with it, and highlights both the continuing validity of the national and the complexities attendant on border-crossing mobilities.

The transnational incorporates a variety of relations of power between national groups, calling attention to the dangers of the homogenizing tendencies of globalization while recognizing ongoing inequalities between territories (Newman 9). Evoking Mary Louise Pratt's notion of borders as "contact zones" (1991) via Kathleen Newman's work, Meeuf and Raphael envision transnational cinema as a contact zone in which connections are forged between

Marion Cotillard

Diane Kruger

Kristen Stewart

peoples and localities which both reflect and transcend global inequalities (3). Elizabeth Ezra argues that the transnational focuses on the movement of bodies and objects across borders, whereas the ultimate goal of globalization is to make those dividing lines unreadable, invisible (1–2). Yet, the transnational is not always attached to the national. Writing specifically about transnational cinema, Song Hwee Lim argues that while some contemporary trends in the industry are transnational precisely because they are deeply national, other phenomena do not arise out of any single country but instead have transnational traits that, crucially, do not make recourse to national agendas. These "help us rethink the transnational *without* the national" (1).

In sum, there seems to have evolved a tendency to position the transnational somewhere between the national and the global. The term suggests that national boundaries cannot contain people's ways of relating to the world anymore while admitting that the nation continues to be a reality in our lives. It evokes both a dissatisfaction with the ways in which economic neoliberal realities have colonized the concept of globalization and anxieties about technology and the world risk society (Beck) and, more positively, the impulse to make visible a variety of social and cultural engagements across borders in an era of intensified mobilities. The transnational, then, describes a more modest reality than the global, even a response to anxieties and frustrations with global trends that seem to benefit only a few.

Transnational stars embody some of these cultural meanings. They may bear strong marks of national identities as they cross borders and relocate within different geographies, and, sometimes, as a result of multiple crossings, they may come to inhabit an in-between territory in which national markers have become debilitated. This chapter discusses three transnational stars who can also be considered global stars, but, I would argue, they are global in a different way, or for different reasons, than they are transnational. Marion Cotillard, Kristen Stewart, and Diane Kruger, three actors that had come to international visibility in the previous decade but whose screen personae and celebrity status became established in the 2010s, are Hollywood stars, even if the intensity of their respective radiance on the global screens may not be identical. Each have their own specificities in relation to the global and the transnational. Yet, in the three cases, those meanings that locate them within "transnational culture" became apparent in the 2010s and turned them into complex exemplars of a transnational decade.

☆☆☆☆☆☆☆☆☆☆ Marion Cotillard

Marion Cotillard had already crossed the Atlantic at least twice before her phenomenal success in *La Môme* (2007) to appear in Tim Burton's *Big Fish* (2003) and Ridley Scott's *A Good Year* (2006), but her performance as Edith Piaf and her subsequent accolades, including the first Academy Award for Best Actress in history for a French-speaking part, brought her to immediate global stardom. It also cemented her acting method, variously described as "impersonation," "immersion," and "inner work," which ran counter to the traditional association of the Hollywood star with the predominance of the actor over the part (Sandeau 2020, 8–12). In his analysis of the construction of Cotillard's star persona in this film, Jules Sandeau argues that while playing a very French icon—later reinforced with her work as Dior ambassador in a series of short films directed by prestigious auteurs—it was the readability of her Frenchness for U.S. audiences, her association with certain Hollywood acting traditions, and her adaptability to Hollywood genres that facilitated her integration in the U.S. star system. At the same time, her Hollywood stardom consolidated her status as a national icon in France (6), and even her Parisianness—"la veritable Parisienne" (Choulant 98). She joined the pantheon of French stars referred to by surname only: Adjani, Deneuve, Bardot, Cotillard (85).

Therefore, in Cotillard's case, the global and the national are firmly welded, her Frenchness a central part of her star persona.

Ginette Vincendeau summarizes that persona, foregrounding both her acting parts and her offscreen celebrity: her traditional Hollywood glamour, her understated, subtle acting, her naturalistic performances, her melancholy, bittersweet character, her sex appeal, her soft voice and gentle smile, and her large blue eyes, often filled with tears (47–48), to which Sandeau adds her image of "tormented French woman" (12). *Allied* (2016), to date the only Hollywood mainstream production in which she has played the lead, alongside Brad Pitt, displays her classical glamour and, at the same time, showcases the main ingredients of her image: in turns subdued and passionate, guarded and sympathetic, ambiguous and genuine. Her character, whose "real" name we never know, is wholly defined by her playacting abilities. A shot of her in her bathroom in London shows her image twice, through reflections in mirrors, with her back to us. In this game of levels of performance, she remains unknowable even as we learn to discern the "authenticity" of the emotions she plays. As she explains to Pitt's Max, "I keep the emotions real. That's why it works," a statement that is also meant to describe Cotillard's acting method. This method, reminiscent of but not identical with Stanislavski's and Lee Strasberg's Method, is part of her global celebrity: the training, the research, the physical transformation, the lip-synching, the discipline, and the intensity. Stardom appears to be closely linked, in Cotillard's case, with the excellence of her performance.

In Hollywood, this excellence has been given little scope, in spite of her relatively auspicious part in Michael Mann's *Public Enemies* (2008), her first film after *La Môme*. In this high-profile biopic of John Dillinger (Johnny Depp), she gradually comes into her own, culminating with a final close-up that conveys, perhaps more forcefully than Depp's performance, the reasons why we should admire a gangster like Dillinger. Yet Cotillard's Billie Frechette (French father, Native American mother) remains a secondary character, setting the pattern for the majority of her Hollywood output in the 2010s. Apart from *Allied* and *The Immigrant* (2013), Cotillard has played mostly secondary parts that rely heavily on traditional French and/or female stereotypes, often generic villains, as in her two blockbusters of the early years of the decade: *Inception* (2010) and *The Dark Knight Rises* (2012). It is symptomatic, for instance, that in the latter's narrative her character Miranda pales in comparison with that of Catwoman, played by fellow Hollywood star, homegrown Anne Hathaway, both in terms of centrality and complexity. It is as if her stardom, highlighted mostly in magazines, TV shows, fashion-icon appearances, and even music videos, does not find a continuation on the global cinema screens. With one or two exceptions—to *The Immigrant* and *Allied* we could add her moving, understated performance in *Contagion* (2011) and her glamour and humor in Woody Allen's *Midnight in Paris* (2011)—most of her complex roles of the decade have come from films produced elsewhere: in France, *Les petits mouchoirs* (2010) and *De rouille et d'os* (2012), among others; in Belgium, *Deux jours, une nuit* (2014); in the UK, *Macbeth* (2015); and in Canada, *Juste la fin du monde* (2016). Vincendeau wonders whether these two separate trajectories—two Marion Cotillards, as she puts it: the American celebrity and the French actor—exist. For this critic she always remains a star, no matter what the film is (2018, 47), but the tension remains; compare, for instance, her colorless part in the Batman movie with her stunning performance as whale trainer Stephanie in *De rouille et d'os*, both released in 2012; or her scientist Sofia in the frustrating video game adaptation *Assassin's Creed* and her compassionate performance as outsider Catherine in *Juste la fin du monde*, both 2017.

For Vincendeau, an important reason for her access to a global dimension is her proficiency in the use of the English language (46–47). In Cotillard's case, this is linked with her engagement with intercultural communication, cosmopolitan attitudes, and border crossings. *Allied* displays her ability to cross borders and navigate between cultures, but it is not just her English but the panoply of different languages and accents that she activates in her films from the 2010s that largely define her transnational dimension as a star. In *Blood Ties* (2013), she plays Italian American prostitute Monica. Even though Cotillard reportedly could not speak the language, it was her choice to make her character Italian (Choulant 165), and she is equally effective when she speaks the language as when she speaks English with an Italian New York accent. In *The Immigrant* she is Polish, which she apparently speaks with a faint German accent, because her character Ewa comes from Silesia (Choulant 160). This is undoubtedly part of her thorough approach to her job but, in cultural terms, it translates into a performance of respect for diversity and a strong desire to make the Other visible and human, particularly in an environment, like the film industry, which has often reduced "foreigners" and migrants to demeaning stereotypes. An otherwise insignificant detail in *Assassin's Creed* gives a measure of her attitude: her character Sofia pronounces "Andalucía," the name of the southern Spanish region where part of the action takes place, in perfect Spanish, whereas her father, played by Jeremy Irons, does not even bother. Not easily noticeable and certainly not part of the story, this little touch speaks about her approach to linguistic and cultural diversity, to highlighting instead of homogenizing difference. This ethical commitment to acknowledging the Other both as complex and as different may be linked with

The face of European precarity: Marion Cotillard in *Deux jours, une nuit* (Luc and Jean-Pierre Dardenne, Canal+, 2014). Digital frame enlargement.

another common feature of her characters: their compassion, impressively displayed in her subtle revision of Lady Macbeth as not only ruthless and ambitious but also empathetic and intensely sensitive in *Macbeth,* and in Catherine, her character in *Juste la fin du monde,* who is often framed in close-ups that highlight her eyes, through which she transmits infinite sympathy and understanding toward the members of the extremely dysfunctional family to whom she is linked by marriage with one of the sons.

The diversity of her linguistic registers extends to her French-speaking roles. In the comedy *Rock'n Roll* (2017), she plays Marion, married to Guillaume (Guillaume Canet), a parody of the real-life couple. She spends much of the first part of the film speaking French with a Canadian accent to her family in preparation for the shoot of her next film in Canada. This, like other elements of the film's plot, is a parody of her by then famous acting method. When she comes back from the shoot, she has dropped her Canadian accent and, asked by Guillaume, she explains her disappointment at the director's decision to have the actors speak with their own accents. This is a direct reference to *Juste la fin du monde,* a film that appears to have been central to her career in the 2010s. Released two years before *Rock'n Roll,* it is a Canadian-French production directed by Canadian Xavier Dolan, a story that takes place in Québec (and was shot in Québec) with an impressive cast of French actors (Cotillard, Nathalie Baye, Vincent Cassel, Léa Seydoux, and Gaspard Ulliel), all speaking French with a French accent. Dolan's decision contributes to the consciously sought, unsettling defamiliarization of the story, but it must have more than unsettled the star, too, who had her later character speak with the accent she wanted and must have practiced hard to use.

The compassion, based on her own uncertainties, that Cotillard's character displays in the Dolan film mutates into a combination of extreme vulnerability and worker solidarity in *Deux jours, une nuit* ("vaillante comme une guerrière, fragile come le verre," in the words of Isabelle Regnier, 2014). Jean-Pierre and Luc Dardenne, universally acknowledged as part of the most exclusive pantheon of twenty-first-century European auteurs, are, in the words of critic A. O. Scott, "faithful chroniclers of a European working class in crisis" (2014) and excel at rendering "everyday lives in close-up and mid-gesture" (Stevens 65), a method that has, with a few exceptions, led them to work with nonprofessional actors. As she did in *De rouille et d'os* and continued to do in most of her films in French for the rest of the decade, here Cotillard divests herself of her star cloak and adapts her acting to the Dardennes' naturalistic requirements to convey not only the fragility that is the consequence of postcrisis precarity but also a stunning other-projection that leads her to constantly empathize with those that have decided to take her job away from her. The very firm sense of locatedness provided by the Dardennes' habitual space—the industrial areas of Seraing, their hometown in southern Belgium—highlights that the film tells a transnational European story about the victims of savage neoliberalism. But Cotillard does this by honoring the geography of the film as she expands her linguistic versatility to the slight Belgian working-class accent of protagonist Sandra. The character's empathy also resonates with transnational issues as formulated above: attention to geopolitical specificities, acknowledgment of inequalities, and the desire to forge connections across borders through recognition of and foregrounding of the other's difference.

Beyond the global reach of her star persona, Cotillard's acting finds a concrete 2010s manifestation not only in the variety of national, cultural, and social identities conjured up in her parts but also, more specifically, in her embodiment of Francophone diversity through French-speaking parts that evoke French, Belgian, and Canadian perspectives, a diverse cultural and linguistic community symbolically brought together by her star persona. In general, in the course of the 2010s, Cotillard, while consolidating her status as global star, constructed a transnational awareness, made up of the various national identities made visible in her performances and of the various border crossings that she invited spectators to engage in, both by following her career and by immersing themselves in her films, thus countering the homogenizing tendencies of the mainstream film culture in which she has been, since *La Môme*, an important player.

Anxiety on the move: Kristen Stewart in *Personal Shopper* (Olivier Assayas, Canal+, 2016). Digital frame enlargement.

☆☆☆☆☆☆☆☆☆☆ Kristen Stewart

Like Cotillard with *La Môme*, Kristen Stewart's access to global stardom happened all of a sudden as a consequence of the phenomenal success of *Twilight* in 2008. Yet, although only eighteen at the time of the film's release, the actor had already had a long career in Hollywood, starting (apart from two small uncredited parts) with Rose Troche's *The Safety of Objects* in 2001 and coming to visibility, if not yet stardom, in her two-hander with Jodie Foster as the latter's daughter in David Fincher's *Panic Room* (2002), a movie that was released when she was not quite twelve years old. Part of her trademark performance style was already in place in the combination of fragility, insecurity, intelligence, and poise shown by her character, Sarah Altman. Six years and some fifteen films later, she became the centerpiece of the *Twilight* phenomenon in the first installment of the cinematic adaptation of Stephenie Meyer's four-novel saga. Another four films followed in four years, but both the personality of Bella and the screen construction of Stewart's star persona were already fully formed in the first one: Bella is a romantic model for teenage heterosexual women who, while almost solely defined by the love of a man (well, a male vampire), remains the dominant subject of desire, something that in mainstream cinema was and continues to be more the exception than the rule. The films are about her fantasies, her quiet power, her comfortable femininity, her gauche pose, her plain clothes, and the combination of independence from and love for her parents. She achieves this through an acting style based on understatement, conveyed through her quick and quiet delivery, her short lines uttered with the slightest of emphases, hardly moving her lips, often with her eyes down, shy, rejecting attention.

Building on *Twilight*, Stewart's films of the 2010s intensify her rebelliousness, her respect for and celebration of difference, her marginality, and, according to Graham Fuller, her embodiment of "cosmic dread" (23). For this critic, writing on the occasion of the release of *Personal Shopper* (2017), she is the actor of her generation, her post-Bella parts offering numerous entries into the modern condition and suggesting a "neurotic package" that marries "cool" and "uncool" (23–24; see also James). For Shonni Enelow, she is not on her own: actors like Jennifer Lawrence, Rooney Mara, Michael B. Jordan, and Oscar Isaac share her "emotional retrenchment and wariness" (2016), a style of acting that the author also relates to the anxieties of the decade. Of the approximately twenty feature films in which she appeared in the course of the 2010s, I will briefly mention three parts, not necessarily her most popular, which illustrate her onscreen persona as it developed in the post-*Twilight* years. In *Camp X-Ray* (2014), she plays Cole, a young private in the U.S. Army doing a turn in Guantanamo. She develops a close relationship with one of the prisoners, Ali (Payman Maadi), who was arrested eight years ago in Germany for no other reason than being an Arab. With echoes of her "screen mother" Jodie Foster's Clarice Starling in *The Silence of the Lambs* (1991), Stewart is constantly onscreen, often in close-up, allowing the viewer to concentrate on the details of her facial performance and delivery: she speaks in fast, short lines, with a lot of pauses in between, rushing to finish sentences, seemingly out of embarrassment, often stopping to look up or away before answering. She is permanently restless, agitated, troubled. In this case, the trouble is directed at the unfairness of the prisoners' lot, and develops into understanding and compassion for others, a feature that became part of the Stewart screen persona in the course of the decade. In *Still Alice* (2014), she is Lydia, the daughter of a distinguished Columbia linguistics professor played by Julianne Moore, who is diagnosed with early-onset Alzheimer's. A Cordelia-type character, she moves from black sheep to prodigal daughter and excels at conveying humanity, generosity, and compassion through a harsh, contrary, apparently uncompromising personality. She is empathetic and resourceful, her rebelliousness compounded here, as elsewhere, by a softness in her delivery and in her eyes. Finally, in the multiprotagonist film *Anesthesia* (2015), about a group of New York intellectuals, ridiculously smart and well educated, Stewart plays graduate student Sophie and embodies professor Walter Zarrow's (Sam Waterston) view of a bleak contemporary world, violent, godless, sunk in relativism, and alienated by technological progress. Sophie is smart but tormented, brilliant but extremely distressed. What the three films show is that, *pace* Enelow, who finds her "undemonstrative" (2016), Stewart manages to both appear emotionally restrained *and* capable of expressing great affection and, when required, emotional intensity, even though her performance style continues to be minimalistic. A close-up during her last conversation with Zarrow encapsulates a simultaneity of the understated passion that characterizes her mature acting style and the generational anguish of which she has become a prime cinematic embodiment.

These three films, like the majority of her other performances, are Hollywood films. Unlike the other two case studies in this article, Stewart speaks to global preoccupations through a recognizable contemporary U.S. identity. Like most U.S. stars, she became a global star with global cultural resonances without cinematically leaving her country. This is what makes her two mid-decade European films both exceptional and exemplary of the pervasiveness of transnational trajectories in contemporary cinema. *Clouds of Sils Maria* (2014) and *Personal Shopper*, both directed by Olivier Assayas, bring about a journey across the Atlantic in which, counter to the general direction taken by actors and filmmakers, she follows in the steps of earlier U.S. female stars, from Clara Bow to Jean Seberg (whom she played in the biopic *Seberg*, 2019)—perhaps a very limited transnational pedigree, compared with Cotillard and Kruger, yet, given the cultural reach of her persona and the explicit transnationality of the two films, this brief journey to Europe proves far-reaching and symptomatic of twenty-first-century mobilities.

Sils Maria and *Personal Shopper* have an open trans-European vocation, both in terms of production and narrative. *Sils Maria* is a French-German-Swiss co-production in which French, German (including Swiss German), and English as linguae francae are spoken. *Personal Shopper* is a French-German-Czech-Belgian co-production whose characters speak French and German, although in this case English is more overwhelmingly dominant given that Stewart is present in almost every shot and speaks English throughout. The story of *Sils Maria* concerns a very exclusive central European cultural elite, and most of its action is set in Sils Maria, a wealthy mountain village only nine kilometers away from the famous skiing resort of St. Moritz. *Personal Shopper* is set in Paris and, for brief spells, in London and Oman. The film zeroes in on affluent areas of the two European capitals. It is difficult to spot a working- or lower-middle-class character in either film: *Sils Maria* brings together a group of extremely cultured theater and film people from France, Germany, and Switzerland, and *Personal Shopper* is set in the fashion world which Mary Harrod has accurately called "globally consumable Eurotrash" (2020, 90), the world of celebrity culture, embodied by Maureen's (Stewart) employer Kyra (played by Austrian Nora von Waldstätten).

Perhaps unexpectedly, Kristen Stewart takes to these apparently remote worlds like a duck to water. She plays Valentine in *Sils Maria* and Maureen in *Personal Shopper*, both personal assistants to other women, in the former to Juliette Binoche's prestigious theater actor and film star Maria Enders and in the latter to global celebrity Kyra. Without abandoning Stewart's signature reticence and permanent agitation, Valentine and Maureen navigate these affluent European environments with ease and competence. The skills the actor brings to both jobs have to do with her mobility and familiarity with communications technologies and social networks. In *Sils Maria* we first see her traveling with Maria by train from Paris to Zurich through the Alps, two mobile phones in her hands, constantly on the move, constantly on the phone, constantly hooked on the internet, very much unlike the more traditional intellectuals and artists that surround her. This is exacerbated and metaphorized in *Personal Shopper*, where the old train is replaced by the high-speed Eurostar in a central scene, and where much of the story is developed through WhatsApp, text messages, and other modern technologies. When she is not traveling to London, Maureen is riding her moped through the streets of Paris or using buses or the tube, constantly on the move.

In *Sils Maria*, after her sudden disappearance not just from the narrative but literally from the frame as she and Maria climb to the top of a mountain, Valentine is replaced at the center of the story by the young Hollywood star Jo-Ann Ellis (Chloë Grace Moretz), who becomes Maria's nemesis. Ellis's Hollywoodian irruption among the cultural elite and the threat she poses to the cultural values of European high art may be seen as metaphor for Stewart's perplexing centrality in these two European films. Like Ellis in the film's diegesis, Stewart is the global Hollywood star that infiltrates the trans-European film of a French auteur and, by extension, high European culture. Even though her characters are, ironically, secondary players in the lives of two celebrities, Stewart dominates both films. The moment she appears onscreen, the European characters start speaking English as a matter of course, as if there were no question of her speaking German or French, handing her the advantage of the native speaker. Her linguistic superiority allows her to dominate verbal exchanges and, as a consequence, turn her into our main point of entry into the fictional worlds and the social, emotional, psychological, and philosophical debates of the films. At the same time, however, neither Maureen nor Valentine reminds us of the usual stereotype of the arrogant, overpowering American abroad. In keeping with her screen persona, she is humble, often insecure, and empathetic. She embodies technological prowess but also revels in her capacity to adapt to a very demanding environment.

In *Sils Maria*, Valentine disappears when she and Maria are finally about to witness the Maloja Snake, a meteorological phenomenon whereby clouds coming from the nearby Italian mountains wind through the Maloja Pass like a snake, submerging the area in a dangerous and paralyzing fog. Yet, seen from above, it is a rare wonder, a spectacle for the privileged few. In his chapter on the two films, Murray Pomerance sees this malevolent, torturous, delicate, and evanescent cloud as a condensation of the film's powerful themes: the Snake is Time, embodying precariously yet magnificently the strange effects of age—yesterday and tomorrow—in the relationship between Maria and Valentine; and it is also a visual expression of the yesterday and tomorrow of eighteenth-century travel and exploration—the search for the "beautiful stranger" that is Valentine in the film (2020, 138, 142–143). But in its spatial specificity, the Maloja Snakes also evokes the elusive transnationality—threatened, dangerous, beautiful—of the geopolitical space of the film: a Europe disconcertingly personified in the Hollywood star. Through Stewart's star presence, then, the two films speak to important trends in the redefinition of the European cultural project and call to mind Harrod, Liz, and Timoshkina's view that the idea of European cinema must be found in the interstices of the national and that it needs to be re-imagined along transgeographical lines (16).

In sum, the ideological goal of Assayas's two films appears to revolve around the transnational fantasy that, through Stewart's screen persona, an enhanced border-crossing culture may be installed in the old Europe, one that goes beyond continental boundaries, if only to welcome "the American friend." The privileged European scenarios in which the stories are set seriously compromise the cosmopolitan aspirations of this project. Yet Stewart manages, however ambivalently, to expand beyond the United States her own project of constructing a global image, one that is devoid of the more openly imperialistic aspects of her country's cultural identity, resulting, in these films, in a powerful if compromised message of transnational hope.

☆☆☆☆☆☆☆★★★ Diane Kruger

In the little-seen *Frankie* (2005), the first of three films in which Kruger collaborated with French director Fabienne Berthaud, a narcissistic photographer asks his makeup artist to turn Frankie (Kruger), a model he is photographing in a makeshift studio session in Paris, more transparent. This demand evokes Richard Dyer's study of whiteness and his argument that in Western culture, whiteness has been invisible. The assumption is, for him, that whites are human beings whereas other races are something else (1997, 2–9). Yet here, the invisibility of whiteness, when applied to women, clearly has other connotations, not of power but of powerlessness. In retrospect, this association of Kruger's whiteness with transparency seems crucial to understanding some of the cultural meanings of her stardom. She had come to international attention the previous year playing Helen of Troy in the epic blockbuster *Troy* (2004), alongside stars Brad Pitt, Orlando Bloom, and Eric Bana. The film does little to change the classical view of the mythological character as a blank recipient of male desire, the traditional object of exchange between men in which the object matters little (Sedgwick). *Frankie* is autobiographical in that Kruger was indeed a model when she started her film career. When, years later, she became a recognizable star, she remained an occasional model, advertising various products for brands like Calvin Klein, Chanel, Martell Cognac and Nestlé among others, the modeling often seeming to predominate over the acting in public perception. Sharing a generalized surprise about her stunning performance in *Aus dem Nichts* (2017), Johanna Schneller explains: "She's primarily known for her flawless skin and stunning fashion sense" (2018). Helen of Troy's generic beauty became attached to the model's generic beauty as the actor's trajectory continued to be marked by the translucence demanded by the fictional photographer in *Frankie*. Notions of charisma and uniqueness traditionally attached to stars (Dyer 1979, 34–37; 1986, 9) were, in Kruger's case, both linked to Helen's status as "the most beautiful woman in the world" and compromised by this genericness.

In the films, this translucid quality is not only a consequence of her embodiment of traditional notions of white femininity but often coincides with the absence in her persona of strong marks of national identity. In *Troy,* heroes and secondary characters, including the other women, are firmly anchored in national identities—Menelaus of Sparta, Paris and Hector of Troy, Phthian Achilles. Helen, however, takes on the national identity first of her husband as Helen of Sparta and then of her lover as Helen of Troy. Born, according to *The Iliad* and *The Odyssey,* of Zeus and Leda, she has no country. It seems fitting that the filmmakers chose for the part a then little-known actor who had been born in Germany, studied in London, and lived in Paris (and would later become a U.S. citizen). Discussing the female police detectives of the Swedish-Danish series *Bron/Broen* (2011–2018), its U.S. adaptation *The Bridge* (2013–2014, one of whom is played by Kruger), and the later French-British spinoff *The Tunnel* (2013–2018), Janet McCabe underlines their physical similarities and common character traits—the flaxen hair and flowing locks, "fragile but unflinching, familiar yet enigmatic"—which cue them as figures of the border (303). McCabe goes one step further in that she associates characteristics of white femininity with the border. As Kruger's career developed and transnational-by-default parts proliferated, this borderliness became an essential part of her star persona, and approximated Kruger to Lim's description of those cinematic phenomena that do not arise from any single country, actively forsaking the national (1). In the 2010s, Kruger became a signifier of the intensification of the transnational turn in cinema while simultaneously illustrating the continuing power of the national to define identity, including a star's persona.

Kruger made *National Treasure* (2004) back-to-back with *Troy*. In it she plays Dr. Abigail Chase, not just an ordinary U.S. citizen but one whose job links her closely with the founding fathers and the Declaration of Independence. In a sense the flip side of *Troy*, the film showcases a different side of the character's transnationality: her ability to cross the Atlantic and "become American" whenever the scripts require it. Apart from demonstrating very early in her career her considerable and seldom exploited comic skills, the film also inaugurates the stunning diversity of her characters' national origins as well as her linguistic malleability: here she is and sounds American, but when erudite adventurer Ben Gates (Nicolas Cage) seems to hear a slight Pennsylvania Dutch accent, she corrects him: Saxony German. Like her identity in general, the actor's foreignness is often invisible, but the transnational character of her parts expands in all directions. In *Wicker Park* (2004), she has a Czech mother and a Californian father; in *Frankie*, she was born in Germany and lives in Paris, speaks German to her mother on the phone, and French and English on shoots; she is a Russian princess turned anarchist who speaks perfect French in *Les brigades du tigre* (2006); Austrian, although the film is spoken entirely in English, in *Copying Beethoven* (2006); South African speaking English with a South African accent in *Goodbye Bafana* (2007); and, from nowhere at all since she is a figment of the male protagonist's imagination, a ghost that speaks both French and English in *L'âge des ténèbres* (2007). In *The Hunting Party* (2007), she is a member of a Serbo-Bosnian militia and speaks English with a strong accent from the Balkans, as she does in *Unknown* (2011) as a Bosnian migrant in Berlin. She is a German film star in *Inglourious Basterds* (2009), speaking English with a German accent, and Austrian princess Marie Antoinette in *Les adieux à la reine* (2012). She is an alien in *The Host* (2013) and a caricatured Bavarian physiotherapist who manages, in a brief cameo appearance, to speak German, French, and English with a German accent in *Les garçons et Guillaume, à table!* (2013). In *Maryland* (2015), she is German, lives in the

Côte d'Azur, says home is London, and flies to Canada when she has to find a new home. In *Tout nous sépare,* she was also born in Germany but is French, and she is a Belgian witch with a German accent in her cameo appearance in *Welcome to Marwen* (2018). To end the decade, in *The Operative,* her character, Rachel, was born in London of a British Jewish father who hated Israel and a German mother who went to live in a kibbutz in Israel. She then lived in Canada for a while and is now living in Germany but working for Israel.

In general, her persona in the 2010s is characterized by an intensification of her vertiginous border crossings and, like Cotillard, her alternation between Hollywood and Europe. Her third film with Berthaud, *Sky* (2015), a film in the European tradition of fascination with the United States, particularly the West, and the open road, narrativizes this transatlantic dimension. Kruger plays Romy, a French woman who is attracted to all kinds of Americana—motels, roadside dives, road signs, coyotes, and Las Vegas—leaves her husband on the road, settles down on a border town, befriends a Native American family, and falls in love with Diego (Norman Reedus), a park ranger. At one point, Diego says, "You piss me off with your fucking angel eyes," which highlights not only her Helen-like beauty but also a new quality: her relentlessness, her determination and her inner strength, features that are compounded by her honesty, her righteousness, and her capacity to give love. The Berthaud films suggest the evolution both in her acting style and her cultural iconicity as a foreigner or as a woman without a country, a persona that crystallizes in her two central parts of the decade: border police agent Sonya Cross in the two seasons of *The Bridge* and bereaved widow and mother Katja Sekerci in her first and so far only film made in Germany, *Aus dem Nichts*.

The Bridge is a crime thriller set on the Mexico-U.S. boundary and focuses on the usual topics of drug-related violence, human trafficking, and corruption, but at its heart lies the relationship between Kruger's Sonya Cross, an El Paso police detective, and Marco Ruiz (Demián Bichir), her counterpart in the Juárez police force. Beyond the fireworks of drug cartels and unbridled violence, the series is a story of borders as prime sites for connecting individuals and "borderwork," that is, the activity of ordinary people in bordering processes (Rumford 245–247). McCabe describes the female protagonists of the Swedish-Danish, the U.S., and the French-British series as "disconnected" heroines, detached, socially challenged, but "able to read a crime like no-one else" (303), and she relates this, as we have seen, to their talent to negotiate the border. In this, Sonya has the advantage of Kruger's experience as a transnational star and her familiarity with

Transnational hope, transnational despair: Diane Kruger in *Aus dem Nichts* (Fatih Akin, Warner Bros., 2017). Digital frame enlargement.

borderlands and cross-border mobilities. In the series, Sonya is hard and uncompromising, has no social skills and no empathy, plays by the rules, and follows procedures, but is also reliable, blunt and honest, and a brilliant detective. Here Kruger's familiar combination of inexpressiveness, insecurity, and harshness feeds into the character's unbending fairness that knows nothing of national difference. Although a U.S. citizen, Sonya is at no time moved by national prejudice and develops a strong connection with Marco across borders and drastically different temperaments and personalities. In this case, the apparent rigidity of her persona makes her luminescent rather than invisible, even as it reinforces the nationally unmarked dimension of her transnationality. For once, her weakly defined national allegiance works toward reinforcing both her uniqueness and, in her association with Bichir's character, the productive potential of borderliness in contemporary social relations. The growing friendship between the "brown" detective from the south and the white woman with the flaxen hair from the north speaks to the radical doubleness of the border as a site of both cosmopolitan engagement with the other and dismal social injustice and violence against the weak.

In *The Bridge*, Sonya and Marco's relationship is set in a highly charged geopolitical space, iconically visualized in the Bridge of the Americas, where the story starts. Both characters are embodiments of that particular space and of the potential as well as the cruel realities of its border-crossing location. Kruger's character in *Aus dem Nichts* has similar resonances, even though the space has changed: from one of the most contested sites in America to a Europe in which internal and external borders proliferate, both evoking and constantly hampering the project of a united Europe. For once, Kruger was unanimously praised for her performance as Katja (see, for example, Kenneth Turan, 2017, and Frank Kermode, 2018) and received her first major recognition with the Cannes Palme d'Or for the best female performance of the year. As in *The Bridge*, an important part of this performance is related to her whiteness. In the DVD extras, director Fatih Akin explains that he wanted a very Aryan-looking woman for his heroine, underlining that her whiteness is ideological in a way that expands Dyer's theory. It becomes part of a wide canvas which, although centered in Hamburg, where German Katja lives with her Kurdish Turkish husband Nuri (Numan Acar) and their son Rocco (Rafael Santana), extends to southeastern Turkey, where Nuri and his family are from, and Greece, where the film's final act takes place. This is a map of Europe marked by the inability of many people to see and operate beyond extremely racialized forms of nationalism and by the willingness of a few to incorporate into their very personal experience the idea of transnational Europe. In Akin's film, it is Kruger's "immaculate" Aryan credentials that make her trajectory more visible and her decisions more compelling, as well as more tragic. After the early deaths of her husband and son in a terrorist attack by a neo-Nazi group, only she understands straight away who the authors of the attacks have been, while the police follow a racist logic in their investigation.

The intensity and narrative pervasiveness of her inner distress at the loss of her loved ones and anger at the structural racism which is mortally wounding the European project that she has made her own make her transnationalism inescapable for the spectator: she is all we have to look at in the story, and, given the actor's translucid persona, it is a particularly uncomfortable look. But Kruger's performance in this film goes beyond iconicity as she plunges the depths of her own identity. This is illustrated in two close-ups in the final section. After the young terrorist couple have been acquitted by the German court, she follows them to Greece, where they have fled seeking the protection of an extreme-right Greek group. Katja is bent on revenge and has built a homemade bomb, planted it in the trailer by the beach where the couple are staying, and is waiting for their return to detonate it, hiding behind a bush. The close-up in which she is framed conveys her gradual realization that, in consummating her plan, she will be betraying the transnational rationale of her own identity and, therefore, will also be betraying the memory of her hybrid family. The piercing and subtly changing expressiveness of her eyes narrates her change of mind as she retrieves the bomb before the murderers arrive. Shortly after, we find her sitting outside her rented house, more relaxed, looking out at the sea. Then the camera follows her gaze down as she puts her hand inside her trousers and realizes that, for the first time since the terrorist attack, her period has come. The camera tilts up to focus on her face again, which now conveys, in the minimalist style that by now every member of the audience can read, the understanding that she cannot allow herself the return to normality signified by her period. Without her hybrid family the transnational citizen is nothing, just as without tolerance and solidarity Europe, like the English title of the film, fades. For Katja there is no way back.

Aus dem Nichts represents a culmination of sorts for Diane Kruger, who here manages to make her earlier anonymity the very core of a strong form of identity and, in the process, confirms the cultural relevance of the radical form of transnationalism that she represents. The marginal identity takes center stage in this film. In the DVD extras, Kruger asserts that the story is about grief and any other form of unbearable loss would have done, but in the film this grief has a specific environment, which could be described as the fall of Europe as a transnational project. This is the same Europe that in Kristen Stewart's two European films appeared to be more open to transborder exchanges; the same Europe whose diversity was celebrated in Marion Cotillard's films of the 2010s. The three stars have a global reach because of their association with Hollywood yet, as we have seen, are transnational in the particularities of their mobilities—in the cross-border circuits they draw and the translocal histories they tell. The three of them allow us, through the position of privilege conferred to them by their whiteness, to look beyond the nation in different forms: from Stewart's strongly marked U.S. identity and her simultaneous adaptability in the two Assayas films, to new forms of European openness through Cotillard's conscientious commitment to cultural diversity, to Kruger's bumpy trajectory toward the visibility of a transnational subject denuded of strong marks of national identity.

☆☆☆☆☆☆☆☆☆★ Acknowledgments

Research for this article was funded by the Spanish Ministerio de Economía y Competitividad, research project no. FFI2017-83606-P. I would like to thank María del Mar Azcona and Mary Harrod for their help with this chapter and Jules Sandeau for sharing his article with me before it was published.

Chapter 6

Tilda Swinton

From Avant-Garde Androgyne to *The Avengers*

JENNIFER O'MEARA

Tilda Swinton

The film industry has traded in gossip since the early days of movie stardom. Stories of eccentric actors and their scandalous personal lives have remained central to publications, moving from early fan magazines to tabloid journalism and, in the twenty-first century, celebrity-focused websites. Unlike with many young starlets, Tilda Swinton (born

Katherine Matilda Swinton in 1960) became an appealing subject for such publications only decades into her career. Born in London and raised largely in Scotland, where her father was a lord lieutenant of a nineteenth-century mansion house, Swinton began her acting career in political theater after finishing a degree at Cambridge. Her early film work involved seven collaborations with the radical filmmaker Derek Jarman from 1986 until his death in 1994, as well as the remarkable performance of a gender-shifting aristocrat in Sally Potter's *Orlando* (1993). Swinton's first real foray into mainstream cinema came in 2000 with *The Beach*. Swinton has described this as a key turning point, not necessarily in terms of acting but because it was the first time she was tasked with dressing for a red carpet ("Planet Tilda," *W Magazine*, 21 August 2011). This moment marked the start of her reluctant ascendance to the dual status of film star and fashion icon. By 2008, Swinton had begun to accumulate high-profile awards, including an Academy Award and BAFTA for Best Supporting Actress in *Michael Clayton* (2007). These awards were accompanied by increased press coverage of Swinton's private life, particularly her romantic entanglements, when it was reported that the man who accompanied her to such ceremonies (Sandro Kopp) was her boyfriend, not the father of her children (John Byrne), with whom she still lived in the Highland town of Nairn, Scotland.

For tabloids, the vague details of Swinton's relationships read like a dream: not only could they report on this apparent ménage à trois but the relative ages and occupations of the three participants made for an even better story. With the Scottish playwright Byrne twenty years older than Swinton, and the artist Kopp eighteen years younger, the actress was presumed to be lustfully having her cake and eating it ("Tilda Swinton: Her Toyboy, Elderly Lover and an Intriguing Ménage a Trois," *Daily Mail*, 14 February 2008). In subsequent years, Swinton would go on to detail the much more mundane aspects of this setup: Byrne and Swinton had not been together romantically for years, but they were living together to raise their children, and both had their own—separate—romantic relationships ("Transformer," *BUST Magazine*, June 2010: 67). Yet Swinton entered the 2010s as an eccentric enigma, a reference point for magazine articles with titles like "Liberated in Love: Can Open Marriage Work?" (*Harper's Bazaar*, 13 July 2009). Few could have predicted that by the middle of the decade she would be appearing in a Judd Apatow romantic comedy, *Trainwreck* (2015), or in multiple installments of the Marvel Cinematic Universe, including *Doctor Strange* (2016).

Though appearing in some fifty screen productions prior to 2010, Tilda Swinton's distinctive star presence has gained increased exposure and currency in the past decade. In this period, discourse around the British performer has retained many of the same associations—androgyny, the avant-garde, and an otherworldly timelessness—yet Swinton has simultaneously appeared in more mainstream and auteur-driven productions. As Jackie Stacey notes, Swinton thus demonstrates an "unusual facility to cross between independent and more popular culture forms" (243). This chapter will consider how Swinton has increasingly brought her unique qualities to productions by established auteurs such as Wes Anderson, Luca Guadagnino, Jim Jarmusch, Bong Joon-ho, and Lynne Ramsay. In particular, her roles in U.S.-made films by the likes of Anderson and Jarmusch seem to have served as an important stepping stone for Swinton to dabble in mainstream comedies like *Trainwreck* and in the Marvel superhero franchise, with *Doctor Strange* and *Avengers: Endgame* (2019). Thus, while Stacey rightly identifies "flux and mutability" as some of Swinton's signature qualities (243), her more recent roles will be shown to stabilize and mainstream some of Swinton's edgy elements. As my analysis of related promotional materials will reveal, such unconventional elements are increasingly limited to interviews and media profiles. In these, details of Swinton's eccentric home life in Scotland serve to remind the public that—while she may appear in a film like *Trainwreck* alongside the famously "relatable" Amy Schumer—Swinton is still far removed, physically and metaphysically, from your average film star.

☆☆☆☆☆★★★★★ A Tourist in Hollywood, an Artist at Large

In the aforementioned *Harper's Bazaar* article "Liberated in Love: Can Open Marriage Work?," Swinton's situation is compared to the "romantic experiment" of the early twentieth-century painter Vanessa Bell, sister of Virginia Woolf. Bell lived on her English country estate with her children, her lover, his gay lover, and occasionally the father of her children. Both Swinton's and Bell's alleged living situations are framed as signs of individual thinking, of being unconventional and imaginative: "Open marriages have always fascinated and unsettled us because they threaten our assumptions; they raise questions we prefer not be raised" ("Liberated in Love"). Though Swinton would subsequently clarify that she was not in an open marriage, the associations around such an arrangement would still appear to hold, and they have informed the reception of Swinton in the media ever since. As a performer and artist, Swinton's long and diverse career is largely characterized by her ability to unsettle boundaries and question assumptions, particularly around gender and artistic mediums. As Hilary Radner explains, Swinton has been aptly described by Anderson as a "visual performance artist at large," a label that captures her ability to "cross borders and transgress categories," including those of on- and offscreen performance (401–402) as well as different artistic mediums including theater, film, fine art, and fashion.

In keeping with Swinton's sustained interest in unsettling boundaries, her forays into the Hollywood mainstream can be seen as another dimension of this, a chance to explore the boundary between high and low art. Why can't she appear in a Judd Apatow comedy? Why shouldn't she be a part of the Marvel Cinematic Universe, the highest-grossing film series of all time? Much as Swinton's personal life reveals a natural inclination to think outside the box—to respond to individual circumstances rather than societal expectations—her career demonstrates a remarkable ability to not place oneself in a box, all while literally placing herself in a glass box. In "The Maybe" (Serpentine Gallery 1995) and "The Maybe (reprise)" (MOMA 2013), Swinton as performance artist presents her sleeping self as though a living museum specimen, while gallery attendees can surround her and peer in. As the remainder of the chapter will suggest, this openness to all kinds of roles—and to being seen, as in the glass box, from every angle—has prevented Swinton from being typecast by filmmakers or by herself. This is not to say that Swinton does not bring distinct qualities, or associations, to these diverse roles, but that elements of her essence are used to different effect in different kinds of roles.

An interest in a decentralized career structure is reflected in Swinton's engaging interviews. In a profile in *The Gentlewoman* in 2012, she refers to the independent films *I Am Love* (2009), *Julia* (2008), and *We Need to Talk about Kevin* (2011) as the "three pillars" of her work since the new millennium ("Tilda Swinton," *The Gentlewoman*, Spring and Summer 2012). As she explains, she started working with Luca Guadagnino on *I Am Love* in 2000, with work on *Julia*, "a film that took up five years of my life," beginning around 2003. Swinton describes all other films from the 2000–2012 period as "excursions": "Those industrial films are like family holidays in comparison with what it took to get [*I Am Love*, *Julia*, and *We Need to Talk about Kevin*] made" ("Tilda Swinton"). The reference to these three films as "pillars" suggests how Swinton's diverse career is measured rather than chaotic, reliant on a structure of integrity but with some space for wild ornamentation. As implied by Swinton's description of "industrial films," roles in such productions can be much more contained in terms of both the scale of the role and the timescale of her involvement. Swinton's work on two of her "pillar" films went far beyond acting, since she was a producer on *I Am Love* and an executive producer of *We Need to Talk about Kevin*. She also has producer or executive producer credits for subsequent films in which she appears, including Bong's *Okja* (2017), Mark Cousins's epic documentary *Women Make Film* (2018), and *Memoria* (2021), Thai filmmaker Apichatpong Weerasethakul's first English-language production.

Often describing herself as "a tourist" in Hollywood, Swinton's occasional forays into mainstream roles may also have a financial motivation. Like other actors with a preference for playing the kind of nuanced roles more often on offer in arthouse cinema, Swinton may be tempted by the injection of income that can come from bigger studio productions. Radner also considers finances to be a motivation for Swinton's work as a brand ambassador, "usually paid," for fashion houses and luxury products (406). Symptomatic of Swinton's well-documented status as a fashion icon (see De Perthuis; Radner), she has served as the face for companies like Chanel, the Italian jewelry brand Pomellato, and the cosmetics company NARS. As Radner explains, such collaborations, which typically involve Swinton appearing in advertising campaigns, "add to her relatively meagre income from her film roles (by Hollywood standards)," and may well be necessary for Swinton's household, since "she appears to be the main source of financial support for a bevy of persons surrounding her, including her children, partner, former husband, [and] the village alternative school her children attend" (406).

My suggestion that Swinton takes certain roles purely on the basis of income might appear at odds with other strands of Swinton's persona—her ties to avant-garde and artistic expression, her upper-class family background—yet such a financial impetus might explain the somewhat jarring references Swinton makes to wanting to stop making films altogether: "That's really what I would like the most," she told *The Gentlewoman* in 2012 ("Tilda Swinton"). Swinton even frames her BAFTA- and Golden Globe-nominated performance as numbed mother Eva in *We Need to Talk about Kevin* as secondary to her interest in helping director Lynne Ramsay get the film made. Serving on the project as a producer first and foremost, she explains: "For a long time, I didn't necessarily want to be in it. To be honest with you, I just don't really like doing it. I love actresses like [Renée] Falconetti, who was only ever in one movie. Every film I make is a personal disappointment: I want it to be the last" ("Tilda Swinton"). Swinton's candor is far removed from the gushing gratitude for film opportunities we have come to expect from actors, particularly women. Swinton's reference to Renée Falconetti, the French stage actress who made a single film appearance in Carl Dreyer's *La Passion de Jeanne d'Arc* (1928), may also be telling of her diverse career. While it is much too late for Swinton to take Falconetti's route—of only appearing in one film—she is arguably succeeding in only appearing in each *kind* of role once. And if with every film she does feel that "I want it to be the last," then by shifting into a new kind of character with each film, her idealized interest in singularity is somewhat achieved. Indeed, in discussing her role in *Doctor Strange* in 2016, Swinton explains: "I'm in this game to amuse myself. I don't know how interesting I would find it to repeat. I'm not really interested enough in any sense of craft to hoe a kind of defined row" ("Why 'Doctor Strange' Star Tilda Swinton Wanted to Do a Superhero Movie," *IndieWire*, 4 November 2016). But although Swinton may not repeat her roles in any generic sense, taking a thematic lens to her career reveals how her sustained interest in androgyny is matched by a sustained engagement with issues of ageing and anachronism.

☆☆☆☆☆☆☆☆☆★ Agelessness and Anachronism

Dating back to her first experimental appearances in Jarman's films and *Orlando* through to her roles in American indie productions like *Only Lovers Left Alive* (2013) and *The Grand Budapest Hotel* (2014), Swinton has played characters largely defined by their age or their agelessness. Viewed against this history, her Marvel role as "the Ancient One" seems less of a radical departure; the role is simply another opportunity to portray a character with a complex relationship to time. Much as many of Swinton's performances and characters seem unwilling to follow a prescribed binary of gendered identity, her roles can also involve untethering a character from a fixed time and place. This is particularly the case with *Orlando* and *Only Lovers Left Alive*—roles to which the Ancient One might be tied in a kind of loose trilogy of Swinton-as-time-traveler.

As *Orlando*'s titular character, Swinton plays the aristocrat poet on a journey through some 400 years of English history. Like in the Virginia Woolf novel on which it is based, Orlando begins the film as a man but later transforms into a woman. In the film's most iconic scene, Orlando enters a maze in an eighteenth-century French robe and powdered gray wig. When Orlando exits the maze, she is wigless and wearing radically different period clothing: a Victorian bustle. Through the cinematic magic of costume and editing, Swinton enters the labyrinth in one century but exits in another. And though Swinton only plays one character, Orlando is consistently recontextualized, moving from the 1600s to modern times. The film radically resists the tropes of the costume drama, or historical drama, providing something of an antinarrative that allows for significant commentary on gender politics throughout British history.

Perhaps more so than any other performance, *Orlando* signals how Swinton has become a symbolic figure that demonstrates how the past inflects the present, and vice versa. Stacey grounds her conception of Swinton's "flat affect" performance style in Lauren Berlant's discussion of flatness as "a structuring of 'unfeeling' that belongs to a historical archive, pointing 'back prior to the twentieth century European and American modernists with whom it is usually associated: from Gertrude Stein and Buster Keaton to Andy Warhol and Jackson Pollock"' (Stacey 253; Berlant 197). Stacey considers how Swinton's performance of a flat affect can mean "the present 'becomes historical,"' so that we can understand "Swinton's performance of flat affect as belonging to the historical present" (253–254). Drawing a comparison with Greta Garbo's minimalist performance style in *Queen Christina* (1933), Stacey also argues that Swinton's film career "reworks the temporalities of particular genres of feminine affect that have become so central to our emotional landscapes since the cinema began" and "indicates her capacity to generate readings of her transcendence of time" (247; 249–250). Stacey traces this back to Swinton's early film roles, her collaborations with Jarman, arguing that "Swinton's more general association with Jarman's artistic practices intent on reframing conventional histories of sexuality, such as *Caravaggio* (1986), *The Last of England* (1988) and *Edward II* (1991), contribute to her reputation as a figure whose presence belongs to the project of contesting historical narratives and traditional chronologies and teleologies that have anchored them" (253). Stacey's analysis of Swinton's presentation of a "historical present" focuses on Swinton's early film work with Jarman and her recurring performance art presentation of her sleeping self as a living corpse in "The Maybe" and "The Maybe (reprise)" (250–254). But such a tendency to transcend time by contesting traditional chronologies lingers on into her 2010s film roles, particularly in *Only Lovers Left Alive* and *Doctor Strange*.

Only Lovers Left Alive was Swinton's second time working with the American independent film maverick Jim Jarmusch, with whom she would collaborate again for *The Dead Don't Die* (2019). More so than any other U.S. indie filmmaker of his generation, Jarmusch's work takes a global outlook, frequently filmed in Europe or Asia and starring European performers—as in *The Limits of Control* (2009), in which Swinton plays the cipher-like character "Blonde" in a production filmed in Spain and starring Isaac de Bankolé as a solitary assassin. As signaled by the name, Swinton's character is purposefully enigmatic in a film that foregrounds acts of translation and (mis) communication between a series of characters with labels for monikers, including "Lone Man" (de Bankolé) and "Nude" (Paz de la Huerta). Jarmusch tends to work with the same performers over time, and it took him some seven years to fund and make *Only Lovers Left Alive*. Swinton was attached to it from early on, and Jarmusch credits the project eventually getting made to her optimistic—verging on fatalistic—approach to timing: "Whenever a bump in the road had him ready to abandon the project, Tilda Swinton would insist: 'That's good news, it means that now is not the time. It will happen when it needs to happen'" ("Jim Jarmusch: 'Women Are My Leaders," *The Guardian*, 20 February 2014). Indeed, time, persistence, and patience are central themes of the film.

Only Lovers Left Alive offers a particularly interesting example of Swinton as symbol of cultural anachronism. The vampire film focuses on Adam (Tom Hiddleston) and Eve (Swinton) and seems motivated by a desire to reveal how much knowledge and culture vampires would experience over the long course of their lives. Named after the biblical couple, Adam and Eve are effectively human encyclopedias: they speak many languages and have personal experiences of a diverse range of cultural and scientific movements and historical events. Swinton's role as Eve can be seen as a culmination of her interests in myth and archetype, while a script littered with Middle and Early Modern English and references to Christopher Marlowe provides an interesting addendum to Swinton's controversial decision to leave the prestigious Royal Shakespeare Company back in 1984 (See Goodman 215–228). Anticipating Swinton's role as the Ancient One in *Doctor Strange* and *Avengers: Endgame*, there is an otherworldly power to Eve's anachronistic presence. Delivering terms from Middle English like "my liege lord" and "weskit" with a confident ease, she has something of a magical touch: with an ability to tell how old things are just by touching them, Eve also seems able to absorb the content of books purely by tracing over the words with her finger. And with Adam presented as a rather depressed figure, it is up to Swinton to convey the playful possibilities of vampires using centuries of knowledge to their advantage. In the closing sequence, desperate for blood, Eve politely addresses a Tangiers couple in their native French before revealing her fangs. It is easy to see why Jarmusch and Swinton would be willing to wait seven years to make this a reality. Like a bloodsucking follow-up to *Orlando*, Swinton's intellectual vampire is the epitome of refined timelessness.

Swinton's ageless qualities have also lent themselves well to her increased engagement with modeling and the fashion industry. Since the early 2000s, Swinton has emerged as fashion icon and muse, as in 2003 when the Dutch avant-garde design duo, Viktor & Rolf, sent her down the catwalk followed by an army of Tilda-like clones. Notably, Swinton's

Tilda Swinton as intellectual vampire in *Only Lovers Left Alive* (Jim Jarmusch, Sony Pictures Classics, 2013).

trajectory has worked against the accepted ageism in the industry, particularly when it comes to models. In 2009, the almost fifty-year-old Swinton's modeling stints included the cover and an editorial for *AnOther Magazine* (Spring–Summer 2009), photographed by esteemed photographer Craig McDean, and the Winter issue of *Acne Paper*, photographed by *Vogue Italia* regular Paolo Roversi (Issue 9, October 2009). Both of these shoots confirm Swinton's instinct for wearing dramatic couture shapes and styles and presenting an edgy, offbeat appearance. For *Acne*, she channels Marchesa Luisa Casati, donning a curly brunette wig and the belle époque style of the eccentric, wide-eyed muse. Casati was an Italian heiress and patroness of the arts in early twentieth-century Europe. Like the *Harper's Bazaar* piece on open marriages that groups Swinton with modernist painter Vanessa Bell, Swinton's distinctive appearance and aura lend themselves to moments of cultural time travel, as though Casati and Bell are her true contemporaries. These fashion editorials work to consolidate Swinton's filmic persona as timeless, ageless. In the *Acne* spread in particular, titled "The Lost Album of Marchesa Casati," we can see overlaps with Swinton's elaborate period costumes in films like *Wittgenstein* (1993) and *Orlando*. Swinton's appearances as the Ancient One in the Marvel Cinematic Universe equally build on her on- and offscreen associations with being from another time and, perhaps, another plane altogether.

Swinton's casting as the Ancient One in *Doctor Strange* was initially fraught, with fans of the original Marvel comic (in which the character is a male Tibetan mystic) seeing it as a problematic example of Hollywood's "whitewashing" practices. The president of Marvel Studios and *Doctor Strange*'s director Scott Derrickson repeatedly defended the casting of Swinton, explaining that the role was written especially for her, and the decision to reframe the character as a Celtic rather than Tibetan mystic was partly due to the crude Asian stereotyping of the character in the original comic ("*Doctor Strange* Director Explains Why the Ancient One Was Never Going to Be Asian in the Movie," *Vanity Fair*, 13 October 2016). From my perspective, one with a complete lack of investment in the Marvel Cinematic Universe, the decision to cast Swinton as the now Celtic mystic is a clever use of poetic license. Though not quite Ancient Celtic paganism, Swinton's personal lineage connects her Anglo-Scots family back to medieval Scotland at least. Furthermore, from her early days in theater she has expressed a keen interest in the symbolic power of myth and religious icons, as explored in a thought-provoking interview with Lizbeth Goodman in 1989 (215–224). In particular, Swinton discusses her forthcoming role as *Orlando* and how she intends to find a point of gender identification for the character: "I would play it moment to moment. I'd treat it as myth rather than as realism" (224).

As with her gender-crossing performance in *Orlando*, and numerous times since, Swinton ties her interest in the role of the Ancient One to an opportunity to escape from realism, including traditional configurations of gender. As she surmised soon after her casting was announced, "I have yet to decide exactly where I'm going to place the gender of this character." ("Tilda Swinton Is 'Delighted' to Look Unrecognizable in 'Trainwreck,"' *The Huffington Post*, 15 July 2015). What came to pass is a performance that takes advantage of Swinton's willingness to appear androgynous, but one where her womanhood is also crucial to the character. This includes the scene where Doctor Strange (Benedict Cumberbatch) arrives to meet the Ancient One and assumes they must be the elderly Asian man in the room, with Swinton mistaken as someone merely there to pour the tea. Swinton's look for the film, and her subsequent minor role in *Avengers: Endgame*, is also uncannily similar to the high-fashion spread "Planet Tilda" she shot for *W Magazine* in 2011. As part of the "out-of-this-world" shoot by photographer Tim Walker, Swinton appears bald and wears an androgynous, all-burgundy outfit, composed (according to the fashion credits) of a coat, dress, and pants. The excess of material, all in one color, make it hard to distinguish the garments, while Swinton (who is probably crouching) appears to be hovering over the alien landscape of rural Iceland. Her costumes in *Doctor Strange* mirror the look entirely, from the bald head to the cloak layered over monochrome fabrics in shades of mustard, beige, or burgundy. Looking at the images side by side, one might wonder if Swinton somehow summoned the invitation to play the Ancient One when shooting the magazine spread four years previously.

★★★★★★★★★★ "Shockingly Conventional": Swinton in *Trainwreck*

While the Marvel films repurposed recurring elements of Swinton's persona (androgyny, agelessness) for a mass market, *Trainwreck* allowed her to bridge an arguably bigger gap—to play an everywoman. As Stacey has explored to great effect, Swinton's extreme version of whiteness is central to her onscreen presence and broader public persona (263–266). Lending itself well to her role as a vampire in *Only Lovers Left Alive*, Swinton's paleness also suits her other otherworldly roles, including that of the White Witch in *The Chronicles of Narnia* series (2005–2010) and the corpse of Madame D. in *The Grand Budapest Hotel*: "The whiteness of Swinton's flesh seems to resist the imprint of time, as angel, witch, vampire and corpse. . . . The paleness of her whiteness suggests a vitality sourced from elsewhere" (263). It is precisely because Swinton's pale whiteness has been central to her image that her characterization of the ruthless magazine editor Dianna in *Trainwreck* caused such commotion. As Nina Terrero puts it in an *Entertainment Weekly* article on Swinton's transformation, "Famous for her avant-garde style and bare-bones approach to beauty, Tilda Swinton is unrecognizable—and shockingly conventional—as Dianna" ("Tilda Swinton in Trainwreck: Here's the Scoop on Her Transformation," *Entertainment Weekly*, 21 July 2015). Conventional here refers to her carefully dyed caramel-colored hair, tanned skin, and smoky eye makeup.

Descriptions of Swinton as paradoxically shocking and conventional are best understood within the historical context of her public image. Swinton's 2008 appearance at the Academy Awards (where she won an Oscar for *Michael Clayton*) was described in the *New York Times* as "brazenly pasty, unsustained by rouge and bronzer, a white waif in an ocean of spray-tanned limbs and bobbing plastic torsos" (Alex Kuczynski, "Extreme Makeover," *New York Times*, 13 April 2008). In many respects, public exclamations around Swinton's natural paleness seem unwarranted. She is, after all, of ancient Scottish heritage, and her skin tone would not appear extreme to most in the United Kingdom or Ireland. It is more her unwillingness to mask it with makeup or tanning products that marks her as unconventional—and her appearance as Dianna in *Trainwreck* as "shockingly conventional" by comparison. Swinton's paleness also seems central to her own sense of

Tilda Swinton wearing fake tan and popular hair and makeup trends in *Trainwreck* (Judd Apatow, Universal Pictures, 2015).

self growing up, as when she discussed her early identification with the equally androgynous David Bowie when addressing him in the opening speech of a Bowie exhibit in 2013: "I was a freak like you and even looked a little like you . . . [a] gingery, boney pinkey whitey person" ("Tilda Swinton Praises David Bowie," *Spin*, 22 March 2013).

These various factors all contributed to Swinton's decision that her costume for Dianna should be marked by three popular trends among twenty-first-century Western white women, but far removed from Swinton's normal appearance: a "Tandoori tan," heavy eye makeup, and curtain-like, caramel-colored hair. Swinton complements these external cosmetic elements with various performance strategies—including a number of affectations and gestures that seem removed from Stacey's focus on her "flat affect" (243). Dianna is impatient with her employees, including the film's protagonist, Amy (Amy Schumer), and this is signaled through her face (pained expressions of boredom), her hands (frantic circular gestures for staff members to wrap up things they are saying), and her stomping exits from scenes. As Dianna, Swinton's walk is distinctive and in alignment with other dimensions of her physical transformation. Twice, Dianna makes a swift exit—as though she has better places to be, or more important people to see—and her walk is accompanied by the syncopated rhythm of heavy heels. These sounds, trailing her as she attempts to march out of rooms, belie Dianna's try-hard nature. She is someone who always wears high heels, even if she can't really walk in them; someone who thinks they are the height of fashion, even if her appearance suggests contrivance rather than inherent style.

These qualities extend also to Dianna's hair: Swinton wore a carefully styled wig, which falls over one eye, hiding part of her upper face. While not an uncommon look, it is far removed from Swinton's personal hairstyles in recent years (short hair, often pushed back into a voluminous sculpture) and from unobscured shots of Swinton's intense gaze in the vast majority of her film roles. Her characters' haunting stares and penetrating glares just wouldn't be the same with one eye hidden behind a curtain of hair. Dianna's hair, like her tan and her heavy eye makeup, works as a mask that separates the natural-looking Swinton from the manufactured Dianna. Also significant is the hair and skin coloring of Amy's co-worker Nikki (Vanessa Bayer), another of Dianna's employees. Bayer's pale skin and deep red hair stand out from both Amy and Dianna's tanned, blonde figures. For audience members aware that they are watching a "shockingly conventional" Swinton, Nikki/Bayer serves as a reminder of Swinton's natural coloring, presenting us with a veritable before-and-after transformation within the same shot.

Swinton's portrayal of Dianna, particularly her discussion of the character and the influences for her physical transformation, can be better understood through Stacey's argument that Swinton is often in dialogue "with *femininity as genre*" (259–260), a dialogue Stacey positions against descriptions of Swinton as chameleonlike: "Unlike the animal, which adapts to the tones and textures of its environment, Swinton almost effects the reverse: standing to one side of the generic contexts of her production, she draws them towards her only to formalize their conventionality through her shifting embodiments of them" (259–260). As a public figure, and in the majority of her film presentations, Swinton has sidestepped traditional visual markers of movie star femininity—to present as androgynous, and to present as pale and barely made up on red carpets and publicity materials (even when dressed in high-fashion gowns and clothing). I am particularly interested in Stacey's description of Swinton's drawing of generic contexts "towards her[,] only to formalize their conventionality through her shifting embodiments of them" (259–260). While Stacey is not referring specifically to visual trappings like costume and makeup, a parallel can be drawn here to Swinton's very conscious decision to embody various contemporary feminine beauty trends when designing Dianna's look.

Over the course of Swinton's career, she frequently discusses her interest in helping to shape her character's costumes, describing close consultation with costume designers in order to put together "the disguise," as "the lion's share of my work" ("Only Lovers Left Alive's Tilda Swinton Talks Playing a Vampire," *Daily Dead*, 10 April 2014). The same applied to *Trainwreck*, where she has described the significance of the tan, the commonness of Dianna's physical appearance, and the idea that Dianna models herself on Carine Roitfeld, former editor in chief of *Vogue Paris* (Terrero, "Tilda Swinton in Trainwreck"). Asked about seeing herself as Dianna, Swinton explains the weight of the transformation: "The Tandoori tan. That's probably the most heavily disguised I've ever been, in my life. Forget *The Grand Budapest Hotel* or *Snowpiercer*. And yet, there are women walking down the streets right now, looking like that. It's a desired look, apparently" ("Tilda Swinton Talks Trainwreck, Doctor Strange, the Coen Brothers, and More," *Collider*, 14 July 2015). In another interview, Swinton similarly comments on the attainability of this look: "You just have to go to a big make-up counter in a big department store and you, too, can get that look" ("Tilda Swinton Is 'Delighted' to Look Unrecognizable in 'Trainwreck'"). In Swinton's observations about the commonness of Dianna's look, and the ease with which it can be procured (at any big cosmetics counter), one can sense her bemused distance from such cosmetic choices, and the way it might seem to contribute to the almost prescribed conventions of—as Stacey puts it—"femininity as genre" (259). Swinton chose Dianna's look precisely because it is one she sees regularly, and one audiences can be presumed to recognize too, and by "draw[ing this] towards her" for a rare embodiment she offers a reminder of how easy it would be for Swinton to masquerade as conventional but how unnatural this would be for someone who has always identified as "a freak . . . [a] gingery, boney pinkey whitey person." Thus, despite Dianna's bronzers and tanning products being applied directly to Swinton's skin—with the reference to a Tandoori curry suggesting a lengthy marination—she wears these cosmetics at an ironic distance.

Swinton's role since October 2014 as "the new face" of NARS cosmetics is notably absent in the considerable discussion of Swinton's makeup for the film, including a step-by-step description of the process taken by *Trainwreck*'s makeup artist, Kyra Panchenko, in *Entertainment Weekly*: "The first step toward achieving the Oscar winner's makeover was a daily, hour-long session with self-tanning cream, followed by 'layers and layers' of bronzers on her face and décolletage. 'She's [normally] translucent, and we turned her the color of a coconut shell,' says Panchenko" (Terrero, "Tilda Swinton in Trainwreck"). Such a description, particularly the tonal terminology (bronzers, translucent, the color of a coconut shell), reconfirms the significance of pale whiteness to Swinton's persona, as does Swinton's NARS makeup campaign. The specifics of the NARS look that Swinton modeled, just months before *Trainwreck* was released, are virtual opposites to her makeup as Dianna. NARS's print campaign with Swinton sees her wearing a barely-there look: nude lips and eyeshadow barely darker than her natural complexion. As Ashley Mateo describes: "The stark, neutral palette shows off her striking looks, so all you can focus on is her beauty" ("Tilda Swinton for Nars Isn't Your Typical Beauty Campaign," *Self*, 17 October 2014). The NARS campaign makeup is therefore much more in keeping with Swinton's personal look. It seems noteworthy that neither Swinton nor any critics brought up her recent casting as the face of NARS when discussing her *Trainwreck* makeup at such length. Perhaps Swinton sensed that, much as she seems to distance herself from Dianna's cosmetic choices, NARS would rather not be associated with this overtanned and overbronzed version of Swinton. But, again, Swinton's work as a fashion muse threatens to spill over into the reception of her filmic image.

☆☆☆☆☆☆☆☆☆☆ A Balanced Film-Star Diet

Swinton's description of her "Tandoori tan" in *Trainwreck* is not the only time she resorts to food when discussing her work, with cooking metaphors offering intriguing insights into a career that might be viewed as a multicourse banquet. Swinton refers to the "various ingredients" in her life with Sandro Kopp ("Tilda Swinton Interview," *The Scotsman*, 22 November 2018) and recalls how producer Henry Rosenthal once told her that "being called an underground film star is like being called a jumbo shrimp" ("Tilda Swinton Interview"). Swinton even refers to her work with noted filmmakers in such culinary terms: "I tend to cook stuff up with my friends," elaborating that these include Guadagnino, who directed her in *I Am Love*, *A Bigger Splash* (2015), and *Suspiria* (2018), as well as Bong, who directed Swinton in *Snowpiercer* (2013) and *Okja* (2017) ("Why 'Doctor Strange' Star Tilda Swinton Wanted to Do a Superhero Movie," *IndieWire*, 4 November 2016). Some five years earlier, Swinton similarly explained her ongoing sartorial collaborations with particular designers in this way: "Having them make clothes for me is like being cooked for by someone who knows what you like to eat" ("Planet Tilda"). Food also recurs in media profiles of Swinton, including one focused on Drumduan Upper School, which Swinton co-founded in 2013 to provide a space where her children could continue to experience a nonconventional education. Schooling there includes class trips where students help Swinton cook soup from foraged ingredients like wild garlic and nettles ("A Sentimental Education: Inside the School That Tilda Built," *The Observer*, 14 June 2015).

In another border crossing between Swinton's personal and performed roles, the sensuality of cooking and eating plays a central role in *I Am Love*. In the part of bourgeois homemaker Emma, the film provided Swinton with the opportunity to perform the transportive properties of food. It opens on the preparation of a dinner party at the home of the wealthy Recchi family, Tancredi (Pippo Delbono) and his Russian-born wife, Emma. She supervises the preparation of her son's favorite dish, a Russian fish soup called ukha. Here, food serves as a bond between mother and son and, in a later scene, it comes to establish a bond between Emma and her future lover, Antonio, a young chef. Dining with other Recchi women at Antonio's restaurant, known for a distinctly artful approach to food, Antonio prepares for Emma what Karen de Perthuis describes as "a dish that transports her into a state of sensual retreat from the people and conversation around her" (272). While the itemized foods they are brought include a dish of marinated egg yolks, pea cream, and zucchini flowers, Emma is transported by a plate of prawns (the kind of jumbo shrimp she quite literally compares herself to in a later interview). Swinton is captured in various extreme close-ups as she becomes alert to the flavors and then savors them: wide-eyed anticipation, a slowly chewing mouth, the closed eyes of intense pleasure. Swinton plays the scene like Emma is experiencing a private moment of sexual rapture in the public space of a restaurant.

A year later, and perhaps related to the critical praise for *I Am Love* and Swinton's sensual performance, she was invited to develop a food-infused scent with the French fragrance house État Libre d'Orange. Far removed from the trend of celebrity-branded perfumes by everyone from Elizabeth Taylor to Sarah Jessica Parker, Swinton's scent "Like This" does not bear her name on the title or even within the description ("Like This," *etatlibredorange.com*). And yet, Swinton describes it as an intensely personal homesickness potion, with its predominant notes of ginger, carrot, and orange all based on "the individual smells of [my] house" ("Tilda Swinton," *The Gentlewoman*). Swinton also considers it as something of a self-portrait, another medium in which she can express herself, and so it includes "lots of orange, because I'm a natural ginger" and "pumpkin from my birthday month, November" ("Tilda Swinton").

Much as Swinton appears to take great pleasure from food and cooking metaphors, her overall approach to her career might be conceived of as a food pyramid. Over the course of four decades, she has filled her plate will all kinds of food; and if experimental and independent productions are her staples, then Hollywood productions might be seen as those offerings high in fat, sugar, and salt that one should take only in moderation. But

Swinton does not discount this peak of the pyramid altogether, because to do so would be to miss out on particular experiences, ones that she may not have had a natural taste for but for which she has acquired a certain palate with age.

The full range of Swinton's appetite has not, and could not, be captured in a single essay. For instance, beyond the roles and thematic threads considered here, Swinton's career since the 2010s has also been marked by a sustained engagement with voice-based roles. Her crisp English accent has narrated documentaries like *Letters from Baghdad* (2016) and *Women Make Film: A New Road Movie through Cinema* (2018). She also uses her voice publicly, in more activist roles, from issuing statements of support in defense of Russia's gay community in 2013 to launching a public campaign to raise the funds needed to save Jarman's "Prospect Cottage" in 2020. This crowdfunding campaign was a success, in no small part due to Swinton's involvement ("£3.5M Crowdfunding Campaign Saves Derek Jarman's Kent Home," *The Guardian*, 31 March 2020). In entering the new decade with this continued commitment to Jarman's legacy, Swinton underscores the significance of their collaborations from the 1980s and early 1990s to her career and to her life. It is difficult to predict how Swinton's career will evolve in the 2020s, but there is no doubt that she will always find filmmakers—like Jarman, Jarmusch, Bong, and Guadagnino—who will "cook" with her for as long as they can.

Chapter 7

Tyler Perry

The Multihyphenate Lane Changer

DANIELLE E. WILLIAMS

Tyler Perry

> Hollywood is uncomfortable if you do more than one thing. It makes everybody uncomfortable because you're only supposed to drive in one lane. But, I'm not that type of person. So, I don't know why I can't do several types of things.
>
> —Tyler Perry

In 2010, Tyler Perry ranked number thirty-five on *Entertainment Weekly*'s list of "50 Most Powerful Entertainers." Perry made the list because his films earned a career box office of $451.3 million. When

Entertainment Weekly published this list, Perry had written and produced ten films: *Diary of a Mad Black Woman* (2005), *Madea's Family Reunion* (2006), *Why Did I Get Married?* (2007), *Daddy's Little Girls* (2007), *The Family That Preys* (2008), *Madea Goes to Jail* (2009), *I Can Do Bad All by Myself* (2009), and *Why Did I Get Married Too?* (2010).[1] He directed all of these except *Diary*. *Entertainment Weekly* identified Perry as the "quintessential one-man brand" because of his work as a writer, director, and producer of films, television shows, and plays (Armstrong et al., "The 50 Most Powerful Entertainers," *Entertainment Weekly*, 15 October 2010). The publication points out that Perry lacks "global reach, but his imprint on African-American culture is indelible" (Armstrong et al.).

Even with the amount of success Perry had achieved by 2010, *Entertainment Weekly* still measured Perry within an industry and standard that lacks diversity onscreen and behind the scenes. He took a niche and made an empire. Before Perry's *Diary of a Mad Black Woman* hit theaters, Perry had a successful career as a playwright on the urban theater circuit; his plays generated over $100 million in tickets, $20 million in merchandising, and $30 million in video and DVD sales (Brett Pulley, "A Showbiz Whiz," *Forbes*, 3 October 2005). His primary audience was African American churchgoing women. That loyal audience followed him when he made the transition to film and television.

Stars such as Perry play a key role in representing cultural ideologies and serve "as beacons of the public world. They helped define the Zeitgeist of any particular moment" (Marshall 2010, 36). Perry is a key figure in the history of African American film as well as the film and media industries at large. Tyler Perry is a multihyphenate: he acts, writes, directs, and produces. He is an independent filmmaker who has been able to build his own film and television production studio outside of Hollywood. He maintains creative control and ownership of his works.

From 2010 to 2020, Tyler Perry continued to build his multimedia empire while also expanding his work as an actor by acting in films that he did not write, direct, or produce. Starting with 2009's *Star Trek*, Perry started acting in films that were not his own. This essay examines how Perry's multihyphenate image functions in his roles in *Star Trek*, *Alex Cross* (2012), *Gone Girl* (2014), and *Teenage Mutant Ninja Turtles: Out of the Shadows* (2016), all films which incorporate this behind-the-scenes image as a director, writer, and leader onscreen. Through these roles, Perry expanded his audience and his international presence as a movie star.

One approach to examining African Americans stars' mainstream success is to examine their crossover appeal. Richard Dyer (2004) defines a crossover star as "one who appeals to more than one musical subculture; one who, though rooted in a particular tradition of music with a particular audience, somehow manages to appeal, and sell, beyond the confines of that audience" (64). Dyer identifies Paul Robeson as the first major Black star and examines his crossover appeal from 1925 to 1945. Palmer (2011) uses Dyer's work to examine Will Smith's crossover appeal. Like Robeson, Smith had a multiracial fan base, which allowed Smith to star in science fiction films, "a genre not traditionally associated with either black actors or black audiences" (29). With *I, Robot* (2004), Smith created a bridge between Black masculinity and the sci-fi genre. Smith's star persona as a "likeable, wise-cracking, eminently cool leading man/action hero" enabled his crossover status. Quinn (2013) examines the different strategies Will Smith and Tyler Perry used to become two of the most successful African Americans onscreen and behind the scenes. Both men had cross-platform range with established careers outside of film: Smith started in rap and Perry in theater. Quinn also argues that Smith works within the system and Perry creates his own system.

Tyler Perry is a multihyphenate crossover star. He performs multiple roles behind the scenes. While acting in other films, Perry continued to make his own films, plays, and television shows in what has become known as the "Tyler Perry way." Although Perry's works appeal to an African American audience, his longevity is a result of his crossover success. While Perry does not have the global appeal of other stars of color such as Will Smith or Dwayne Johnson, he has been able to succeed because of his work behind the camera. Perry can cross over to multiracial audiences because he embodies the American values of hard work and sacrifice that resulted in his success.

☆☆☆☆☆☆☆☆☆★ The Tyler Perry Story: House of Perry

Perry started his career as a playwright. In 1992, he left his hometown of New Orleans to pursue his dream in Atlanta, Georgia. Perry self-financed his plays; from 1992 to 1998, he worked multiple jobs to produce *I Know I've Been Changed*, a gospel musical focusing on adult survivors of child abuse. At his lowest point, Perry lived in his car, but by 1998, the play was a hit and the show ran for two years. Perry also directed and starred in the production. During the show's national tour, Perry wrote his next play, *I Can Do Bad All by Myself* (2000), about a woman, Vianne, who discovers that her husband is leaving her for her sister. Vianne moves in with her grandmother, Madea, played by Perry in drag. Madea is a straight-shooting, wisecracking, swearing, smoking, pistol-packing comedic relief figure in Perry's plays. Perry describes her as "the kind of person who will beat the hell out of you one minute and take you to the doctor the next" (quoted in Gerri Hirshey, "Tyler Perry's Brand New Day," *Best Life*, April 2008). Perry's mother, Maxine, and aunt, Mayola, were the inspiration for Madea. The character's name is a "Southern African American portmanteau for 'Mother Dear'" (Love 2013, 285). The character is popular with audiences and appears in his plays *Diary of a Mad Black Woman* (2001), *Madea's Family Reunion* (2002), and *Madea's Class Reunion* (2003). During this time, Perry met with Fox and CBS about making the transition to TV. Fox opted not to pick up his show and Perry ended his deal with CBS because he would not have had complete creative control over his project. Perry then shifted his focus to film.

The financial success of his plays allowed Perry to split the $5 million production cost for *Diary* with Lionsgate, with Perry maintaining complete ownership of the film. *Diary* grossed $50.6 million (boxofficemojo.com). On *Diary*, Perry wrote and served as an executive producer; he did not direct. This would change with his next film, *Madea's Family Reunion* (2006), in which he is credited as the screenwriter, executive producer, and director. Perry made this film for $6 million and it earned $63 million in ticket sales (boxofficemojo.com). The budget for his films is always $20 million or less (Rebecca Rubin, "Tyler Perry Ends 'Madea' Franchise on a Box Office High Note," *Variety*, 4 March 2019). His films average $52 million at the box office.[2]

In 2007, Perry purchased a former Delta corporate campus in Atlanta, Georgia, and turned it into Tyler Perry Studios. The sixty-acre property consists of five soundstages, postproduction facilities, and a theater. On the site, Perry added twelve soundstages named after African American stars such as Sidney Poitier, Quincy Jones, Ruby Dee, and Cicely Tyson.[3] This is the first full-service television and film studio owned and operated by an African American (Margena Christian, "Hallelujer!!! Tyler Perry Aims to Lift Spirits with Laughter and Madea," *Jet*, 23 February 2009; Alex Block, "Tyler Perry, Inc.," *The Hollywood Reporter*, 19 February 2009). In 2009, Perry started 34th Street Films for projects not written or directed by Perry. Perry named it after the film *Miracle on 34th Street* (1947) because Perry describes his life as a "miracle." One of 34th Street Films's first projects was *Precious* (2009), which was acquired after the film's screening at Sundance.[4]

Perry acknowledges the racial inequities within the movie industry and, as a content creator, hires actors of color. According to *Entertainment Weekly*, Perry is the number one employer of Black actors in Hollywood

(Svetky et al., "How Do You Solve a Problem Like Madea?," *Entertainment Weekly*, 20 March 2009). Yet Tyler Perry Studios is located 2,000 miles to the east, in Atlanta. In his acceptance speech for the 2019 Black Entertainment Television (BET) Ultimate Icon Award, Perry discusses his onscreen talent: "When I started hiring Taraji [P. Henson], Viola Davis, and Idris Elba, they couldn't get jobs in this town but God blessed me to be in a position to be able to hire them" (quoted in Rosy Cordero, "The Top 7 Moments from the BET Awards," *Entertainment Weekly*, 24 June 2019). Taraji P. Henson validates Perry's claim. She acted in *Hustle & Flow* (2005) and *The Curious Case of Benjamin Button* (2008), but Perry was the first to value her worth as an actor: "I think the industry knew I was talented. But it's about money. Are you bankable? I had to continuously prove that. I was asking for half a million. I didn't get paid that until I did my first Tyler Perry film. He was the first person who paid me $500,000" (quoted in "Actors on Actors," *Variety*, 4 June 2019). Perry is diversifying Hollywood behind the camera as well:

> To have that many Black people working in this business looking at each other and seeing themselves . . . especially the ones who come from Hollywood. They say, "I've been on sets for years, and I was the only Black face there." To come here and see this—it's all love. (quoted in Roy Johnson, "His Own Man," *Ebony*, August 2011)

Perry claims that at his studio, he works "with people who have Ph.D.s and former inmates. We're all side by side doing what we need to do and I think it's very important to have that kind of experience" (quoted in Jade Scipioni, "Tyler Perry on How He Hires," *CNBC*, 28 January 2020).

Perry does not have to wait for the "perfect" part. He writes it for himself. He does not have to worry about not getting along with the director, because he is the director. With Tyler Perry Studios, he has access to soundstages, sets, wardrobe, and postproduction facilities. Yet Perry made the decision to act in films that were not his own, starting with *Star Trek*.

★★★★★★★★★★ The Heroes

Star Trek was Perry's first non-Perry role, with a minor part as Admiral Richard Barnett, head of the Starfleet Academy. In the film, James Kirk (Chris Pine) has been accused of violating the academy's ethical code of conduct. Before the proceedings begin, Kirk wants to face his accuser directly. Kirk's accuser, Commander Spock (Zachary Quinto), outlines Kirk's violations and Barnett simplifies them for Kirk: "In academic vernacular, you cheated." A distress signal from the planet Vulcan interrupts the hearing as Kirk and the other cadets are called to duty. By the end of the film, Kirk is a hero, and Barnett awards him the title of captain as well as a commendation. The cinematic reboot of the popular franchise was the perfect vehicle for Perry. The role is very similar to Perry's work behind the scenes. Barnett and Perry are men in charge, and both take their jobs seriously. The role gave Perry the opportunity to experience acting on a big-budget production. According to Box Office Mojo, *Star Trek* had a budget of $150 million, which is about seven times the budget of a Perry film. The role gave Perry exposure to a wider audience; the film made $257 million domestic and $127 million international (boxofficemojo.com).

Perry was not a fan of the franchise and did not seek out this role. According to Perry, director J. J. Abrams recruited him:

> I just got a call for the part. A small part. "Would you like to do it?" I'm like, "How long is it?" He's like, "Well, it's going to be about a month." I'm like, "Hmmm, can't do that. Is there a smaller part?" He said, "Well, there's one that's three weeks?" I'm like, "What do you have for one week?" That's how that worked out because I wanted to see if I could work with another director. And I wanted to see the process because the only time I'd ever done it has been on my own set. It was really great. (quoted in Mike Ryan, "Tyler Perry Is Not Afraid to Do What He Wants," *Huffington Post*, 26 June 2012)

Perry talked about the challenges of relinquishing control behind the camera. During filming on *Star Trek*, Perry yelled "cut" and "the whole room turned and looked at [Abrams]. It was my fault. I was screwing up the line and I yelled 'Cut!' Everybody in the room was like, 'Who does this kid think he is?' They all look at J. J. and J. J. had this big smile on his face" (Matthew Belloni and Stephen Galloway, "Q&A: Tyler Perry," *The Hollywood Reporter*, 15 July 2009).

It would be several years before Perry acted in another non-Perry film. However, his next role would not be a cameo but the lead. For his next part, Perry starred in *Alex Cross* (2009). Perry is the second actor to play the role of the African American psychologist adapted from the James Patterson book series of the same name. Morgan Freeman played the role in *Kiss the Girls* (1997) and *Along Came a Spider* (2001). In the 2009 version, Cross is a detective with a PhD in psychology working for the Detroit police department. He has been offered a position with the FBI in Washington, D.C., and his wife is expecting their third child. Cross is observant and notices the slightest details, and his professional acumen allows him to psychoanalyze suspects adeptly. His partner notes how Cross is never wrong in his assessments. Cross and his team are assigned a case involving a hired assassin nicknamed Picasso (because he leaves Cubist-style artwork at the scene of each crime). Cross discovers the murderer's next victim and prevents him from completing his task. Picasso escapes and retaliates by killing a member of Cross's team and Cross's wife. The rest of the film focuses on Cross finding Picasso.

In *Alex Cross*, Perry is an action hero, which is a new role for him. This film gave him a chance to play a character who chases and fight villains. The film's opening scene shows Cross and his team chasing and capturing a rapist. During this pursuit, Cross runs through an abandoned building, climbs a ladder, jumps off stairs, and punches the culprit. While Madea carries a pistol in her purse, Alex Cross uses handguns and shotguns on the job and engages in hand-to-hand combat. For the film, Perry learned Krav Maga, which can be seen in Cross's final battle with Picasso in an old theater converted into a parking garage. In the final sequence between Cross and Picasso, they end up in the ceiling rafters, where Picasso falls to his death.

In an interview with Charlie Rose, Perry talks about being offered parts similar to his own work. *Alex Cross* gave Perry the opportunity to be in an action film: "I have always wanted to do these types of roles but I've never had the opportunity. I've never been offered something that made sense or everything that was offered to me was already in my wheelhouse" (*The Charlie Rose Show*, 19 October 2012). Perry decided to star in *Alex Cross* to expand his global exposure:

> With *Alex Cross*, people say it's off-brand, a little different. But it's on purpose. They release it here, release it internationally, and now my stock has gone up on my own catalogs. Everything is about moving the ship forward. Outside the ship doesn't matter. What's in the ship is mine, and it's going in the direction I think it should go. (quoted in Drew Jabera, "Tyler Perry Runs the Table," *Men's Health*, November 2012)

Star Trek and *Alex Cross* allowed Perry to expand his acting beyond comedy and his popular Madea character. His onscreen performance demonstrates that he can act in science fiction and action films. He told NPR's *Fresh Air* that acting on the film *Alex Cross* was a vacation because he only had to focus his attention on his performance and "to take every bit of energy that usually has to be divided into a million different areas, into just acting" (12 October 2012). Yet Perry continued his role as a multihyphenate. While filming *Alex Cross*, Perry continued work on his "ship." During downtimes on set, Perry wrote a script. In 2012, Perry released two films (*Good Deeds* and *Madea's Witness Protection*) and a play (*Madea Gets a Job*). His series *House of Payne* (2007–2012) ended its run on TBS, and he inked a deal with the Oprah Winfrey Network to create original scripted programming. In 2013, it was announced that Perry had a role in David Fincher's *Gone Girl* (2014). With the part of defense attorney Tanner Bolt, Perry left behind the "good guy" part to play a character with some morally gray areas.

★★★★★★★★★★ The Villains

In *Gone Girl,* Nick Dunne's (Ben Affleck) wife Amy goes missing on their fifth wedding anniversary. Dunne is a suspect of interest and the case receives national media coverage. Bolt first appears onscreen during a cable news program as a correspondent. The host, who clearly believes Dunne is guilty, describes Bolt as "patron saint to wife killers everywhere." Bolt, as an observer, defends Dunne: "Just because this guy isn't walking around weeping, that doesn't mean that he's not hurting." Dunne flies to New York City and convinces Bolt to take his case. Dunne also learns that Bolt's services are not cheap and require a $100,000 retainer. Bolt offers Dunne a "special 'my wife is skilled in the art of vengeance' rate."

Bolt travels to Missouri and prepares Dunne on how to speak to cops and the press. In one of the film's lighter moments, Bolt prepares Dunne for an on-air interview by throwing gummy bears at him every time Dunne looks "smug or annoyed or tense." Bolt's job is to help shift public perception of Dunne from murderer to innocent husband. Bolt's training works and Dunne successfully pulls off a TV interview. Once Amy returns home, Bolt heads back to New York City.

On the *Today Show,* Perry discussed preparing for this role. While reading the script, Perry thought the character was "very Johnnie Cochran-ish, kind of cool and slick. But . . . he's sleazy. Johnnie wasn't sleazy. But he is just a really smart and great attorney. And I wanted to try my hand at it" (30 September 2014). Perry also discussed working with director David Fincher: "I'm a storyteller. That man is a di-re-c-tor. He is amazing. And to watch him work and to watch how he paints his pictures, the tableaus, everything is really just beyond anything I could ever imagine" (quoted in Alicia Rancilo, "Tyler Perry Happy with 'Gone Girl' Role," *The Canadian Press,* 18 December 2013).

As Bolt, Perry is able to present his behind-the-scenes persona as a multihyphenate. Bolt wants Dunne to play the role of an innocent husband who is concerned about his wife's safety. He directs Dunne on what to say and how to say it. Bolt's job is to construct Dunne's narrative and change the public's perceptions of him. Perry does this with every project he writes and directs. He creates works that appeal to his loyal audience. Perry is

Tanner Bolt (Tyler Perry) and Margo Dunne (Carrie Coon) prepping Nick Dunne (Ben Affleck) for his television interview in *Gone Girl* (David Fincher, 20th Century Fox, 2014). Digital frame enlargement.

aware of his fans: "When Black women are down with you and in your corner, you have an ally that will move heaven and earth. When they love you, they will forgive you" (quoted in Susan Fales-Hill, "Walking Tall," *Essence*, November 2012). With Tanner Bolt, Alex Cross, and Admiral Richard Barnett, Perry is aware that his fans might not watch these genres. However, Perry continues to create films and characters that his audience will appreciate and consume. Perry can do both because the success of the Madea franchise has provided him with continued financial security and creative control on his projects.

Perry became part of another franchise with the role of Baxter Stockman in *Teenage Mutant Ninja Turtles: Out of the Shadows* (2016), a character who did not appear in the first film in this rebooted franchise, *Teenage Mutant Ninja Turtles* (2014). Stockman is a scientist whose expertise assists the main villain Shredder, starting with breaking him out of police custody and assisting him with locating the pieces to a device that will open other dimensions. He is a scientific genius with limited social skills. At the beginning of the film, reporter and turtle ally April O'Neil (Megan Fox) believes Stockman is working for Shredder. In order to get the information she needs, she dresses in disguise and approaches him at Grand Central Station as a fan and not a reporter. Stockman invites her to sit down at his table, and the two exchange light banter about the difference between nerds and geeks. The information O'Neil needs is on an electronic device that Stockman passes off to an employee. O'Neil fakes a phone call from her "boyfriend" and tells him that she must leave. Stockman, while not surprised that someone as good-looking as O'Neil has a boyfriend, makes one final

Baxter Stockman (Tyler Perry) synthesizes a mutagenic compound for Shredder in *Teenage Mutant Ninja Turtles: Out of the Shadows* (Dave Green, Nickelodeon Movies, 2016). Digital frame enlargement.

appeal, asking if the boyfriend knows "the difference between pi to the third decimal point and pi to the fifteenth decimal point." Stockman works with Shredder because of the science; he wants to be a legend. Stockman describes the dimensional portal as glorious and he and Shredder will be "gods to future generations." Stockman's journey to scientific glory is cut short when Shredder has his henchmen take Stockman away to Tokyo.

As previously discussed, this role allowed Perry to expand his acting range. He also talks about how this role was an educational opportunity: "Working in this kind of environment . . . I get an opportunity to be a student. I've been doing my own thing for so long, I got a chance to put all that aside and go into someone else's set, sit back, learn and pay attention" (quoted in Mark Daniell, "'Teenage Mutant Ninja Turtles 2': Tyler Perry Joins Fun as the Bad Guy," *Toronto Sun*, 1 June 2016). Perry considered his family when taking the role: "The No. 1 variable for me was to be able to do something that my son could one day watch and enjoy" (quoted in Brian Truitt, "Tyler Perry Breaks Down His 'Ninja Turtles' Supervillain Squad," *USA Today*, 3 June 2016). Perry's son Aman was born in 2014.

Leaving a legacy is something Perry has in common with the Stockman character. As a creative figure, Perry emphasizes the importance of creative control and ownership:

> The thing about using other people's money is they're going to set the rules. So at the beginning I used my money, kept reinvesting in myself. Now I own all my content, as opposed to having someone else own it and me being "work for hire." That's the difference between doing well and having generations of wealth to pass on to your children. (quoted in Drew Jabera, "Tyler Perry Runs the Table," *Men's Health*, November 2012)

Perry built a legacy through Madea and the creation of Tyler Perry Studios. When he created the Madea character, he had no idea what impact the character would have on the audience besides entertaining them with laughter. Madea's commentary about faith, pain, and forgiveness connected with the audience:

> When I got to those life lessons, something happened. There was utter silence in the theaters, and it became so clear to me that the audience was hanging on her every word. I understood very early on that this mostly blue-collar African-American audience was feeling inspired. They were getting answers to a lot of what was going on in our community that no one was talking about. . . . I could lift them with humor and use that laughter as an anesthetic and talk about really deep, sensitive issues that were destroying so many of us—things like rape and molestation and the inability to forgive. (Tyler Perry, "Time to Move on from Madea," *The New York Times*, 3 March 2019)

Perry heard from fans about Madea's influence: "Madea did in two hours what my family hasn't been able to do in 12 years—convince my sister to finally leave an abusive relationship" (Perry, "Time to Move On"). Perry continued to incorporate the character into his plays and films, turning a fan favorite into a franchise.

☆☆☆☆☆☆☆☆☆☆★ Madea's Big Retirement

2019 was a monumental year for Perry. In March, Perry released his final Madea movie, *A Madea Family Funeral*. Madea does not die in the film, but Perry wanted to retire the character. The decision to retire Madea was not easy:

> I wrestled for a while with the question of the right time to end the character. But then I thought—this is the year I'm turning 50. There's much more I want to do, so many more stories I want to tell and more roles I want to play. I was thrilled to be Colin Powell in "Vice" and Tanner Bolt in "Gone Girl," and I'm looking forward to more opportunities like those. But that old broad has been good to me, so who knows—maybe one day I'll tell the story of Madea in the '70s and hire a real actress to play the role. But the time of playing her has come to an end. (Tyler Perry, "Time to Move on from Madea")

A Madea Family Funeral made $27.1 million on the opening weekend and grossed $73.2 million total (boxofficemojo.com). In addition to the film, Perry gave Madea fans one last opportunity to see the beloved character live onstage in *Madea's Farewell Tour*, which ran from January 2019 to February 2020.

The second epic event for Perry that year was the grand opening of Tyler Perry Studios in its new location on 5 October 2019. In 2015, Perry purchased 330 acres of the former Fort McPherson army base located in southwest Atlanta for $30 million (Katie Leslie and Scott Trubey, "Fort McPherson: Fort Deal Closing Appears in Sight," *The Atlanta Journal-Constitution*, 26 April 2015). The acquisition of the property included a historic district of thirty-three acres, which includes forty buildings that are on the National Register of Historic Places. On the site, Perry added twelve soundstages; he maintained the tradition of naming them after iconic African American figures such as Ruby Dee, Ossie Davis, and Diahann Carroll. In addition to the soundstages, the facility's sets include a replica of the White House, a bank, prison yard, farmhouse, cabins, and a commercial jet. Perry also plans to add a six-lane highway (Greg Braxton, "Landmark Turn for Tyler Perry," *Los Angeles Times*, 5 October 2019; Catherine Hong, "Setting the Scenes," *Architectural Digest*, December 2019). The *Los Angeles Times* states Tyler Perry Studios is "larger than Paramount, Warner Bros. and Walt Disney's Burbank studios combined" (Greg Braxton, "Landmark Turn").

Perry sold his old studio lot to Ozzie Areu, the former president of production for Tyler Perry Studios (TPS), and Will Areu, the current president of production for TPS. Areu Bros. Studios is the first Latinx-owned and operated film and TV studio in the United States. Ozzie Areu's vision is similar to Perry's: "Minorities want to see ourselves in different roles—not just the mechanic, the gardener, the maid. . . . I feel I have a unique opportunity to build a media company made up of people who reflect the world that we live in" (quoted in Natalie Jarvie, "So Stories Can Be Told," *Los Angeles Times*, 26 December 2019).

In 2019, Perry joined forces with Tim Palen to create a new production company, Peachtree & Vine. Perry and Palen had worked together since Lionsgate, where Palen was president of worldwide theatrical marketing. He left the company in 2018 to start his own production company. Peachtree & Vine is named after two popular streets in Georgia and California. The company will develop scripted and nonscripted projects for film and TV (Pamela McClintock, "Tyler Perry, Tim Palen Team for New Production Company," *The Hollywood Reporter*, 3 September 2019).

Perry currently has a deal with Viacom to create content for BET as well as other Viacom networks, and subsidiary Paramount Pictures has "exclusive 'first look' rights on any new feature film concepts created by Perry" ("Viacom Announces Multi-year Content Partnership with Tyler Perry," *Business Wire*, 14 July 2017). Perry's *The Oval* and *Sistas* made their debut on October 23, 2019 (BET renewed both series for a second season in 2020). In

September 2019, Viacom launched the streaming service BET+, which includes Perry's plays in its catalog. Perry also created original digital content for BET+ in the form of *Ruthless* (2020), a spin-off of *The Oval*, and *Bruh* (2020). On February 29, 2020, *Young Dylan* premiered on Nickelodeon. Perry is also getting into the streaming business. His film *A Fall from Grace* (2020) debuted on Netflix with over 26 million views in the first week (Patrick Hipes, "Tyler Perry's 'A Fall from Grace,'" *Deadline*, 4 February 2020). In 2020, Perry expanded his presence onscreen in non-Perry projects to TV. He appeared as himself in the mockumentary series *#blackAF* on Netflix. In the series, TV showrunner and creator Kenya Barris plays a fictionalized version of himself. In the fifth episode, Barris reaches out to Perry to discuss how Black creators handle the pressures of creating content for audiences and critics. Barris says after a project comes out, he goes to Rotten Tomatoes to read feedback. Perry informs him: "Let me just tell you about them tomatoes. I don't fuck with them." He says that "rotten" or "fresh" is inconsequential to him. Perry states, "I know that I'm telling stories my folks want to see . . . I superserve my niche . . . I'm telling the stories that I come from. And that's why they're winning because people are recognizing themselves in these stories" (*#blackAF*, "yo, between you and me . . . this is because of slavery").

As of this writing, Perry is working with Angelina Jolie in *Those Who Wish Me Dead* (2021). The film is an adaptation of a book by the same name. The book is a thriller about Jace, a young man who witnesses a murder. To protect him, police change his identity and place him in a wilderness skills program for troubled teens in Montana, but the killers are still after him. *The Hollywood Reporter*, *Deadline*, and *Variety* reported on Perry's casting in the film in an undisclosed role.

With Madea in retirement, it will be interesting to see the types of characters Perry plays in his own works and the works of others. During the 2010s, the success of his projects gave Perry the freedom to expand his onscreen roles. As Perry transforms himself into a Starfleet admiral, detective, lawyer, or scientist, his persona as a public creative figure is present in these roles. There is something in each of these characters that embodies Perry's image of a successful man in charge.

In the 2020s, it appears that Perry will continue to not "stay in his lane." Maintaining the relationship with his current fan base while attracting new ones with each new non-Perry film seems to be in order. Whether he is appreciated for his alacrity as a multihyphenate or is simply revered as an avant-garde artist, it is evident that Tyler Perry is finding ways to pave new roads in the entertainment industry for himself and people of color.

NOTES

Epigraph quoted in Mike Ryan, "Tyler Perry Is Not Afraid to Do What He Wants," *Huffington Post*, 26 June 2012.

1. All of Perry's works start with the phrase "Tyler Perry's" (e.g., *Tyler Perry's Diary of a Mad Black Woman*), which I have omitted throughout this essay.

2. The average is based on nineteen Tyler Perry films. His most successful film to date is *Madea Goes to Jail* ($90 million) and his least successful is *Single Mom's Club* ($15 million).

3. The soundstages are named after Cicely Tyson, Sidney Poitier, Harry Belafonte, Oprah Winfrey, Whoopi Goldberg, Will Smith, Halle Berry, Denzel Washington, Spike Lee, Ruby Dee, Ossie Davis, and Diahann Carroll.

4. Perry teamed up with Lionsgate and Oprah Winfrey's Harpo Productions to distribute the film.

Chapter 8

Jessica Chastain and Michelle Williams

Open Windows

DANIEL VARNDELL

> It is not enough that our face should tell the story of our feelings, if the audience are not let into the secret. . . . We should ensure that the window is wide enough for them to see through, and the latch left sufficiently ajar.
>
> —Robert Speaight, *Acting: Its Idea and Tradition* (1939)

In his 1982 lecture on "The Thought of Movies," Stanley Cavell mused on the "questions" raised by performative moments that move or disturb us in a motion picture, some as subtle as a hand gesture, eye twitch, or pursed lip. Such details are very often critically overlooked, he suggested; while cherished for their effects on the audience, they remain little analyzed (and practically dismissed, writes Steven Rybin, when romanticized away as actorly "magic" without any further ado [3]). Cavell reasoned that this was because great performances vacillate somewhere between the evanescence of a theatrical performance and the permanence of a recording, settling on neither. Here is a key passage:

> If it is part of the grain of film to magnify the feeling and meaning of a moment, it is equally part of it to counter this tendency, and instead to acknowledge the fateful fact of a human life that the significance of its moments is ordinarily not given with the moments as they are lived. . . . It is as if an inherent concealment of significance, as much as its revelation, were part of the governing force of what we mean by film acting (94).

Onstage in a theatrical performance, such moments are not only unique to the nights on which such gestures spark, they remain thereafter only in the memories of those fortunate enough to have noticed them. Cavell is bedeviled, however, by the fact that screen performances are not quite recordings "because there is nothing independent of them to which they owe fidelity,"

Jessica Chastain

Michelle Williams

and yet, "because they are perfectly repeatable" (94), neither are they performances. Such screen performances linger in our memories while also offering themselves to be seen again.

For Murray Pomerance, this idea can be explored using Roland Barthes's distinction between the *studium* (appreciation, taste) and the *punctum* (point, detail) of the photographic image. Apropos cinema, Pomerance writes that the *studium* can be conceived as a viewer's route through and mapping of the geography of a scene, their navigation of the film world. The cinematic *punctum*, however, marks an "obstruction of route and routine, precisely in the sense that when I encounter it my eye is stopped in its peregrination, is derailed, is thrown into the pure experience of gazing and meditating without gaining the benefit of an accretion of knowledge" (*Johnny Depp* 109–110). The cinematic *punctum* is a wounding detail that derails one's journey, or as Barthes put it, "That accident which pricks me (but also bruises me, is poignant to me)" (quoted in Pomerance, *Johnny Depp*, 109). Rybin turns the screw on this idea by pointing out that if a critic has been sufficiently "pricked" by a performative moment-as-*punctum* as to be "bruised," that is, moved to write about it in the first place, then they themselves are implicated, even revealed, in what they might write about (4). Rybin argues that we ought to take the actor's "magic" seriously (that is, without quote marks) (3) while avoiding the danger of falling too hard for the *punctum*, of losing sight of the actor who bruised us.

In this chapter I look at two performative *puncta* that "pricked" and "bruised" me in two films: *Zero Dark Thirty* (2012) and *All the Money in the World* (2017) featuring Jessica Chastain and Michelle Williams, respectively. Both actresses give stellar performances throughout these films (as, indeed, they have given throughout the decade of the 2010s), but it is here, in these moments, that they do "something" to open up to existential questioning. It is a questioning limited not just to their characters, nor even to the roles their characters play in the wider dramas; they give philosophical expression to broader complexities about performance per se, including the window such performances open onto the actors themselves. Both play characters who are required to be tough, indeed, to toughen up in a world of tough men. Both are stoic, not to say taciturn, in the face of terrifying situations in which they must think and act lest horrible things occur. Yet their final expressions communicate more than the release of emotion following the ordeal during which each must keep herself together (the return to normalcy in which her guard can finally be lowered). Their gestures and expressions movingly, even hauntingly bespeak an opening onto the ordeal of "being" as such, in which such expressions mark a *punctum* within the drama. Such moments, I will argue, not only constitute the "thought of the movies" that so moved scholars like Cavell, Pomerance, and Rybin (among others); they are moments that both reflect thought (a thinking subject) and move us to reflect on thought (subject us to thinking).

☆☆☆☆☆☆☆☆★ Chastain's Haunted Eyes

Despite her delicate, Botticelli-like features, Jessica Chastain has a "ferocious will to achieve," writes Ben Dickinson; with her "often haunted-looking eyes, pale complexion, and gorgeous red mane—which in ambient light can make her appear almost as if lit from within," she can project everything from "icy hauteur" as Melissa in *The Martian* (2015) and as the eponymous *Miss Sloane* (2016) to "loving warmth" as Mrs. O'Brien in *The Tree of Life* (2011) and as Antonina in *The Zookeeper's Wife* (2017) or "unstable equilibrium and high intelligence in between" as Maya in *Zero Dark Thirty* and as Anna in *A Most Violent Year* (2014) ("Jessica Chastain Is Using Her Versatility to Get Women's Stories Told," *Elle.com*, 26 November 2017). If early roles in *Take Shelter* (2011), *The Tree of Life*, and *The Help* (2011) quickly highlighted Chastain's acting talent and propelled her from theater to film acting, her performance as Maya in *Zero Dark Thirty* confirmed her as a star. Kathryn Bigelow's film explores the decade-long manhunt for Osama bin Laden—leader of the terrorist organization responsible for the September 11 attacks in New York and Washington, D.C.—by following the CIA operative "Maya," whose grit and determination to locate and capture this modern-day bogeyman challenges her moral sensibility, imperils her life, and risks her credibility. She fights tooth and nail to pursue leads and evade assassination attempts while battling her male superiors, each of whom sees the mission as a means (to promotion) rather than an end in itself. The scene I want to focus on comes right at the end of the movie, in which Maya is called upon to identify bin Laden's corpse after a successful raid on his compound, following which she must confront the sudden vacuum of meaning that his death—the culmination of a decade of work and struggle—represents.

The scene follows a long, by turns breathtaking and disquieting, sequence depicting a raid on a heavily secured and guarded compound in Pakistan by a squadron of elite U.S. marines who, as they sit in a helicopter recovering in silence from their mission, slowly come to terms with the historical and political enormity of what they've done, the body of bin Laden lying in a body bag between them. As they make their descent to a nearby "black site" (a secret U.S. base somewhere in the region), a cut reveals Maya watching anxiously from the ground as dust and sand swirl. When they land it will be her duty to identify bin Laden's body, thereby authenticating his death as the government awaits confirmation back in the United States. Many political careers hang on this moment, but for Maya it is the point up to which her entire professional life has been focused. We know this because in an earlier scene, Maya had been questioned by the CIA director (James Gandolfini) about the degree of certainty she held that this target was, indeed, the location of bin Laden. While her careerist male colleagues (their political futures entering into their calculations of the risk) had demurred that they were between sixty and eighty percent sure, Maya immediately (and firmly) declared herself "one hundred percent" certain, drawing an admiring, wry smile from the director who, impressed by her gutsiness, asks her in private what she'd done before investigating bin Laden. "Nothing," Maya replies, winning him over. There was nothing before bin Laden; he has been her raison d'être. For what will she strive now he is gone?

From the very first scene in the film (set ten years prior to this mission), Bigelow has depicted Maya, at various stages of her investigation, as a woman continually refining and galvanizing her position as she confronts a series of obstacles. First, her moral principles, as when she looks upon the torture by a CIA interrogator (Jason Clark) of a terror suspect (Reda Kateb) who, beaten, exhausted, and sexually humiliated, looks in desperation to her, having detected in her reaction a trace of disgust. As the suspect hoarsely decries his treatment as inhumane and implores her for help, a taciturn look comes over Maya's face as she coldly asserts that he can help himself by helping them with their investigation (it is arguably this reaction from Maya that finally deflates any glimmer of hope in the suspect's bruised and swollen eyes).[1] Second, her traumatization and grief, as when she is nearly killed in a terror attack along with a cherished colleague (Jennifer Ehle), who is, indeed, later killed in a car bombing. Maya finds her resolve following both events not only undiminished but intensified; she more firmly advocates for decisive action among her male colleagues. The third obstacle is sexism. Maya finds herself marginalized by her male colleagues when, having produced quality intelligence, she is continually sidelined as they speak on her behalf to give cagey reports based on her insights (in two such scenes, Maya quickly loses patience with the politicking and interrupts to give more honest, more *hawkish,* assessments). And fourth, her nerve. When she is finally given the green light by the CIA director to move on her intel and is invited to brief the marines, she quickly earns not only their respect but their confidence as one of them (Joel Edgerton) declares that his faith in the mission has been secured by the strength of her conviction.

From that early scene in which she is (rather patronizingly) handled by the CIA interrogator who questions if she has the stomach to witness torture, through multiple scenes in which she confronts a series of sneering, intractable male superiors (played by Kyle Chandler, Daniel Lapaine, and Mark Strong), Maya earns, challenges, and at times undermines (and in one scene even threatens) their authority with her single-mindedness and strength of will. Her authority rests now on this operation's success, and so it comes down to this scene, this unveiling and identification of the object-cause of her pursuit.

Out of the bluish darkness of this sultry night and into the dusty yellow light illuminating the base (offering a sharp contrast to the luminosity of the bright green night vision used in the previous scene), Maya watches as the helicopter lands and the marines disembark with their quarry. As they unpack and begin the process of cataloguing their haul (files, hard drives, and cassettes), it is now Maya who moves dazedly through the bustling room as the marines efficiently follow procedure, barely containing their relief at the success of the mission with back slapping and howls of delight. Bigelow uses a handheld camera to track Maya's face as she tries to take in and process what she is seeing. In this scene, Chastain darts her eyes around the room in a manner that we haven't seen before: different from the lowering of her eyes in disgust (and shame) during the torture scenes; different from the vacant expression on her face after learning of the death of her friend; different from her blazing anger at being informed that a lead has gone cold and resources withdrawn; and markedly different from the steely glare she uses to penetrate and break down her patronizing male superiors. As she reaches the end of the tent, Bigelow switches perspective so the camera is now from Maya's POV, and, as the blurred bodies of soldiers darting and bustling about their work begin to clear, she sees the wrapped corpse of the man they believe to be bin Laden. "One moment, please," a voice breaks in, revealed through a cut to be a general speaking on the phone (with, we might presume, the CIA director who, in turn, waits to brief the president). Maya no longer needs to shout to be heard among the clamor of careerist men, no longer needs to interject to have her opinions taken seriously. It is her word on which they hang, and as she is ushered to the corpse by the general, her eyes transfixed on the body bag, she briefly (*almost* beseechingly) looks up at this man (who, unlike the other marines, is older, graying, even paternal) before returning her gaze to the bag. However, it is her authority, her responsibility, and any instinct to pass this buck quickly vanishes as she slowly unzips the bag while the soldier reiterates to the top brass on the other end of the line that they must please wait yet

Jessica Chastain as Maya in *Zero Dark Thirty* (Kathryn Bigelow, Sony Pictures Classics, 2012). Digital frame enlargement.

another moment. Maya looks down at the bloodied bearded face for a few seconds before giving a curt but decisive nod, at which the general peels away to confirm that the "agency expert" has issued a positive identification (adding "one hundred percent" in an echo of Maya's earlier statement). Maya, however, returns her gaze to the figure in the bag.

It is at this point that Chastain's facial expression now passes through a series of subtle shifts indicating the range of feeling and the complexity of her reflections on this moment in her character's life. We see numbness and a sense of unreality, the tremor of nervousness (and even a quiver of disgust), all fighting against the sudden heaviness of a deferred fatigue. She turns and leaves the tent, almost staggering outside while assuming the same blank stare, her mouth slightly agape. She closes her eyes and lifts her face up to the stars—or perhaps it is to the heavens she looks (after all, momentous moments such as these often occasion recourse to a long disavowed deity, called upon to make sense of the insensible).

The more one looks at Chastain's face, the more one seems able to detect emotions. Are they all really present in her face, or am I reading them into it? This is the conundrum described by Andrew Klevan as the "fluency of film performance," which not only resists the concretizing effect of a critical description; it risks a proliferation of meaning in excess of the moment itself. For Klevan, one must contend with meaning as "shifting" (33), as "suspended" (35), as "fleeting" (37), as "embedded" (39), as "mistaking" (42), and as "slippery" (44); meaning, that is, as "living." It is this very depth and elusiveness, however, that interests me, because if we might be tempted to pass this range of emotion Maya tries to settle after herself, having faced the abject countenance of her life's work, if we seek refuge as does she in the night air outside the tent, then Bigelow doesn't linger on such a resolution or make the mistake of thinking that this is where her movie will end.

A jarring cut (facilitated by a sound prelap of the hull of a large aircraft noisily descending) reveals Maya waiting to be transported away from the black site as the new dawn breaks over the horizon. A pilot shortly emerges to welcome her onboard, inviting her to sit wherever she likes given she is the only passenger (to which he ventures to add that she must be "pretty important"). Maya busies herself with the seatbelt but looks up sharply when the pilot asks her where she wants to go. Cutting to face Maya in medium close-up, Bigelow's camera—which has been in near constant handheld movement throughout the film—is suddenly still. Maya does not answer. Rather, as she turns her head, her eyes glaze as she stares once more into the abyss before refocusing to finally release a little of her pent-up emotion as she quietly sheds a tear. About what is she crying? She clearly doesn't have an answer to the pilot's question, which is about more than her immediate travel plans. It is a question that resonates with the CIA director's earlier question regarding what Maya had been doing before her epic hunt for bin Laden. The answer she'd given then was, "Nothing," and its counterpart, now, seems to be, "Nowhere." Or at least that's what it seems.

Almost as soon as that tear reaches her jawline and her haunted eyes cast around the aircraft interior as if searching it for an answer, Chastain refocuses her gaze once more and, with the score swelling, seems on the verge of a new focal point. Bigelow, however, cuts to the credits. The film leaves so many questions as to what could possibly succeed an obsession like this, but for me the key to a "living meaning" is precisely this lack of definition, the sense not of closing down but of opening up. Onto . . . what? The destination is irrelevant. What is important is that Maya is opening back up at all. "If questioning is a way of desiring," writes Adam Phillips, "answering must be akin to satisfying, a meeting of desire" (176). However, given psychoanalysis continually emphasizes that desire *cannot* be satisfied, "it is misleading—somehow baffling or distracting—to be too interested in answers. The patient must," Phillips concludes, "learn to enjoy desiring, without needing satisfaction" (177–178). This is what is suggested, I claim, and wordlessly so, in Chastain's subtle modulation of her facial expressions, in that shift from the blankly staring, roving eyes which, after shedding a single tear and centering once more on the aircraft in which she is seated, seem to settle, seem to recover from the unspeakable loss that the death of bin Laden represents—both the loss of a target to pursue and the loss of who she was in pursuing him. The image of "living meaning" is, in this sense, nothing less than an image of futurity, of recovering from a *punctum* in order to navigate oneself in a new world—of welcoming that which is yet to come. It is what Arthur Schopenhauer called an affirmation of the will to go on: "If in comprehending the world you start from the thing in itself, from the will to live, you discover that its kernel, its point of greatest concentration, is the act of generation" (63–64). Here, as in so many other great performances, Chastain's focalization of her haunted eyes becomes the concentrated expression of volition itself.

☆☆☆☆☆☆☆☆★ Williams's Trembling Lips

Kyle Buchanan issued something of an understatement when he described Michelle Williams's career as "curious." She is "private but well-known," simultaneously regarded as one of the best actresses of her generation "and yet, somehow, she is underrated" ("Michelle Williams Is Ready to Lead," Vulture.com, 10 January 2018). Having come of age as Jen on the "youthquake" TV show *Dawson's Creek,* Buchanan continues, as well as raising the daughter she had with the late actor Heath Ledger, she has largely shied away from big-budget films. She instead favors powerful performances in independent productions (as Randi in *Manchester by the Sea* [2016] and as Elaine in *Wonderstruck* [2017], for example), earning Oscar nominations (for Cindy in *Blue Valentine* [2010] and for her iconic Marilyn Monroe in *My Week with Marilyn* [2011]), and especially her collaborations with Kelly Reichardt (as Emily in *Meek's Cutoff* [2010] and as Gina in *Certain Women* [2016]), as well as award-winning Broadway productions (as Una in *Blackbird,* for which she won a Tony). Yet, all too often, Buchanan concludes, "she leaves you wanting more" ("Michelle Williams Is Ready to Lead"). Until 2017's *All the Money in the World,* that is, in which Williams plays Gail Getty, a woman married into and divorced out of the family of a wealthy oil tycoon, John Paul Getty (Christopher Plummer), who was at the time (the 1970s) the richest man who had ever lived. Gail finds herself in an impossible situation when her teenage son, John Paul Getty III (Charlie Plummer), is kidnapped by a gang in Italy only to discover that, upon asking Getty for the ransom money, he refuses to pay. Caught between a rock and a hard place, Gail must work with an ex-CIA security consultant, Fletcher Chase (Mark Wahlberg), to convince Getty to change his mind as well as play for time with the increasingly frustrated hostage takers—headed by the courteous and kindly "Cinquanta" (Romain Duris). Gail must work against a background of growing public discontent at the Gettys' apparent miserliness, a perception exacerbated when she refuses to cry for her missing son during a press conference. In an interview, director Ridley Scott observed that it was this latter quality that drew him to Williams for the role: "She suits me down to the ground because she is not sentimental. . . . To get a tear out of her? Impossible, but if it comes, it comes for the right reason, and you have to earn it" (quoted in "Michelle Williams Is Ready to Lead").

We are introduced to Gail as she takes a phone call from Cinquanta informing her that he has her son, to which she responds with an exhale of relief (having mistaken the kidnapper's meaning). "Er, no," Cinquanta avers, unaware that his considerate and polite manner on the phone is in stark contrast to Gail's experience of discourtesy and venom in her dealings with Getty. As it dawns on Gail that this man Cinquanta is, in fact, holding her son hostage, she steels herself. It is this very shift that characterizes the key performative moments throughout the film. At first, Gail thinks the call might be a joke, but quickly adjusts to the desperate situation. She is not unflappable, as such, but adept at adapting quickly to each new development, each new unreasonable demand from the kidnappers, and even more unreasonable reactions from Getty. Against and around these stubborn men, Gail must move patiently and nimbly. She is castigated for her apparent lack of overt emotion when presented to the media. "They want me to cry?" she asks following a disastrous appearance before cameras. "Your son is kidnapped!" responds an incredulous Italian detective when Gail then quips that with all the hostage negotiation equipment crammed into her kitchen, she has no room to cook. "How can you think of eating?" he chides. But Gail is merely being pragmatic. Soon after, having had the kidnapping dismissed by Getty's consultant, Chase, Gail receives the news that they have recovered the charred remains of a body they suspect is Paul. En route to identifying the body, Gail is quaking with rage as she stares out of the window, covering her mouth with the back of her hand. She controls her voice lest it break as Chase miserably attempts to apologize for the mistakes he made in his initial investigation. "Show . . . me," she gasps when confronted by the body, seizing Chase's hand as he moves to identify it. Gail dismisses Chase's (rather patronizing) gesture to spare her agony, and when the charred remains are revealed to be one of the dead kidnappers, she briefly bursts with relief, gasping "It's not him!" before quickly settling to press on with the investigation. This is not to say that Gail won't erupt. In a later scene, Chase lies to Cinquanta on the phone, suggesting that Paul is just a delinquent disowned by his grandfather (a power play to negotiate a smaller, more manageable ransom), Gail wrests the phone from him and, finding the kidnapper has hung up in disgust, smashes the phone over Chase's head. She soon expresses remorse, however, and tosses him a cloth with which to tend his bloodied forehead. In such scenes, Gail either maintains or quickly recovers her poise.

In a wonderful moment—one that gets to the heart of this tension that Williams presents with such virtuosity in this film—Gail suddenly remembers a gift Getty gave to Paul when he was a young boy: a priceless statuette of a minotaur dating (so Getty has informed them) from the sixth century. Its value, Getty casually observed, is over a million dollars. However, the sudden, urgent joy animating Gail's face soon disappears when she is informed by an evaluator at Sotheby's in Rome—with whom she'd been hoping for a quick sale—that the minotaur is, in fact, little more than a trinket of the kind sold to tourists. At which blow Gail remains silent, her head already bowed slightly and her eyes looking away (perhaps because on some level she was already wary, even incredulous, that Getty would bestow such a princely gift). Williams briefly raises her eyes before lowering them (a little cognitive dissonance now kicking in) and, again raising her eyes to meet the assessor's, she lets her bottom lip wobble momentarily. Rallying, Gail offers a more assured, if somewhat unconvincing retort: "J. Paul Getty is the foremost collector in the world. Do you *really* think you know better than he does?" Her clipped diction, which David Edelstein describes as "sharp, with a hint of North Shore (i.e., old money) Long Island and perhaps a Kennedy or two," is at once haughty *and* vulnerable ("Christopher Plummer Is Getting Headlines for *All the Money in the World*, but It's Michelle Williams Who Deserves Them," *New York Magazine*, 20 December 2017, via Vulture.com). Gail quickly leaves Sotheby's to seek out an expert at a rival museum, only for her eye to be caught by something in the gift shop. Stunned, she walks slowly in as Scott cuts to show, behind the back of a cheerful cashier, row upon row of the same minotaur statue being sold for fifteen dollars apiece. A half-hysterical smirk flashes across Gail's face as she finally confronts her gullibility reflected in these replicas—recognizing her own, though still clasped preciously to her breast, as worthless.

Her Ariadne's thread severed, Gail must get a grip on herself as this latest blow (compounded by humiliation) leaves her deflated. She stumbles out of the shop, that ironic smirk combining with sharp intakes of indignant breath as she attempts to regain control of her raging emotions. In a state of near hyperventilation, Gail half sits, half collapses onto the floor and brings her hand up against her head. Scott shoots Williams from behind as her shoulders shudder in what we initially take to be a release of the tears "held back" during the press conference. However, as the reverse shot of Gail's face reveals, she is in fact laughing at the utter absurdity of her situation.

Gail's struggle to maintain a steady equilibrium in the face of such absurdity is the driving force of the film. Apart from Cinquanta (who is in many ways Gail's counterpart among the hostage takers), she alone is responsible for managing these inflexible men, calcified in their relative positions of power. The situation decisively shifts when, having been sold to the mafia after months of fruitless deliberation, Paul's ear is sliced off by his new, more ruthless, captors and mailed to a local newspaper, who requests that Gail identify the accompanying image as Paul. Her lips purse and her body briefly sags as she confirms it is him, but after touching (to the horror of the waiting forensic team!) the photograph depicting Paul's mutilated face, Gail still refuses to break down, responding instead with a show of defiant determination by pointing out that this means "he's alive," if nothing else (keen viewers will notice those lips, anxiously pursed once again). The newspapermen inform her they wish to publish the image (defending their decision on the grounds that "it's news"). After curtly reasoning that it's *his* ear . . . it's *our* ear, Gail recognizes that, given the paper can publish with or without her permission, she might as well take advantage of the fifty thousand dollars they are offering. As she purses her lips to suppress the urge to speak her mind, a different idea flashes across her eyes. "Pay me in newspapers," she demands, newly animated—a thousand copies, all adorned with Paul's maimed face, to be sent, she brightens, to the Getty mansion. "Now you're thinking like Getty," Chase later points out.

Williams plays Gail as always holding something back or keeping something in. It is more meaningful, then, when Gail is finally reunited with her son after Getty is convinced (by the newspaper ploy) to pay the ransom. As mother and son embrace in the back of Chase's car, tears stream down Gail's face as Chase observes this tender moment in the rearview mirror. This tearful reunion is nicely intercut with Getty desperately clutching an expensive oil painting, *Beautiful Child* (the million-dollar purchase of which he'd secured during his grandson's hostage crisis), as he succumbs to the effects of a deadly stroke. As he dies alone, we see (through Plummer's incredible performance) the terror of a man recognizing too late the consequences of his materialistic life

As with *Zero Dark Thirty*, however, any sense that this moment of resolution will lead to closure is belied by two further scenes in the film. In the penultimate scene, Gail is informed by Getty's (now obsequious) lawyers that in light of the patriarch's death she is to become the chief executive of the Getty Trust (and hence the Getty fortune, including his vast assets) until such time as his grandchildren come of age to inherit the wealth for themselves—news of which Gail takes with the same smirking sense of absurdity wrought by life as a Getty (Williams holds this irony in the corners of her mouth). In the final scene of the film, then, we find Gail busying herself around the Getty mansion, instructing a flurry of handlers as they carefully (and not so carefully) remove countless priceless paintings and invaluable artifacts from the estate. She appears completely at ease and in her depth as she directs the men, offering some instruction, cautioning others. As Chase arrives to bid her farewell, she attempts to convince him to remain in their employment, expressing regret when he reaffirms his intention to leave (doubtless wanting nothing more to do with the infernal Gettys). He leaves with Paul, whose youthful, boyish smile barely conceals the strains of a young man who will be forever haunted by the months spent in captivity wondering why he had been forsaken by his own kin. It is here that we get what is for me the defining moment in Williams's performance.

Gail remains in the hall (shot from behind in a medium shot), seemingly lost in thought as she gazes at a series of expensive-looking marble busts. She slightly turns her body and cocks her head, as if scrutinizing the busts for something we cannot quite see. "Miss Getty?" a man with a clipboard interjects, interrupting Gail's distracted contemplation. "Is there anything we can help you with?" She replies, softly: "No thank you, I'm fine. I have everything I need," at which Scott cuts to a perspective of the busts—as if from their blank gaze. Gail's head remains turned away, watching as the man withdraws, only turning back to the busts once he is gone. She resumes her vacant inspection (now in close-up), and we detect a certain shift in her look, a slight frown indicating increasing disquiet, the cause of which neither we, nor she, seems able to place. The diegetic sound of a clock ticks away in this now deserted hallway, as if measuring the beats of Gail's unsettled thought.

This disturbance in her eyes moves to her bottom lip which, almost imperceptibly, begins to tremble (recalling the moment with the evaluator at Sotheby's). As Gail once more reorients her head—as if searching for a different angle from which to make sense of, to see anew this object that is disturbing her—a single violin enters on the soundtrack, intensifying the unease currently gripping her. The strange look deepens as Scott finally cuts to an eyeline match revealing . . . a bust of John Paul Getty, his stern eyes glowering in watchful suspicion—still sneering, still scolding from beyond the grave. The violins—almost a slowed-down version of Bernard Herrmann's shrieking score from the shower scene in *Psycho* (1960)—rise

Michelle Williams in *All the Money in the World* (Ridley Scott, Sony Pictures, 2017). Digital frame enlargement.

further as Scott cuts back to Gail. Williams's face now registers a series of minor, fleeting expressions: her eyes twitch, her jaw tightens, her lip even curls. She trembles with . . . what? Contempt? Disgust? Nothing is clear beyond the fact that she is profoundly, even existentially, unsettled at the sight of this man from whom, even with his death, she finds no release. Then, right at the moment Gail seems on the verge of failing to contain whatever terrible emotion this disturbing thought gives rise to, Scott cuts to black and the credits roll.

The power of Williams's performance is somehow held in those trembling lips, which remind me of Jacques Derrida's description of trembling as more than a mere sensation. It is, wrote he, a signal, a symptom even, of something that has already taken place, of violence that having passed through the body threatens to erupt once more.

> Most often we neither know what is coming upon us nor see its origin; it therefore remains a secret. We are afraid of the fear, we anguish over the anguish, and we tremble. We tremble in that strange repetition that ties an irrefutable past (a shock has been felt, a traumatism has already affected us) to a future that cannot be anticipated (152).

As I have illustrated, Williams's performance throughout this film is filled with attempts to remain or recover her composure. She smirks or places a hand over her mouth to stifle a scream. She brings a phone sharply down to the receiver only to delicately replace it. She pauses or slowly takes a breath before speaking. In this final moment, however, the trembling lower lip marks a sudden, unexpected loss of composure, unexpected because this decomposition of form occurs right at the very moment her authority has been confirmed and her son's safety assured.

The moment clearly resonates with the Chastain scene on the aircraft. Both exemplify what Klevan meant by "living meaning," that is, as an expression of meaning itself, as if developing, like a Polaroid, but from which Scott, as does Bigelow, will cut before any firm contours can take shape, before definition of the final mood or emotion can be confirmed. Any number of things might be disturbing Gail in this moment. Is it the vacant expression that refuses to lift from her son's still and perhaps forever haunted face? Is it the eagerness, even urgency, in Chase's desire to leave—not just in the sense that his departure denies the Hollywood convention of leaving open the possibility of a budding romance between them, but in the lingering sense that he declined her offer a little too sharply, polite but just a little too formal? Perhaps Gail is thinking of Chase's earlier backhanded compliment—"Now you're thinking like Getty." As she now thinks and stands in for Getty, quite comfortably assuming the authority he once wielded so mulishly, is her own character in the Getty mold, after all?

☆☆☆☆☆☆☆☆☆☆ Open Windows

In her essay on the "contested ending," Barbara Klinger writes that the feminist power and potential of a final scene that struggles to resolve its inherent ambiguity is diminished by an "either/or" interpretation, "since its value lies in its vividly complex manipulation of cinematic conventions that typically regulate the depiction of femininity." By contrast, Klinger concludes, "indeterminate endings can animate the interpretive enterprise, while also . . . suggesting that female-centred narratives worth their salt will refuse to settle their issues of identity in any way that could be mistaken for complacency" (138). While Klinger is discussing *The Piano* (1993) (which pushes irresolution to a postmodern extreme), these scenes in *Zero* and *Money* in many ways achieve something much more nuanced, perhaps even more effective, by concentrating that powerful indeterminacy into the performances of two mesmerizing female stars who, in these scenes, come face-to-face with the blank, immobile (and hence unresponsive) faces of oppressive patriarchy. We couldn't be further from the complacency in which such films tend to find resolution with the removal of such antagonists. Hence, in confronting these dead patriarchs, Maya and Gail not only react to the uncertain consequence of their demise; they are responding to, thinking through, even, the uncertainty of their own instinctive responses (an eye that tears, a lip that trembles) such paradigm shifts provoke. In such small gestures we see nothing less than the power of a cinematic performance to move us emotionally and intellectually: we see the "ordeal of being" itself. What Chastain and Williams's performances mark in these moments are points of interruption, even irruption (*puncta*) that force them (and by extension us) to think again, to confront new questions. They are not just images of thinking (i.e., characters seized by a thought) but images *of* thought itself, of characters caught in the existential freedom of thought (condemned to freedom, as Sartre would say). For Murray Pomerance, thought is "[m]ore intimate than flesh, more complex than organs, more devious than muscles" (*Moment of Action*, 2016, 137). "When a character's *mind* is the thing being acted," Pomerance continues,

> the performer comes in front of us bearing a secret she can never reveal, yet a secret we presume to divine. . . . What stands before us, ultimately, is the character living with the intimate experience of personal thought, the character mentally touching the self, which is to say, the performer being accepted as a thinker through a pantomime of thought. (*Moment of Action*, 2016, 146, pronoun changed)

For their part, Chastain and Williams present themselves as alive and alert to such "pantomimes of thought" (as not many actors, Pomerance writes, do). "This is how I want you to see me," Chastain mused during an interview, "but also, you're also getting to know me and my vulnerabilities as well, because they can't help but come through" (quoted in Ray Rahman, "Jessica Chastain Shows Her Cards on *Molly's Game*, Poker, and Idris Elba," *Entertainment Weekly*, 10 August 2017). But we mustn't think that this "coming through" can be taken for granted. When asked where she thought her career was heading, Williams gave a smile and replied that "I feel like this opening has been created where we can recreate the world" (quoted in "Michelle Williams Is Ready to Lead"). With a clear nod to recent empowerments for women in the film industry—achieved in no small part thanks to the efforts of stars like Williams and Chastain—such "openings" don't just reflect on the film world but the outside world, too. They are the pricking *puncta* that interrupt the forward, unthinking thrust to leave a bruise, to remind us to pay heed to the moments that free and bind us all. Such bruises quickly heal but linger long and abidingly in the memory.

NOTES

1. I don't have the space to get into it here, but this film doesn't in my opinion deserve the charge that it defends torture under circumstances (such as these) of national security threats. For me, the presence of Chastain in the film—her gaze *as such* (which is taken over in the compound assault scene by Hakim [Fares Fares])—renders such depictions more ambiguous than is often assumed.

Chapter 9

The Predicaments of Queer Stardom

Ben Whishaw, Zachary Quinto, Ezra Miller

KYLE STEVENS

Hollywood has yet to give us an A-list gay male movie star. Yet in the 2010s there emerged a handful of gay actors in Hollywood movies who publicly identified their nonheterosexuality, such as the subjects of this essay, Ben Whishaw, Zachary Quinto, and Ezra Miller. These openly queer white waifs have claims to stardom and have graced mainstream Anglophone screens, yet they may not be considered household names, at least outside of the domiciles of queer folks. That is, they *are* stars in the queer subcultural sphere. They thus afford new opportunities for thinking about stardom, and queer stardom. Traditionally, these have been to focus on independent queer stars such as Divine (whose sexual identity was downplayed in favor of his status as "freak," as Dan Harries contends) or to look back with promissory nostalgia for unrealized futures where actors such as Rock Hudson and Anthony Perkins—later confirmed homosexuals—could have been open to the public and their fans. Film worlds and genres may not have risen up around Whishaw, Quinto, and Miller, as they have not been given star *vehicles,* but each has been a supporting actor in major Hollywood franchises and may claim a general cultural recognizability due to appearances in independent films. This quality of both knownness and unknownness—itself perhaps queer in the attention economy that marked the decade—suggests a third predicament when considering queer stardom. A star, by definition, must enjoy widespread cultural celebrity, suggesting that a figure cannot be properly dubbed a star if beloved only by a niche audience. Yet to that niche audience the actor is indubitably a star. While there is significant variation in the careers of Whishaw, Quinto, and Miller—as well as Miller's gender nonconformity in contrast with Whishaw's and Quinto's cisgender identity—we can see patterns across their work, such as supporting roles in globally dominant film franchises and character types,

Ben Whishaw

patterns that illuminate ways their queerness functions narratively and in films' receptions, and the vexed position of queer stardom more broadly.[1]

But in order to understand precisely the advances that these three actors made, it is necessary to briefly look at the history of Hollywood's queer actors in the past few decades, as the visibility and acceptance of queer people dramatically increased in U.S. culture generally. Coming of age in the late 1990s, I recall in the summer of 1999 eagerly, if abashedly, collecting articles touting Rupert Everett as "Hollywood's first gay movie star" after his turn in a supporting—and gay—role in *My Best Friend's Wedding*. Seeing an "out" gay actor in a gay role in a mainstream Hollywood hit with Julia Roberts, the biggest star of the day, was arguably unprecedented. It felt like a sea change. Of course, there have long been white male actors rumored to be men who have sex with men in the industry (Anton Walbrook, Cary Grant), as well as those rumored to be totally closeted (John Travolta, Hugh Jackman), and audiences were pretty sure about Nathan Lane's personal preferences when he appeared in 1996's *The Birdcage*, but Lane did not receive the star treatment in the media, presumably because he lacked Everett's conventional good looks.[2] Everett, however, was given "a promotion to leading-man status" and upheld as a sign of Hollywood's progress on LGBT representation, which, at the time, was largely evaluated in terms of white gay and lesbian representation (Liane Bonin, "Rupert Everett Rejects His Status as a Gay Icon," *Entertainment Weekly*, 17 June 1999, Ew.com).

Zachary Quinto

Everett was to star as a romantic heterosexual lead in *An Ideal Husband* (1999) and as Madonna's gay best friend in John Schlesinger's *The Next Best Thing* (2000). The pressure was on to prove that gay actors could not only be stars but move between straight and gay roles; yet both films bombed at the box office, Everett's career fizzled, and Hollywood had an exemplary case to show that audiences did not, in fact, want a gay movie star. It seemed that straight audiences could not see past knowledge of the actor's sexuality onscreen. Everett himself was aware of this bind: "What am I supposed to do, get down on all fours and worship everyone because they accept me?" he complained. "If people enjoy what I do, I feel gratified. But if I have to start thinking of feeling that way because I'm a homosexual, I think that's a bit sick. I'd be insulted" (quoted in Bonin). A question of realism as criterion has haunted the casting of queer actors in a way that it has not straight ones, and leads to a predicament: resemble a typical leading man and suffer straight audiences' fears that queerness may be visibly undetectable, and in turn, become stripped of stardom, or do not resemble a leading man and do not become a star.

A decade later in 2009, *Brokeback Mountain*, cast with straight male stars in highly public heterosexual relationships, was supposed to herald another major step forward in queer male representation. But there have been only a handful of LGBTQ-themed films distributed by Hollywood in the 2010s, such as *The Imitation Game* (2014), *Battle of the Sexes* (2017), *Love, Simon* (2018), *Green Book* (2018), *Bohemian Rhapsody* (2018), and *Rocketman* (2019);

Ezra Miller

none have had openly queer actors in leading roles. Independent Anglophone queer-themed films that received reasonably wide release, such as *The Kids Are All Right* (2010), *Weekend* (2011), *Albert Nobbs* (2011), *Carol* (2015), *Moonlight* (2016), *God's Own Country* (2017), *Call Me by Your Name* (2017), *Disobedience* (2017), *Can You Ever Forgive Me?* (2018), and *The Favourite* (2018), do not feature actors who were openly queer at the time of their release, either. This stands in stark opposition to television, which has been far more welcoming to queer performers. Actors such as Matt Bomer,

Cheyenne Jackson, Neil Patrick Harris, and Billy Porter, who occasionally find work on the big screen, are largely known for TV roles. Indeed, the welcomed presence of queer actors in queer roles may be one of the few ways to distinguish cinema and television today.[3]

Move actors such as Jodie Foster and Ian McKellen have gone public as participants in same-sex relationships, but after the peak of their careers, and their relatively advanced age renders their sexuality "safe" in the context of our gerontophobic society. Kristen Stewart is now a bona fide movie star, out in the heyday of her career. She is thus the only A-list queer star working frequently in movies today; conventionally beautiful queer women have less often been the target of the homophobia that is the legacy of the culture wars of the 1980s and 1990s (when conservative politicians vilified gays for the nation's woes, in large part because white gays were propped up by liberals in an appeal to respectability politics to try to secure funding for AIDS research and resources).

Significantly, Stewart's dating life has been subject to heightened media reports and cultural interest, such as her relationship with singer Annie Clark, known professionally as St. Vincent. Theorists of Hollywood stardom such as Janet Staiger and Richard deCordova have demonstrated that publicity discourse and fictional personalities mesh with a star's persona, and that revelations of personal romantic life have been at the heart of such publicity discourse. DeCordova writes: "The star system continually set us out on an investigation that is, both in its methods (eliciting confessions and unveiling secrets) and in its promised result (revealing the sexual as the ultimate, ulterior truth of the player's identity), closely tied to the construction and deployment of sexuality in modern times" (quoted in Anderson, 6). Mark Lynn Anderson has similarly argued that "sexual identity, in large measure, accounts for our fascination with the star" (7). Seen this way, Hollywood stardom has *needed* some sort of closet, some peephole through which to peer in the hope of discovering sexual truths (and the amorous conclusions that extend from them). DeCordova even connects the rhetorical structures by which we make sense of both sexuality and stardom, pointing out that "the dynamic of secrecy and confession, concealment and revelation, that supports discourse on sexuality supports discourse on stars as well" (Anderson 75). This brings us to another predicament. When queer stars disclose their sexual preferences, which are usually seen as essential identities and so the endpoints of discourse, they offer a disappointing epistemological excess—we know too much about them (at least until there are a sufficient number of queer stars that we might wonder who may be paired as lovers). So again, we have a dilemma:

remain closeted and not become a queer star, or come out and not be a star. It is Whishaw, Quinto, and Miller, I will now show, who are innovating ways around such dilemmas.

☆☆☆☆☆☆☆☆☆★ Ben Whishaw: Forging a Path

I will focus first, and in most depth, on Whishaw. He arrived on the scene years before the other two, and his groundbreaking career established patterns for the other two actors. But in order to understand how the British actor's persona functioned in the 2010s, we must again look backward and appreciate how his career was built in the 2000s, when his emotionality and physical appearance was more challenging for audiences and critics to appreciate, as their eyes had yet to be exposed to a range of queer bodies in other media. Whishaw's first feature film appearance was at the age of twenty-one, playing a victim of homosexual sexual abuse in *My Brother Tom* (2001). He then appeared as a working-class smarm mixed up in the cocaine business in *Layer Cake* (2004). He only came to international prominence with *Run Lola Run* director Tom Tykwer's 2006 film, *Perfume*, a 65-million-dollar drama and one of the most expensive German films to that date. He plays Grenouille, an orphaned boy who possesses a supernatural sense of smell despite giving off no scent himself. Grenouille's obsession with creating the perfect perfume leads him to murder several individuals in order to condense and combine their odorous essences.

Whishaw made most critics uncomfortable. Prominent reviewers focused more on his physical appearance than his talents. The *New York Times* called him "wan and jug-eared" (A. O. Scott, "The Sweet Smell of Life That Drives Him to Kill," *The New York Times*, 27 December 2006). The *Guardian* wrote that he was "intensely gaunt" (Peter Bradshaw, "*Perfume: The Story of a Murderer*," *The Guardian*, 21 December 2006, theguardian .com), while Boyd van Hoeji found:

> Whishaw is a revelation in a very difficult role that is mostly mute and certainly ugly. His slight, lanky body seems to suggest he was an extra in Tim Burton's *The Corpse Bride*, and his eyes are ablaze with an unnatural intensity that is perfectly suited to the one obsessive quest that Grenouille feels he has to fulfill. (Boyd van Hoeji, "Review: *Perfume: The Story of a Murderer*," *European -Films.net*, 17 September 2006, accessed via archive.org)

Female critics were more at ease with Whishaw's physicality. Lisa Schwarzbaum, for example, found that "Whishaw somehow gives his entire begrimed, sinewy body over to the thrall of sniffing" ("Movie Review: *Perfume: The Story of a Murderer*," *Entertainment Weekly*, 3 January 2007, Ew.com).

Most tellingly, however, is the opinion of the only gay critic I know of who wrote for a major venue at the time, Michael Koresky, who called Whishaw "seductive" and "alternately teeny-bopper cute and revoltingly wastrel-ish" ("Heaven Scent: Tom Tykwer's *Perfume: The Story of a Murderer*," IndieWire .com, 27 December 2006).

It is not hard to trace critics' discomfort with the fact that Whishaw feels queer in a story that itself has a queer sensibility. Grenouille is an alien in this world, understanding it through a sense—and sensuality—unlike others. For someone guided by scent to have no scent is to be invisible: in but not of the world, like the historical queer. Tykwer, who tells us the search for the right actor "took nearly one year, and hundreds of meetings," dramatizes Grenouille's psychotic-sexual impulses as deeply erotic, though they are not about sex acts (Brian Brooks, "IndieWire Interview: Tom Tykwer, Director of *Perfume: The Story of a Murderer*," IndieWire.com, 2 January 2007). The story culminates in Grenouille's execution; yet before he dies, he unleashes his masterful perfume, a perfume that stimulates the crowd to such carnal arousal that the entire town has an immediate orgy, eradicating lines of social difference in the service of pleasure. We see in this narrative arc a pattern in which the queer actor–character teaches the remainder of the social world, to which they are an outsider, how to feel.

The next year, Todd Haynes cast Whishaw as queer poet Arthur Rimbaud in his star-studded experimental biopic of Bob Dylan, *I'm Not There* (2007). And in 2008, Whishaw took on one of the most notable queer male roles in Western literature, Sebastian in *Brideshead Revisited* (Julian Jarrold), another character with a heightened aesthetic sensibility who is discarded once he shares his talents with the characters possessed with the privileges of normativity. The bravery of Whishaw's Sebastian in this adaptation of Evelyn Waugh's story solidified him as a monument among gay audiences. It was a shocking, thrilling turn. Sebastian is introduced swanning on a punt, a queer dandy supreme, then discussing his teddy bear Aloysius while delicately peeling a plover's egg. We see him see how the other boys judge him, but he does not shift or cease his behavior. He knows who he is. Later, when his body is on display in a swim costume, Whishaw slightly increases the drama of Sebastian's walk, crossing one foot in front of the other, the antithesis of an "appropriately" butch walk. The inherent defensiveness in the presentation of one's sense of dignity, a presentation that results in heightening one's gestures, is familiar, I suspect, to many queer audience members. Whishaw's Sebastian exhibits high-queer behavior without ever falling into camp or parody. Never had we seen such authenticity in the voice, the tilt of the head, the tipsy wrists, the way the eyes darted about the room, which is passed off as witty and alert in order to mask the sense of imminent danger entailed in any act of self-expression.

As Sebastian is proven to be too sensitive for this world and shunted off to an asylum for his homosexuality, Whishaw plays him becoming unhinged, tears flowing with a density very rarely seen from a male actor onscreen. It is a brutally physical cry, and Whishaw miraculously (especially in a British context) does not apologize for it, does not seek a way to play "trying not to cry" (for more on the masculinist critical celebration of emotional restraint, see chapter 4 of Stevens 2015). Whishaw displays the queer knowledge that painful emotions are not fatal. It is not they but their causes that are to be feared. The sheer rightness of the pain and indignation suffered by Whishaw's Sebastian, expressed deeply yet without weakness, allows him to emerge as the story's moral center, the one capable of standing up to the knotted threads of religion, family, and tradition.

Jane Campion understood how to use Whishaw's presence, casting him as John Keats in her telling of the tragic romance between Fanny Brawne (Abbie Cornish) and the fragile poet, *Bright Star* (2009). The film opens with a visual meditation on what has traditionally been considered women's labor and expression, needlepoint work. In extreme close-ups, we see the violence of the needle pushing and poking fabric, penetrating it, leaving torn and messy fibers everywhere, fibers that disappear when seen at arm's length. The real protagonist of Campion's story is Fanny, and it is quickly established that the character's care for fashion and "flounce" is dismissed in this traditionally gendered world. Fanny's hope arrives in the form of Keats, a lollipop of cheekbones and David Cassidy hair, who ruptures the binarist gendered logic that subtends the misogyny threatening to trap Fanny. He, however, confesses: "I'm not sure I have the right feelings toward women." Nevertheless, she pursues him because "he's not like other men." In fact, Fanny falls for Keats because he exhibits the characteristics traditionally associated with queer men, including his understanding of "the shape of beauty." Hence, Campion's film offers audiences, particularly female audiences, the fantasy of wooing a queer man (the main obstacle to their union is Keats's infatuation with the macho John Browne), and knowing that a queer actor is in the role may well heighten the thrill of such an onscreen victory. In the end, the world cannot abide so sensitive a soul as Keats's, and the promise of Whishaw's mortal thinness is delivered. Whishaw's performance is again full of tears, and he does not *build* to a single emotional climax, as has been the dominant structure of straight male actors' performances since talkies began. (One cannot help but consider the antipatriarchal quality of female and queer actors' ability

Ben Whishaw's Ariel embodies the epicene in *The Tempest* (Julie Taymor, Walt Disney Studios Motion Pictures, 2010). Digital frame enlargement.

to deliver multiple emotional climaxes as deeply rooted in psychosexual loyalties.)

By the 2010s, Whishaw's persona charted a space beyond "leading man" conventionality. Unlike stars such as Tilda Swinton who were celebrated for their androgynous appearance and performances, Whishaw operates outside of cishet expectations altogether—not androgynous for combining masculine and feminine traits but epicene, displaying neither particularly masculine nor feminine properties. This quality of the epicene can be seen in his scenes in Julie Taymor's adaptation of Shakespeare's *The Tempest* (2010). Whishaw plays Ariel, the "airy spirit" at a remove from all things fleshy and profane (juxtaposed with the butch, earthly, sexual Caliban). Taymor and Whishaw's iteration is otherworldly. Whishaw's brows are shaved, he wears no clothes, has a smooth pubis area—an absence of genitalia not coded as lack—and occasionally, barely-there breasts. Indeed, the character is itself ambiguously present, often rendered translucent through visual effects. Whether fluttering through the forest or descending as a harpy, Ariel remains more idea than physical presence, a quality that, CGI aside, is intrinsic to Whishaw's slight frame and odd beauty. Critics called Whishaw's Ariel "genderless" (Quarmby 386)—a contrast to the androgyny of Helen Mirren's Prospero in the film—and noted that "Taymor has opted for the unisex look and cast Ben Whishaw," as if the one follows the other (Harry Haun, "Julie Taymor Spins a Shakespearean Web for New "Tempest Film," Playbill.com, 20 December 2010).

In 2012, Whishaw appeared in two Hollywood tentpole productions: the Wachowskis' *Cloud Atlas* and the James Bond film *Skyfall*. In *Cloud Atlas*, he again plays a sensitive aesthete, Robert Frobischer, a pianist in the 1930s who must hide his love for a man (though he also sleeps with a female character played by Halle Berry). Robert, in fact, composes the "Cloud Atlas Suite" which hovers over the whole movie, echoing character emotions and guiding audience sentiment. In *Skyfall*, Whishaw plays Q, the iconic head of the team of inventors who supply Bond with his state-of-the-art defensive gadgets. (Bond is played by Daniel Craig, with whom Whishaw also worked on *Layer Cake* and *Enduring Love* [2004]). Q is introduced in a museum, again associating Whishaw with aesthetics, and, moreover, immediately advises the radically heterosexual Bond on a painting that Bond seems unable to grasp: "Always makes me feel a little melancholy . . . the inevitability of dying, don't you think . . . what do you see?" Equally significantly, although Q wears a hoodie that one may expect of any "techie," he also wears well-tailored plaid pants, a subtle fashion historical-specific sign to queer audiences searching for representational possibilities. Unlike Qs of the past who deliver jet packs and explosive boom boxes, tested in spectacular fashion in a laboratory, this Q hands Bond a very small gun and a stamp-sized gizmo that can emit a distress signal. Seeing Bond's disappointment, Q offers, "What were you expecting? An exploding pen? We don't really go for that anymore." The metaphor is not to be missed. This Q will not perpetuate macho standards of weaponry rooted in ostentatious displays of hetero-phallic power. This shift becomes more significant as we discover that this installment of the franchise delivers its most explicitly queer-coded male villain. As played by Javier Bardem, Raoul Silva is stereotypically mincing, flamboyant. Moreover, Silva's queerness is not just about gendered actions; he molests Bond. When he has Bond bound, he touches his chest, and his hand wanders up Bond's thigh. This queerness-as-threat is in implicit juxtaposition with the sexless Q: male effeminacy is bad but epicene is okay, the film seems to say via Whishaw.

Following the prestige of appearing in the high-profile Bond series in the 2010s, Whishaw pursued a fascinating array of characters in film and television, many of them gay or queer. In 2014, he played the lead in *Lilting*, Hong Khaou's moving and tender study of a gay man who takes on the difficult task of caring for his dead Chinese lover's traditional mother. Whishaw also appeared in Yorgos Lanthimos's independent hit *The Lobster* in 2014, which darkly skewers enforced heterosexuality and couplehood by critiquing the social impulse to identify people as romantic numerals. In its fictional hotel setting, individuals are encouraged to find mates with similar traumas. In a movie baroque with irony, Whishaw plays a straight man who performs a sort of passing by self-inflicting nosebleeds in order to seduce a woman.

2014 also saw, or rather heard, Whishaw's performance as the voice of the titular bear in the box-office hit *Paddington*. In this film and its 2017 award-winning sequel, the winsome ursine hero is available to be read as a metaphor for social and political differences, not least of which is the figure of the immigrant, as Paddington moves to the United Kingdom from the jungle and suffers various xenophobic attitudes. Paddington can also be read as a queer figure, or at least as a figure that blurs boundaries of social identities. Beyond being a bear in a world of humans, at times he seems to be childlike, not just in his naivete but in needing to be cared for; yet he is also regarded as an adult who can go to a men's prison, subject to all the discriminations afforded there. But, even if seemingly fragile, Paddington triumphs through the strength of his intuitions and convictions, convictions that arise from his *nature* (emphasized by his nonhumanness) as an especially sensitive creature, attuned to beautiful things in the world, such as marmalade, and beautiful ways of being in the world, such as kind. Paddington is thus in many ways a quintessential Whishavian role: an especially sensitive creature who is smaller than everyone else, yet whose aesthetic sensibilities afford not only his survival but require he teach the rest of the world how to be more sensitive, too.

Space prohibits discussion of all of Whishaw's screen performances in the 2010s, not to mention his work onstage, but he went on to play not only Q in the Bond sequels but supporting roles in *Suffragette* (2015), *In the Heart of the Sea* (2015), *Mary Poppins Returns* (2018), and *The Personal Life of David Copperfield* (2019). He also played a supporting role as a gay lover in the Academy Award–winning, if bland, *The Danish Girl* (2015), another instance of refusing to cast queer actors in queer roles, in this case casting cishet Eddie Redmayne as historical trans woman Lili Elbe. Whishaw also played gay characters in excellent television miniseries that further ratified his persona. In *London Spy*, he played Danny, an "ordinary" Londoner suffering the indignities of life as an automated worker who becomes an amateur sleuth after his one-night stand goes missing. What is significant about this detective story is that it supplants the fetishization of clues and facts with the fetishization of trust in instinctive feeling. Danny's intuition about spaces and people guides him. In the historical fiction *A Very English Scandal*, Whishaw played Norman Scott with a degree of queer male effeminacy rarely seen on-screen, and for which he won a BAFTA, Emmy, and Golden Globe.

☆☆☆☆☆☆☆☆☆☆ Zachary Quinto: Embracing Emotion

Quinto came to prominence for queer audiences when he starred as the hilarious best friend of Tori Spelling in her semi-autobiographical sitcom *So NoTORIous* (2006), at a time when gay characters, especially campy ones, were still relatively rare on TV. Quinto was also cast that year as the villain Sylar in the TV show *Heroes* (2006–2010), which was popular enough to make him a household name. In 2009, Quinto made the leap to the big screen, and in a big way, by taking up the role of Spock in J. J. Abrams's reboot *Star Trek*. The next year he came out officially, though his very public support of LGBT causes was widely known and reported, leading to much speculation. But when previously asked about his sexual orientation, he gave "artist's dodge" answers that neither confirmed nor denied his self-identified sexual orientation. Coming out in 2010 jeopardized his position in the new franchise intended to achieve global blockbuster success, risking not only his career but a lucrative one at that.

Star Trek was a huge success, grossing almost $260 million domestically, more than enough to launch the Starship *Enterprise*'s story into sequels. Those landed in the form of *Star Trek into Darkness* in 2013 and *Star Trek Beyond* in 2016. Spock is half-human and half-Vulcan, and the narrative defines the species here as emotional and rational, respectively. A young and comparatively effeminate Spock is shown being forced to learn to control his emotions as he is bullied by macho Vulcan teenagers. Next, when we are introduced to the older Spock as played by Quinto, it is in conversation with his mother, who tells him, "As always . . . whoever you choose to be . . . you will have a proud mother." Particularly in 2009, the discourse of pride in lifestyle *choice* was heavily queer-coded language, certainly highlighted by Quinto's presence. Having a gay actor play Spock also underscores the awkwardness of the heterosexual romance with Uhura (Zoe Saldana). He can play straight precisely because he need not play straight. That is, even though Spock may be heterosexual, he isn't straight-acting. He need never perform desire to begin with, as that is outside the purview of his half-Vulcan identity. Moreover, Quinto emphasizes that Spock's decision to abandon his home planet and join the Federation is a choice not to discount his human side. While still presented as hesitant to emote, Quinto's Spock cries easily and expresses friendship easily. In fact, the franchise's Captain Kirk, played by Chris Pine, is portrayed as excessively emotional and desirous. He must learn from Spock how to *better* control his emotions, not how to relinquish emotionality altogether. This is something of a departure from the classic TV and film series. There, Leonard Nimoy's Spock

Zachary Quinto does not shy away from making his Spock emotional as he weeps for Captain Kirk in *Star Trek into Darkness* (J. J. Abrams, Paramount Pictures, 2013). Digital frame enlargement.

often failed to understand human emotion altogether. In a series of complex narrative moves, Nimoy returns as Spock in the 2010s franchise, and so audiences are explicitly invited to compare Nimoy's stoic Spock with Quinto's more sensitive performance.

Quinto starred alongside James Franco in *I Am Michael* (2015), based on the life of Michael Glatze, a gay activist who finds Christianity and denounces homosexuality. The film is a rare account of stark ideological conversion, and Glatze's description of his pursuit of self-discovery echoes the rhetoric of queer liberalism in challenging ways. Quinto plays Glatze's lover, Bennett, whose ability to handle changes in life, career, and love is juxtaposed with Glatze's existential angst and obsessiveness. The film ends tragically because Glatze lacks Bennett's maturity. In this way, even in stories about gayness, the gay actor continues to play the emotional and moral center.

☆☆☆☆☆☆☆☆☆☆ Ezra Miller: The Future Is Genderqueer

Unlike Whishaw and Quinto, Miller does not identify as gay. While Miller came out as queer in 2012, the public largely regarded that identity in terms of sexuality, as he described being in relationships with other boys as far back as kindergarten. It was not until 2018 that he publicly laid claim to a more expansive and profound notion of "queer," defining the term as "an umbrella of non-identification" to a *Playboy* interviewer. In that same interview, Miller received a great deal of attention not just for appearing in fishnet stockings, size-fourteen pumps, and bunny ears but for his openness about sexual traumas in the industry and his polyamorous lifestyle, a formation he dubs his "polycule" (Ryan Gajewski, "The Magic of Ezra Miller," *Playboy*, 15 November 2018, accessed via playboy.com). Miller has also become known for his extravagant, and decidedly queer, red-carpet looks: wearing lip gloss to the premiere of *Justice League* (2017); showing up in leopard-print short shorts with "slut" emblazoned on his cheek to a Saint Laurent fashion show; waltzing up the steps to the Met Gala in a surrealist, androgynous tuxedo number with five photorealistic eyes painted on his face that make it difficult to determine where his body ends and fashion begins; or sliding along in a full-length, black, puffer-coat gown, complete with hood, to the Paris premiere of *Fantastic Beasts: The Crimes of Grindelwald* (2018).

Miller's first feature film role was in the 2008 indie *Afterschool*, where he played a high school student who, it is slowly revealed, murdered classmates. The following year he was cast in another independent film, *City Island*, playing a heterosexual teenager with a fat and feederist fetish. In 2010, Miller starred in another small-budget film that did not receive much attention, *Beware the Gonzo*, playing a mercenary high school newspaper editor, and a supporting role as a gay son in *Every Day*. 2011 brought Miller his big break, playing the titular son opposite Tilda Swinton in Lynne Ramsay's brilliant *We Need to Talk about Kevin*. Although another low-budget film that did not receive a wide release, the movie garnered much attention due to positive reviews and various awards for Ramsay and Swinton from critics' groups. The film follows Swinton's character dealing with the aftermath of having mothered a son who locked his classmates in the gymnasium and murdered them with a bow and arrow. It is largely a portrait of the complexity of motherhood, but Miller's powerful, and powerfully sinister, performance signaled to the world an actor of unusual depth and commitment. That Miller was repeatedly cast in roles with such dark themes—stories of social outsiders or to those with misshapen psyches—demonstrates his talent for empathy as well as intelligence, an understanding of others beyond his own experience.

In *The Perks of Being a Wallflower* (2012), Miller plays Patrick, the type of dance-loving, scarf-wearing gay best friend character well established in the 1990s and 2000s by mostly heterosexual actors (with the exception of Everett in *My Best Friend's Wedding*). But the intensity of Miller's gaze, the cock of his wrists, the slight swish to his walk that was more apparent in scenes with characters Patrick trusted—these aspects rendered the type darker and more authentic than was typical. As Patrick, Miller seems to be all planes and angles, cheekbones catching light amid a mop of shoulder-length, tousled hair. Unlike previous incarnations of the type, Miller imbues Patrick with sexuality, too, a sexuality not on the page. We never see Patrick do more than kiss a boy—and when it's his football player boyfriend, the two sit on a bed leaning in, bodies implausibly distant—but in Miller's hands Patrick is sexy. He preens around, and when he wears a tuxedo and white scarf, there is an androgynous, erotic quality reminiscent of Marlene Dietrich in *Morocco* (1930).

The Perks of Being a Wallflower won the GLAAD Award for Outstanding Film in wide release and the Independent Spirit Award for Best First Feature for director Stephen Chbosky. Miller won "Best Breakthrough Performance" at the MTV Movie Awards (when that meant something), Best Supporting Actor from the Boston Society of Film Critics, the Hollywood Film Festival, and the Santa Barbara Film Festival, and a handful of nominations from other organizations, cementing his status as an up-and-comer in film culture at large, as well as his bona fide stardom among queer audiences with very few actors to embrace as one of their own. (*Perks, Cloud Atlas*, and the animated film *ParaNorman* were, I believe, the only widely released films in 2012 to feature gay characters—and none of them leads.)

In *Fantastic Beasts and Where to Find Them*, a spin-off of and oblique prequel to the *Harry Potter* series, audiences follow the travels of "magizoologist" Newt Scamander, a wizard who attempts to secure and protect magical animals. Aside from various bureaucratic and romantic subplots, the core conflict of the narrative concerns attacks being made on London by an obscurus, a dark swirl of evil magic. Miller plays Credence Barebone, who, it turns out, is an obscurial (one who produces the obscurus), as it results not from any malicious intentions but from the prohibition of the expression of a witch or wizard's magic (in this case, by Credence's orthodox, antimagic family). The metaphor for the queer experience is practically manifest. Indeed, when vying for the role, Miller wrote a letter to director David Yates and producer David Hayman attesting to understand the character because

> it's the story for me and a thousand lost friends. . . . And that's not just things that are reflected metaphors in real, vital and—seemingly at least—a little intentional ways for the LGBTIA community, but also for communities who are not neurotypical, or people who are creative, people who are sensitive, people who are anything. . . . People who are nerds, people who are punks and bicycle addicts and, and, contemporary pirates and people who live on the fringes, who are marginalized. . . . Really a lot of these are metaphors that can be reflected. (Brendan Haley, "The Queer Metaphor behind Ezra Miller's *Fantastic Beasts* Character," *Pride.com*, 15 November 2018)

Ezra Miller's Credence is so full of desire for Colin Farrell's Percival that he can barely look at him in *Fantastic Beasts and Where to Find Them* (David Yates, Warner Bros. Pictures, 2016). Digital frame enlargement.

That Miller would feel the need to argue that the obscurus metaphor can be extended *beyond* queer identities suggests just how obvious that metaphor is. The explicitly gay subtext was commented upon by most critics, and was the subject of thinkpieces itself (see Haley, and also Jeffrey Bloomer, "J. K. Rowling's *Fantastic Beasts* Flirts with Gay Allegory. Its Sequels Should Go All the Way," *Slate.com,* 28 November 2016).

For his part, in playing Credence Miller attested to being very lonely, going without sex and company for long periods. The sadness of Credence is certainly visible on-screen, such that when he is tempted to do the bidding of villain Percival (later revealed to be the legendarily powerful and nefarious wizard Grindelwald), played by the fetching Colin Farrell, there is no question that Miller will obey. Miller and Farrell are often filmed in intimate two-shots, and when Percival cups Credence's face in his hands, Miller expertly plays the adolescent longing Credence feels by struggling to lift his eyes to meet Percival's gaze, staring instead at his lips; the desire is palpable.

☆☆☆☆☆☆☆☆☆☆ Conclusion

By way of conclusion, and connecting themes across the stardoms of Whishaw, Quinto, and Miller, consider the clavicle, the body's only truly lateral-lying bone. This is a bone not easily visible in the biggest cishet male Hollywood stars of the 2010s, such as with the brigade of Chrises (Pine, Pratt, Evans, and Hemsworth) that populate superhero movies, or in Daniel Craig's Bond, whose pecs overtake it. One might also note the blondeness of this macho bunch, which stands in stark contrast to our three queer stars' dark brunette litheness. All three are *thin,* pliable and slender as fronds on a weeping willow that lives by the water. Their bodies are usually put on display, with lighting to highlight the clavicle, and perhaps the visibility of this bony, rigid, corporeal horizon asks us to rethink how these queer stars bridge head and heart, mind and body.

As we have seen, in each franchise, the queer actor plays the Other to the straight lead. Whishaw functions as a physical contrast to Bond but also an emotional one. Q understands melancholy and is the only character uncharmed by Bond's wisecracks. Quinto's Spock is physically distinct from Pine's shorter, voluptuous Kirk and, as the human-Vulcan trained in controlling his emotions, teaches him how to temper his mercurial nature. In *Fantastic Beasts,* Miller's Credence does not yet understand how to control his feelings; even still, his example helps teach the straight characters to express their love for one another. And it is no minor point that when Grindelwald is revealed, he is a harsh blonde. It would seem that, just as the narratives need these foils, so, too, do the cishet male stars need queer counterparts. The correlations among body types, queerness, and character types suggest a cultural shift in perceptions of queer bodies on-screen.

In the decades before the 2010s, and especially before the advent of preexposure prophylaxis medications to prevent the transmission of HIV, queer male bodies (or those perceived as male, as in the characters Miller plays) were subject to heightened scrutiny. Extreme thinness could signal disease, impending death. Similarly, there is a long homophobic tradition of perceiving queer men as effeminate, as sissies, which was usually by definition related to a lack of the assumed musculature appropriate to a properly masculine, cishet man. Hence, in the 1980s and 1990s gay male body types emphasized muscle and the appearance of male masculinity and health—motivated in no small part by the need to court public opinion in order to secure funding to fight HIV/AIDS and stay alive. In this context, thinness appears as a choice, a refusal of traumatic inheritance. It may function as a type with which popular audiences are comfortable: not the threat that Rupert Everett posed, that a queerness may not be visibly signified, but a reassurance that queers are fragile-bodied, easily broken. As Richard Dyer suggests in his account of the representation of male queerness in the twentieth century, and particularly of the dominant type he labels "the sad young man" figure, the melancholic waif is the suicidal type.[4] Thus, his demise, whether in the tradition of literature and film which typically ends in queer death or in real-world hate crimes, is not shocking. He was already near death.

But I want to see the slender forms of Whishaw, Quinto, and Miller as moving beyond such stereotypes and histories, operating in new contexts only possible in the 2010s. (Although the U.S. Supreme Court struck down same-sex sodomy laws in 2003, the decision to end the Defense of Marriage Act in 2015 marked a moment of wider cultural acceptance for gay and lesbian forms of being, though that of course did not include many queer and trans forms.) Unlike the ever-bulking Hemsworth, or Henry Cavill, who grow in size from film to film, in the case of these three actors their thinness makes them, ironically, big enough. There is a confidence in a refusal to take up space, in being small and feeling grand—or even, in fact, sundering body shape from self-esteem.

Changes in body type affect our perception of these stars as erotic objects and as objects of potential identification, situated as they are in relation to dominant ideas of conventional white male attractiveness both within the films and for the ideological and historical context of the audience. Finding a star beautiful is, of course, an ultimately subjective matter, and one that is perhaps especially so for queer audiences. Dyer writes: "Actual reading practices are always more complicated and insecure than this, but desiring both to be the object of desire and to want the subject of desire structures the text of lesbian/gay fantasy" (134). Central to the fantasy of "the sad young man" was that "to be homosexual was both irremediably sad and overwhelmingly desirable" (116). The desire to both have and be the object of one's desires is not a desire that usually enters into discourse about heterosexual spectatorship and stardom (although it certainly could, as could differing schemes of activity and passivity rather than the typical schematics that assume the male-active and female-passive binaries). Miller is the most conventionally attractive of the three, but nevertheless the unconventional beauty of these stars affords queer spectators the opportunity to regard a star as an erotic object without the concomitant impulse to want to look like that star. Speaking as a gay male audience member, I do not particularly want to look like Miller, though I find him beautiful. I do not particularly want to move like Quinto, though I find him elegant. I do not particularly want to speak like Whishaw, though I find him erudite. I do not particularly want to react like each, though I find them soulful. There is freedom in this separation, the ability to sink into the pleasures of desire without the accompanying (and often painful) demand to reflect upon one's sociopolitical identity. How freeing to be able to desire an onscreen object without the accompanying bewitching tangle of processes—again, many of them painful—entailed by identification? This is not to discount that many queer spectators desire, say, Ben Affleck, Idris Elba, or Brad Pitt without wanting to *be* them. Yet it is hard to dismiss the cultural atmosphere that encourages viewers to see them as icons of a maleness and masculinity to which one *ought* to aspire. Hence, in the queer's experience of them on-screen, there is often a quality of resistance rather than mere absence of identification. (The queer does not aspire to assimilation.)

Dyer's historical category helps us contextualize other patterns in Whishaw's, Quinto's, and Miller's careers, too, particularly the sadness and youth that he names as endemic to the stereotypical representation of white queerness. Dyer recalls seeing a sad young man type and the concomitant longing: "A wish that I could both be him and have him with his 'earnest face and handsome physique'" (116). Queer audiences, Dyer suggests, identified with the glamour of unlovability. After all, few attitudes are more relatable than believing one does not deserve love, and few postures demand greater attention than suffering. As we have seen, in the 2000s Whishaw was repeatedly cast as the epitome of the sad young man. But as social acceptance towards white gays developed, we saw changes in this stereotypy. Credence is sad but the arc is to redeem that sadness; Spock begins as a sad, bullied boy but learns to control his emotions; Q begins as an expert at perceiving melancholy but is ultimately shown to also have control over his expression of feeling.

Yet luxuriating in one's sadness, even if overcome narratively, is a privilege inextricable from these actors' whiteness. Only white suffering is offered by these figures as a spectacle, and so it would seem that queers must be white lest audiences worry they are suffering not just due to queerness and be reminded of the atrocities of racism. Within the Anglo-American context, Dyer argues that "there is something specifically white about the stereotype" (124). He points out that "even James Baldwin [made] his sad young David in *Giovanni's Room* white," and describes how much of the literature featuring sad young men stressed the figure's whiteness against characters of color. This results in an association of queer masculinity with white sensitivity, and, in turn, "the sad young man becomes part of much wider constructions of white identity in terms of suffering (the burden of which becomes the badge of [their] superiority)" (124). (For Dyer, superiority is not tantamount to power: "Power in contemporary society habitually passes itself off as embodied in the normal as opposed to the superior" [824].)

The image of suffering as a burden that carries the weight of moral justice, marking gays as victims of an unjust system and therefore above it, is embodied into the 2000s, particularly by Whishaw. But in the 2010s, we see him, Quinto, and Miller moving in a new direction, away from the ubiquitous melancholy that plagued the depiction of the queer white male; away from the "romantic-pornographic" emotional tone of the sad young men, the queer male stars queer culture often claims but who were of course not publicly so, such as James Dean or Anthony Perkins, and hopefully on to forge new types. As the youngest, perhaps it makes sense that Miller is most vociferously challenging the norms, strictures, and expectations of male stars. Maybe one day, if the stars align, we will have A-list queer male stars who have access to the full spectrum of onscreen affects, and be considered objects of desire, loci of identification—or not. Yet in all three we might see possible futures outside of established types. The 2020s will determine whether queer actors can overcome the predicaments into which audiences and industries have bound them, and whether films can accommodate new forms of being and belonging.

NOTES

1. Given that we have not yet had an out, nonwhite male actor achieve what we might properly call stardom in Hollywood films, my discussion of queer actors is limited to white actors, a fact to which I will return. Though not discussions of stardom per se, to read about Black queer representation, see Gerstner and Mercer, and for Asian queer representation, Hoang. See Negra for a discussion of nonwhite female stardom. See McRuer for a discussion of the representation of queer disability. See Schoonover and Galt for a discussion of queer representation beyond Hollywood.

2. Readers might consider the presence of queer characters in sitcoms like *Soap* (1977) or *Ellen*, the latter having the titular character come out in 1997. Significantly for my discussion of queer males, TV showcased characters dealing with the AIDS crisis in mainstream venues more frequently than Hollywood did via made-for-TV movies like *An Early Frost* (1985) and *And the Band Played On* (1993). The TV show *Pose* (2018) is noteworthy for employing queer and trans actors of color. For more on queer television, see Villarejo and Martin.

3. Histories of Hollywood stardom, such as Michael Newton's *Show People: A History of the Film Star*, do not include discussions of openly queer actors.

4. Ryan Powell has recently written about the persistence of this figure in the 2010s in terms of narrative characters.

Chapter 10

Timothée Chalamet

Refashioning Hollywood Masculinity

MATT CONNOLLY

On 28 February 2020, the *New York Times* ran a column by author Teddy Wayne entitled "Raising a Nontoxic Man." In it, Wayne sees himself as situated between two distinct archetypes of male role models: "It may be that my generational position, somewhere between the Gary Cooper and Timothée Chalamet paradigms of manhood, is the source of my anxiety." That same day, the *Huffington Post*'s Jenna Amatulli published a story summarizing the latest episode of "Hiking with Kevin," a YouTube series in which comedian Kevin Nealon interviews celebrities as they tromp together along outdoor walking paths ("Courteney Cox Has a Suggestion for Who Could Be Joey in a Recast 'Friends'"). The episode in question featured actress Courteney Cox, who at one point was asked by Nealon who she would cast in a remake of *Friends* (1994–2004), the beloved NBC sitcom that effectively launched her career. Cox thought for a moment before offering her replacement for the show's goofball lothario originally played by Matt LeBlanc: "Well, Timothée Chalamet can be Joey."

It is a striking confluence of observations. How, exactly, is it the case that the same actor at the same point in his career can be simultaneously held up as an exemplar of enlightened modern manhood and championed as the inheritor of a role most accurately characterized as a womanizing (albeit comic) lunkhead? What is it about Chalamet that not only elicits effusive praise from contemporaries but so often places him at the center of larger conversations and contradictions about the role and nature of celebrity masculinity?

This essay argues that Chalamet's career and the public fascination that he has engendered since his breakout role in *Call Me by Your Name* (2017) rest upon a negotiation between two different yet interconnected modes of contemporary male celebrity. On the one hand, Chalamet embodies prodigious acting talent, marked by a physical grace and emotional intensity that has led several critics to describe his abilities in generation-defining terms.

Timothée Chalamet

Along with these kudos have come expectations from some commentators and industry figures that Chalamet will mirror the persona and follow the career paths forged by serious-minded male celebrity-performers as varied as James Dean, Daniel Day-Lewis, and Leonardo DiCaprio. On the other hand, Chalamet has come to personify a relationship to masculinity marked by emotional vulnerability, sartorial androgyny, and a strong link with films that center female and/or queer experience. While some contemporary stars have drawn acclaim for portraying queer characters while markedly not carrying over those roles' connotations into their public personas, Chalamet acquired a passionate fan base in part for being able to occupy a more ambiguous space of gender performance both on- and offscreen. This is not to say that Chalamet seamlessly knits together the roles of "serious young thespian" and "new masculinity idol." Indeed, it's the ambiguities of embodying these roles—sometimes effortlessly, sometimes haltingly—that has framed Chalamet as not just a sterling performer but a figure of fascination in an era of ever-shifting ideals surrounding masculine power, privilege, and behavior.

★★★★★★★★★★ Chalamet in the James Dean Mold

While the seemingly sudden nature of Chalamet's fame was a key element of his initial stardom, the years of professional work that preceded his rapid rise offer insight into the initial perceptions that the public had of Chalamet. Born on 27 December 1995, Chalamet grew up in the Hell's Kitchen neighborhood of New York City in a family steeped in film, television, and the performing arts. His mother, Nicole Flender, is a former Broadway actress and dancer, and other family members have worked as television directors, producers, and screenwriters (Timothée's father, Marc Chalamet, is an editor for UNICEF). Both Chalamet and his sister attended New York's prestigious Fiorello H. LaGuardia High School of Music & Art and Performing Arts, whose alums include not only Chalamet's mother and uncle but such stars as Al Pacino, Jennifer Aniston, and Billy Dee Williams. This combination of familial and educational influence led Chalamet to become involved in the arts at a young age.

Chalamet's earliest roles were in short narrative films or television episodes that placed him in decidedly gruesome situations: a Hansel-like little boy beheaded by a witch in *Sweet Tooth* (aka *Butcher's Hill*, 2008); the tortured ward of a psychotic carnival performer in *Clown* (2008); and a young murder victim on a 2009 episode of *Law & Order* (1990–2010). In what would become a bit of a casting trend for Chalamet, he also played the younger version of the male protagonist in the CBS TV movie *Loving Leah* (2009). A three-year pause from the screen followed, broken in 2012 by multi-episode guest stints on *Royal Pains* (2009–2016) as the gawky nephew of one of the lead character's sometimes girlfriend, and in *Homeland* (2011–2020) as the brooding son of the vice president. This oscillation between genial and moody teendom would similarly define Chalamet's film performances into 2014, which included roles as a disillusioned sign twirler in the short *Spinners*, the youthful iteration of a put-upon townie in *Worst Friends*, a bullying high school football player in Jason Reitman's *Men, Women & Children*, and (most notably) the adolescent version of the son of Matthew McConaughey's galactic voyager in Christopher Nolan's *Interstellar*. The prominence of the latter two roles also gave Chalamet some of his first media coverage as a performer. *Teen Vogue* deemed the young actor a "James Dean reincarnate . . . [that] has an air of mystery and an old-school charm" while simultaneously possessing a mature outlook on stardom as evidenced by his studies of cultural anthropology at Columbia University (Liana Weston, "The New Wave," October 2014).

Chalamet would cut short his time at Columbia after his freshman year to pursue acting more fully, though these subsequent roles initially failed to capitalize on the relative prominence of Nolan's film. He continued to be cast throughout 2015 as adolescents defined either by precocity (as with the teleporting farmer's son in the independent fantasy drama *One & Two*) or comic sullenness (see his moody, hormonal teen in *Love the Coopers*). By 2016, however, Chalamet's burgeoning reputation as a soulful, self-aware talent deftly sketching portraits of troubled youth began to come into sharper focus. This shift first occurred away from the screen, when Chalamet was cast as the gifted but self-destructive prep school student at the center of *Prodigal Son*, John Patrick Shanley's autobiographical play that premiered off-Broadway in February 2016. Critics praised Chalamet's ability to capture a roiling mixture of intelligence, intensity, and adolescent yearning, with the *New Criterion*'s Kyle Smith describing him as "a soulful sloucher in the James Dean mold" ("Minding the Gaps," March 2016, 34). A supporting role as (yet again) the wayward adolescent iteration of James Franco's haunted adult author in *The Adderall Diaries* (2016) did not leave an impression on reviewers, but Chalamet received some of his most positive notices to date for his turn as a talented if underachieving high school actor in *Miss Stevens* (2016). Multiple reviewers noted Chalamet's promise as a performer, with Stephen Holden of the *New York Times* describing the actor as akin to "a younger, more high-strung James Dean" ("A Chaperone Flirts with Temptation," 16 September 2016, C7). These comparisons to

Dean established a set of loose associations around Chalamet—actorly skill, intensity, and youthful beauty—that would be amplified exponentially with the release of his next film.

☆☆☆☆☆☆☆☆☆★ Breaking Through in the #MeToo Moment

Much of the rhetoric surrounding Chalamet's performance in *Call Me by Your Name* positioned the young actor as both an out-of-nowhere discovery and a singularly well-suited celebrity for the moment—"a zeitgeistian lightning strike," in the words of *Call Me by Your Name* co-star Armie Hammer ("The New Power of New York List," *Variety*, 2 October 2018, 50). This section examines each of these overlapping ideas. It first analyzes how Chalamet both embodied and adapted the persona of the Dean-esque actor wunderkind. Then, it considers how his ascendancy coincided with the #MeToo era of Hollywood reckoning surrounding male sexual predation and power, which Chalamet navigated in ways that came to define his public persona as much as his acting prowess and purported star presence.

While his rise to critical and cultural notoriety rested in part on his sheer onscreen ubiquity in 2017—with supporting roles in the coming-of-age dramedy *Lady Bird* and revisionist Western *Hostiles*—it was his lead performance in Luca Guadagnino's queer romance that powered Chalamet's sudden and intense fame. Set in picturesque northern Italy in the summer of 1983, *Call Me by Your Name* centers on seventeen-year-old Elio (Chalamet) as he experiences an emotional and erotic awakening when he has a brief but life-changing affair with his father's twenty-four-year-old graduate assistant Oliver (Hammer). The film premiered in January 2017 at the Sundance Film Festival. Adjectives like "extraordinary," "sensational," and "star-making" quickly attached themselves to Chalamet's performance, which reviewers singled out (in echoes of earlier praise for his work in *Prodigal Son* and *Miss Stevens*) for its combination of preternatural confidence and striking emotional transparency—"petulance, balletic physicality and a new kind of goofball naturalism," as Ryan Gilbey put it in the *New Statesman* ("Rumbles in the Jungle," 24 February–2 March 2017, 52). Two scenes drew particular attention. The first (faithfully adapted from the passage in André Aciman's novel on which the film is based) showcases Elio's carnal encounter with a particularly ripe peach. The moment would not be seen as among Chalamet's bravura acting moments so much as a striking example of his commitment to illuminating Elio's unruly sexual desires. The second, on the other hand, served as the cornerstone of Chalamet's critical acclaim—a "minutes-long and wordless final shot, another rare close-up of Elio," as described by the *Hollywood Reporter*'s Boyd van Hoeij, "so mesmerizing that it immediately cements [Chalamet's] status as one of the world's brightest young talents" ("'Call Me by Your Name': Film Review Sundance 2017," 23 January 2017).

Critics continued to laud Chalamet's performance as the film worked its way through many of the year's major film festivals—including Berlin, New York, and Toronto—before arriving in U.S. theaters on 24 November 2017. His other 2017 film roles, meanwhile, served to bolster Chalamet's near constant presence in American movie theaters, with *Lady Bird, Call Me by Your Name,* and *Hostiles* all theatrically released in the United States within a seven-week period. Some reviewers found particular resonance between the actor's work in *Call Me by Your Name* and his gently comic portrayal of a blasé high school poser in *Lady Bird*. "Elio is something of an extension of the actor's hilariously pretentious character in the recent film 'Lady Bird,'" noted the *Washington Post*'s Ann Hornaday, "another teenager with pedantic ideas about his own depth and seriousness" ("'Call Me by Your Name' Is among the Best Movies of the Year," 14 December 2017). Still, it was Chalamet's work as Elio that ultimately drove not only this chorus of critical praise but an ever-growing collection of year-end accolades: breakthrough actor and performance honors from the Gotham Awards and the National Board of Review; best actor statues from the New York Film Critics Circle, the Los Angeles Film Critics Circle, and the Independent Spirit Awards; and best actor nominations from the Golden Globes (in drama), BAFTA, and the Screen Actors Guild. On 23 January 2018, Chalamet became at the age of twenty-two the third-youngest person ever nominated for an Academy Award for Best Actor. As Daniel Riley of *GQ* put it, "This young actor is very good, maybe the best in a long time, maybe even a sort of genius" ("The Arrival of Timothée Chalamet," 14 February 2018).

Chalamet at once contributed to and undercut these grandiose media narratives through two overlapping strategies of self-presentation—self-deprecation and an emphasis on himself as a "star as fan." In interviews, he gamely poked fun at the by then infamous "peach scene" in *Call Me by Your Name,* or would playfully deflate notions of his own burgeoning superstardom. One can see both of these at work in an interview with actor Daniel Kaluuya, when Chalamet recounted how "somebody dropped a bag of peach candies in front of me at Chipotle the other day" and ran off. "That's one for the memoir," Kaluuya quipped, to which Chalamet added, "One for the memoir, yeah exactly. The memoir that four people will buy" ("Timothée Chalamet and Daniel Kaluuya," *Variety,* 30 November 2017, 12–13). At the same time, Chalamet remained emphatic in interviews, acceptance speeches, and red-carpet press junkets about discussing the actors, filmmakers, hip-hop stars, and other artists he looked up to. "It sounds cheesy," he told Riley of *GQ*, "but I think of myself as an actor third, an artist second, and a fan first." This not only led to many a starstruck moment at awards shows but was further amplified by publications that interviewed Chalamet using some of these very idols—a conversation with *Interstellar* co-star Matthew McConaughey in *Interview*, or an extended exchange with singer Frank Ocean in *VMan* (Matthew McConaughey, "Timothée Chalamet," June 2017, 42–44, 118; "Throwback Thursday: Frank Ocean Interviews Timothée Chalamet in VMan39," 16 April 2020). Taken together, these elements at once further endeared Chalamet to the public and underscored the seriousness of his artistry through an implicit comparison with the breeziness and humility of his star persona.

Of course, Chalamet did not rise to prominence in a cultural vacuum. Both the natures of his star-making roles and the historical moment of his public ascendancy posed challenges to the relatively smooth, apolitical narrative of "talented young actor makes good." How he addressed these would not negate the aforementioned emphasis on actorly prowess so much as inflect and complicate it, ultimately producing a public image that was inextricably bound up with "millennial" ideas about gender, sexuality, and politics.

In publicizing *Call Me by Your Name*, Chalamet (who, by all public accounts, identifies as heterosexual) worked to convincingly describe his connection to queer-identified Elio in a manner that neither overstepped the boundaries of his own experience nor came across as defensive of his own sexual orientation. Both Chalamet and Hammer emphasized the comfort they felt in physically intimate scenes with one another, with an oft noted anecdote about how the two actors "just got so into" making out during an early scene that crew members had to pull them apart (Patrick Ryan, "Timothée Chalamet, Armie Hammer Had an Epic Makeout Session Filming 'Call Me by Your Name,'" *USA Today*, 22 November 2017). On the question of how Chalamet personally connected to his character, he framed Elio's journey as an illustrative example for all men, telling *Newsweek*'s Anna Menta, "I love the idea that young guys—particularly Americans because I feel the mental health dialogue is less repressed in Europe the way it is here—will see this movie and see there's nothing wrong with being themselves" ("Timothée Chalamet on 'Call Me by Your Name,' Vulnerability and That Peach Scene," 29 December 2017). This championing of a casually fluid and emotionally transparent vision of masculinity—combined with Chalamet's own striking physical beauty and increasingly

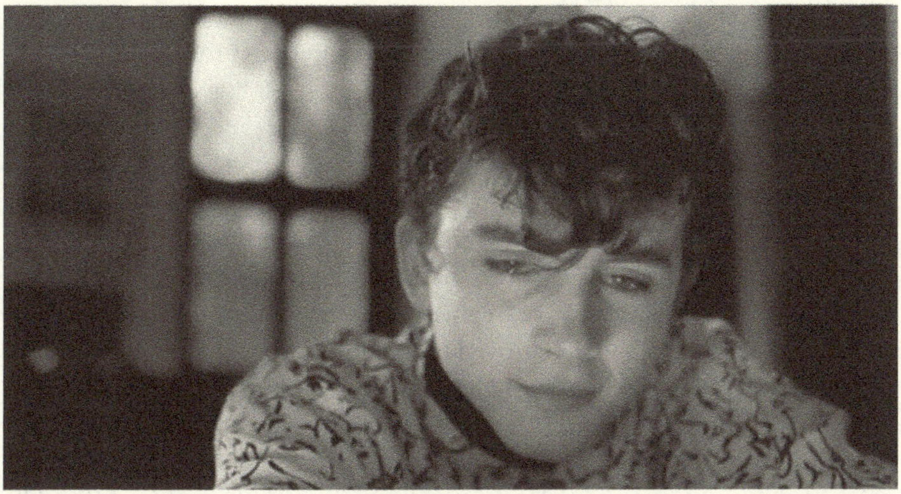

Suddenly, last summer: Timothée Chalamet in *Call Me by Your Name* (Luca Guadagnino, Sony Pictures Classics, 2017). Digital frame enlargement.

androgynous sartorial choices, which will be discussed in the next section—left an impression on the actor's young admirers. In the words of one fan named Luke, "It's so refreshing to see a straight male in the spotlight who doesn't feel the need to constantly reinforce his masculinity" (Steven Blum, "The Queer Kids Who Can't Get Over 'Call Me by Your Name,'" *MELMagazine,* 9 January 2018).

The year 2017 also offered two specific political and cultural contexts that would indelibly shape Chalamet's public persona—the aftermath of the 2016 presidential election and the #MeToo movement. The 2017 Sundance Film Festival overlapped with the inauguration of Donald Trump, fueling an aura of protest that manifested in ways both literal (a demonstration in the streets of Park City in solidarity with the Women's March in Washington, D.C.) and symbolic (the framing of Sundance titles that foregrounded sexual, ethnic, or racial diversity as implicit rejections of Trump's revanchist political ideology). With its emphasis on queer love and eroticism, *Call Me by Your Name* became a potent example of the latter—a trend that continued all the way to the 2018 Academy Awards ceremony, when host Jimmy Kimmel joked that "we don't make films like *Call Me by Your Name* for money. We make them to upset [vice president] Mike Pence." Both *Call Me by Your Name* and *Lady Bird* ultimately figured in a cinematic refutation of the presidential administration by the end of 2017, with *Variety* reporter Steven Gaydos noting the films—a "celebration of gay love" and a "passionate ode to youthful female empowerment," respectively—within a larger article on "speaking truth to power via cinema" entitled "Might as Well Trump" (18 December 2017, 6–7). Chalamet's prominent roles within both broadly aligned him with a larger feeling of Trump-era resistance within Hollywood.

Additionally, when reporting by the *New York Times* and the *New Yorker* in October 2017 exposed the history of sexual misconduct, assault, and rape allegations against powerful producer Harvey Weinstein, the subsequent nationwide reckoning on gender discrimination and sexual power that became known as the #MeToo movement had (among other consequences) profound effects on industry self-conception throughout the remainder of the 2017 Oscar race. Chalamet proved largely adept at discussing questions of male misconduct and privilege, relaying conversations that he had with his sister (an actress and dancer) about her experiences as a woman in the performing arts and affirming his generation's duty to correct the systemic inequities of the current system. These comments were bolstered by his public affiliation with both Greta Gerwig and Saoirse Ronan (director and star, respectively, of *Lady Bird*), as seen in a joint interview that Chalamet and Ronan gave to the *New York Times*. After Ronan offered an account of how working under Gerwig "changed my perspective on what I might achieve" as a potential female filmmaker, Chalamet put his commitments to practice when he told Ronan, "I'd act in a movie you directed in three seconds" (Philip Galanes, "Coming of Age on the Big Screen," 3 February 2018, AR1).

Indeed, the one discordant note in that interview—and in Chalamet's relationship to #MeToo politics generally—occurred when the subject of Woody Allen came up. Chalamet had been cast in Allen's then latest project, *A Rainy Day in New York* (2019), in August 2017. By then, long-standing accusations of sexual molestation alleged by Allen's adoptive daughter Dylan Farrow had returned to the public discourse, leading an increasing number of actors who had worked on past Allen films to dissociate themselves from the director. (Allen has long denied Farrow's allegations; the film itself received a belated release in the United States in October 2020.) Given his much remarked upon authenticity in interviews, Chalamet's responses to queries about working with Allen proved notably stilted, vaguely referencing a future moment when he would discuss the issue and occasionally using his participation in films with positive sexual representation as a kind of shield. "It's going to be important for me to talk about that," he said when the *Village Voice*'s Alex Frank brought up the Allen allegations, "but *Call Me by Your Name* is a movie about consent and love and it's depicted in such a beautiful way that I don't want to let anything take away from that right now" ("Timothée Chalamet's New York State of Mind," 12 January 2018). He gave versions of this response throughout the end of 2017 and the beginning of 2018 and reportedly consulted with Gerwig (a former Allen cast member who would dissociate herself from the director shortly before Chalamet) on how to address the issue (Chris Gardner, "Gerwig Advises Chalamet on How to Handle Woody Allen," *Hollywood Reporter*, 25 January 2018).

Finally, in an Instagram post on 15 January 2018, Chalamet wrote that, while he had previously "chosen projects from the perspective of a young actor trying to walk in the footsteps of more seasoned actors I admire," he now understood that "a good role isn't the only criteria for accepting a job." He announced that he would donate the entirety of his salary from *A Rainy Day in New York* to three charities: TIME'S UP (an organization founded in response to the #MeToo movement), the LGBT Community Center in New York, and RAINN (the Rape, Abuse & Incest National Network).

This immediately distinguished Chalamet as an actor willing to take a decisive stance (albeit after a time) on Allen's status in Hollywood and, by extension, affirm the validity of #MeToo beyond supportive public statements. It would be all the more notable as Chalamet continued to operate within an awards-season ecosystem that included an expected Best Actor nominee accused of sexual misconduct (James Franco, who ultimately was not nominated for his work in *The Disaster Artist* [2017]) and an eventual Best Actor winner who had long-standing domestic violence allegations made against him (Gary Oldman, who won out over Chalamet for his turn in *Darkest Hour* [2017]). Beyond this, however, both Chalamet's framing of his decision and the specific charities he donated to worked to solidify a public persona that merges actorly ambition with social consciousness. His initial understanding of the Allen role as following "in the footsteps of more seasoned actors I admire" links up with Chalamet's "star as fan" identity while underscoring his seriousness as an actor, modeling a career path on esteemed older colleagues by collaborating with renowned auteurs. That such a path has been complicated by the revelations of #MeToo—"a good role isn't the only criteria for accepting a job"—does not negate Chalamet's ambitions so much as broaden them, marrying social ethics with professional aspiration. Furthermore, he donated not only to two charities explicitly tied to gender equity and the combating of sexual violence but also to an organization specializing in queer equality and social support. It neither besmirches Chalamet's intentions nor ignores the positive impact of his actions to point out that a donation to the LGBT Community Center in New York had little practical connection to the Allen allegations but does speak to Chalamet's broader affiliations with LGBTQ issues as exemplified by his association with *Call Me by Your Name*. In this way, the donation both addresses the specific issue of his affiliation with Allen and reflects a wider commitment to issues of gender, sexuality, and social justice.

All of these developments placed Chalamet in the unique position of being both widely beloved and at-least somewhat politicized. Goodwill towards him following his Best Actor loss continued thanks to his genial public appearances and dashing good looks, as reflected in a winking series of *New Yorker* cartoons entitled "Timothée Chalamet Made Me Do It" (Olivia de Recat, 4 April 2018). (A sample caption reads: "I broke up with my boyfriend because he didn't possess the bemused, self-effacing, and impossibly tender charm that Timothée possesses. Also, his hair wasn't tousled enough.") At the same time, these apolitical charms had become more explicitly intertwined with culturally relevant (and sometimes contentious) issues of sexuality, gender, and politics. A *Wall Street Journal* profile of Dallas Sonnier (a film producer catering to audiences that "Hollywood has unwisely left behind") finds Sonnier using the actor as a de facto stand-in for all things disconnected from red-state tastes: "If I text [his target audience members] the name of, let's say, Timothée Chalamet, they don't know who the hell he is. . . . They haven't seen 'Lady Bird,' and they certainly haven't seen 'Call Me By Your Name'" (Erich Schwartzel, "A Texan Rewrites Hollywood Script for Trump's America," 16 May 2018, A1). And as the next two years of his career attest, Chalamet's star persona would only grow more attached to progressive ideas about masculinity and gender performance even as he tentatively attempted to pursue previously trodden paths to male Hollywood stardom.

★★★★★★★★★★ Harnessing Male Stardom in a Gender-Fluid Era

The two years after Chalamet's Oscar loss illuminate both the intensified linkage of his star identity with a "new" form of contemporary masculinity and the complex interplay that such a persona had with the actor's seeming goals of sustained critical and commercial success as a Hollywood leading man. This section will first consider how the aforementioned associations of Chalamet with a softer, more fluid form of maleness coalesced at the same moment as his performance in *Beautiful Boy* (2018) sought to solidify his "once in a generation" actorly reputation. Then, it will briefly compare the responses to Chalamet's two 2019 performances—his bid for a kind of "leading man upgrade" in *The King* and his supporting-turn immersion into the female-led world of *Little Women*. Affiliations with femininity and gender fluidity were not unwittingly "thrust upon" Chalamet any more than the desire for a more "conventional" form of male celebrity exclusively drove the actor's decision-making. Rather, his more recent screen work and public persona prove relevant for how both Chalamet and the wider culture seem to be laboring to meld these two elements in a manner by turns innovative and vexing.

In the months after the 2018 Academy Awards ceremony, writers moved from broadly linking Chalamet with "new masculinity" to seeing him as a chief embodiment of it. A 2018 essay in the *New York Times*'s *T* magazine, for instance, posited that the lithe, unprepossessing Chalamet and other actors of his ilk offered "a new answer to the problem of what makes a man" (Nick Haramis, "The Age of the Twink," 20 May 2018, 34). This also proved a central thesis in a lengthy interview with singer Harry Styles published in November 2018. The two men discussed their expansive conceptions of masculinity, with Chalamet at one point observing that "there isn't a specific notion, or jean size, or muscle shirt, or affectation, or eyebrow raise, or dissolution, or drug use that you have to take part in to be masculine." The interview's introduction, meanwhile, describes Chalamet as a kind of cultural redeemer for a new generation: "In a post #MeToo world, Timothée Chalamet represents the change we want to see in the film industry. He's sensitive, honest, thoughtful, polite, goofy, and self-aware. He's in touch with his feminine side, and he smiles. A lot" ("Timothée Chalamet in Conversation with Harry Styles: The Hottest Actor on the Planet Interviewed by Music's Most Charismatic Pop Star," *i-D Magazine*, 1 November 2018). Hollywood itself seemed to agree. In a 2018 article in *Vulture* (aptly titled "Timothée Chalamet Is the Perfect Movie Star for 2018"), Chris Lee asked industry insiders about the actor's appeal. Respondents emphasized Chalamet's emotionality, sensitivity, and androgyny as key markers of his success. Perhaps more striking was a comparison that one unnamed producer made between the actor and Leonardo DiCaprio. Chalamet had often been appraised in relation to DiCaprio's early career, with obvious similarities including their boyish good looks, acknowledged acting prowess, and passionate teen fan bases. The interviewed producer, however, drew a clear distinction on the basis of masculinity: "Leonardo DiCaprio is alpha. He's alpha in the way he runs his life, in the performances he gives; he's alpha in the choices he makes. When Timothée walked out of the room, he was beta for me. Maybe in this era, the male movie star that is a little more compassionate, that has that softness, will be rewarded."

Perhaps no series of decisions made by Chalamet further framed the actor as manifesting shifting standards of gender presentation than those regarding fashion. To be clear, Chalamet (who acts as his own stylist) had become known as a clothes-conscious celebrity on the publicity circuit for

Call Me by Your Name. Editors at *GQ* commented in November 2017, for example, that the "young gun is on a menswear roll" and is "not afraid to take risks either, like wearing top-to-toe velvet or popping the collar on a DB blazer" ("Timothée Chalamet Is Making *All* the Right First Impressions on the Red Carpet," 29 November 2017). Throughout the latter half of 2018, however, Chalamet's sartorial choices became increasingly bold, including a bright red ensemble designed by Virgil Abloh for the Los Angeles premiere of *Beautiful Boy* and an Alexander McQueen floral suit for the 2018 London Film Festival. If U.S. *GQ* applauded his fashion "risks" in 2017, U.K. *GQ* in 2018 named him their third best dressed man of the year, deeming him "a bona fide red-carpet hero . . . regularly opting for a series of slim fits in bursting colours or bold patterns" ("The 50 Best-Dressed Men of 2019," 2 December 2018). Nor did these clothing choices escape a larger analysis of how they related to Chalamet as an avatar for shifting conceptions of gender presentation. In an overview of 2018 men's fashion, Stephen Doig of the *Daily Telegraph* followed his approval of Chalamet showing "how a millennial should 'do' suiting" with a broader comment: "Call it the snowflake-effect if you like, but the younger generation of actors aren't preoccupied with how masculine and action-hero ready a suit can make them look, either" ("Handsome Morning Suits and Ever-Experimental Ezra Miller: The Best Dressed Men of 2018," 28 December 2018).

Of course, Chalamet also continued to act, releasing two films between July and October 2018. While his work as a gawky teenager turned small-time drug dealer in *Hot Summer Nights* elicited little critical or popular interest, his role as Nic Sheff—the real-life author who struggled as an adolescent with methamphetamine addiction—in *Beautiful Boy* had inspired Oscar anticipation since the previous year. *Beautiful Boy* premiered at the 2018 Toronto International Film Festival, which prompted a series of largely positive (and occasionally ecstatic) reviews for Chalamet's performance that continued through the film's theatrical release on 12 October 2018. Kenneth Turan of the *Los Angeles Times* claimed that Chalamet "might be the male actor of his generation," adding, "With moments reminiscent of James Dean, the ne plus ultra of these roles, Chalamet both echoes the best of what's come before and makes the part his own, allowing us to feel we've never seen a character like this" ("'Beautiful Boy': Rare Portrait in Familiar Tale," 12 October 2018, E6). This "confirmation of greatness" narrative—at once evoking and building upon the previous year's coverage—seemed to manifest in Chalamet's own self-presentation as well. He continued to express humility and fan praise for his co-stars, in this case Steve Carell, who played Nic's father in *Beautiful Boy*. Chalamet also once again showed his knack for social media–friendly moments, as when he agreed to sign peaches and (somewhat less explicably) hamburgers handed to him by admirers in Toronto. *Beautiful Boy*, however, received a somewhat muted critical response overall. Despite garnering nominations from the Golden Globes, SAG, and BAFTA, Chalamet failed to receive a widely expected second Academy Award nomination.

If there was a moment when Chalamet the millennial-masculinity icon seemed to eclipse (or at least more permanently imbue) Chalamet the Dean-esque actor-of-a-generation, it occurred at the 2019 Golden Globe Awards. What became one of the major stories of the evening was not Chalamet's loss of Best Supporting Actor but what he had on: an all-black outfit over which he wore a beaded black harness designed by Abloh for Louis Vuitton. The ensemble's glittering bedazzlements and seeming link to queer and BDSM sexual cultures at once continued and amplified Chalamet's established associations with LGBTQ allyship and increasingly outré designer fashion. It solidified Chalamet's reputation as an androgyny-embracing sartorial maverick, with the *Sunday Times*'s Raven Smith deeming Chalamet "the cherub of nu-masculinity Hollywood" for his outfit ("All Hail the Harness," 17 March 2019, 38). At the same time, reactions to Chalamet's look seemed to reveal some limits of how far the actor was willing to associate himself with the subcultures his fashion choices alluded to. Asked about his Golden Globes ensemble on a 2019 episode of *The Ellen DeGeneres Show*, Chalamet responded in a flustered, even myopic fashion: "I thought it was a bib. They told me it was a bib. I had a friend send me a thing that, like, sex-dungeon culture is a thing where you wear harnesses. I didn't do it for that reason." Guy Lodge of *The Guardian* noted the resonances between Chalamet's "bib" and the more explicitly kink-identified leather harness worn by gay figure skater Adam Rippon at the 2018 Academy Awards and pointedly commented that Chalamet's "obliviousness is testament to the fashion world's successful rebranding of the harness as Yolo bro-wear" ("How the Bondage Harness Was Rebranded as Red Carpet-Wear," 28 January 2019, 2).

This striking if somewhat inelegant negotiation with nonnormative gender and sexuality speaks to Chalamet's seemingly larger desire to balance the opportunities afforded a burgeoning young male star and the responsibilities and pleasures connected to a more "enlightened" form of masculine celebrity. His two 2019 film roles offer a brief but telling snapshot of Chalamet's current public persona. To use the crude if illustrative terms of the aforementioned Hollywood producer, they showcased the "alpha" and "beta" instincts being mediated through and around his star image.

The possibilities and boundaries of the former could be seen in his work in *The King*, an adaptation of three Shakespeare plays (*Henry IV, Parts 1* and *2*, and *Henry V*) with Chalamet as the titular would-be monarch. The actor would receive some of the more mixed reviews of his career for his performance, with both positive and negative assessments often basing their judgment on an implicit understanding of the role as a test of Chalamet's stature, star power, and ability to project masculine command. "When you take an actor who looks like this and cast him as a young king," argued Owen Gleiberman of *Variety* in a positive notice, "it's not just about how fascinating the role is—the film is capturing the elevation of his stardom" ("Venice Film Review: Timothée Chalamet in 'The King,'" 2 September 2019). Writing in *Vulture*, meanwhile, David Edelstein observed that the actor's "Prince Hal looks like a bony, whey-faced, lank-haired Tim Burton protagonist, an emo rich boy who angrily tells his father he has no interest in the throne" ("In *The King*, Timothée Chalamet's Emo Angst Is Underwhelming," 10 October 2019). For his part, Chalamet made little attempt to "butch up" his public appearance to accord with a metanarrative of masculine ascension through the Hollywood ranks. He wore one of his most androgynous looks to date to the film's Venice premiere—"a pale gray silk-and-satin suit" with an external cummerbund—and, "asked how he felt being at the festival for the first time, Chalamet answered with a reference to last year's most iconic Lido arrival: 'I feel like Lady Gaga on the boat'" (Justin Chang, "Venice International Film Festival: They're Best Seen on the Big Screen," *Los Angeles Times*, 6 September 2019, E1). The film was seen as a kind of false start to Chalamet's movement into mature stardom—"the perfect boy-to-man transitional role but Chalamet didn't quite pull it off" (Steve Rose, "Move Over, R-Patz: How Timothée Chalamet Became the Movie Star of His Generation," *The Guardian*, 1 June 2020).

Ironically, Chalamet achieved more critical success that year in a role designed to undercut male centrality and play up gender fluidity. His Laurie, the friend and would-be love interest of protagonist Jo March (Saoirse Ronan) in Greta Gerwig's adaptation of *Little Women*, built upon his preexisting professional and personal affiliations with the two women. Gerwig herself conceived of Chalamet's Laurie through the lens of androgyny. She told *Hollywood Reporter*'s Bryn Elise Sandberg that she cast Chalamet in part because "[Timothée] is handsome but he's also beautiful, and Saoirse is beautiful but she's also handsome" ("Little Women," 11 December 2019). This muddling of gender boundaries was further underscored by having

Handsome and beautiful: Timothée Chalamet and Saoirse Ronan in *Little Women* (Greta Gerwig, Columbia Pictures, 2019). Digital frame enlargement.

Laurie and Jo occasionally wear versions of the same items of clothing across scenes. And in an instance of Chalamet's own sartorial reputation bleeding into the film, costume designer Jacqueline Durran told *Vulture*'s Devon Ivie that when fitting Chalamet's wardrobe, "I'd tell him, *Look at these things, this is what you got, how would you wear it?* That's how we went on and got the flavor of Timothée into the style of the clothes" (emphasis in original; "Timothée Chalamet's Little Women Outfits Are Anachronistic, Just for His Fans," 17 December 2019). Chalamet received generally strong reviews for the performance, even if many critics saw it as a largely expected extension of his star persona. "Chalamet is delightful as an emo, millennial spin on Laurie," noted the *New York Post*'s Sara Stewart, while Tom Shone of the *Sunday Times* described Chalamet as "doe-eyed and floppy-haired, with his slight, puckish figure . . . an elfin Day-Lewis" ("'Little Women' Movie Review: Greta Gerwig's Film Is a Big Deal," 18 December 2019; "Mad about the Girls," 22 December 2019, 14). It's a performance, in short, whose strengths seem to rely upon Chalamet's embrace of a more recessive and gentler embodiment of masculine stardom. Gerwig framed the very presence of Chalamet in the film as a rejection of typical male-celebrity prerogatives: "She recalls her astonishment when Chalamet, a fast-rising movie star with his pick of vehicles, eagerly took a supporting role in a film about four women. 'I think it speaks to a different generation, because he said, "Why wouldn't I?"' Gerwig recalls" (Ann Hornaday, "A Film Not for Women Only," *Washington Post,* 20 December 2019, C1).

☆☆☆☆☆☆☆☆☆☆ "I Want to Be a Beautiful Boy"

Chalamet's reputation as an actor who backs up statements of gender equity with tangible action could be seen at the 2020 Academy Awards ceremony, when he co-presented Best Adapted Screenplay with Natalie Portman. The actress wore a dress embroidered with the names of female filmmakers (including Gerwig) who were seemingly passed over within the year's all-male Best Director category. On 11 February 2020, Portman posted a photo on Instagram of her and Chalamet at the ceremony, noting in the caption that "he's so incredibly talented, so fun and so smart—and a third of the films he's been in have been directed by women!" While this is a true and laudable statement, it's worth noting that a look at Chalamet's current completed and anticipated projects reveal a slate of high-profile titles, all directed by male auteurs: Wes Anderson's *The French Dispatch*, Denis Villeneuve's *Dune*, and Adam McKay's *Don't Look Up*, all currently scheduled for release in 2021; followed by a re-teaming with Guadagnino for the director's next film, *Bones & All*. He will potentially inherit a franchise when he takes on the titular role in *Wonka*, a prequel currently slated for 2023 that will explore the early years of the fictional chocolatier. Regardless of the individual titles' merits, they collectively point to a perhaps more standard pathway ending in (to use the *Guardian*'s aforementioned phrase) that "perfect boy-to-man transitional role" than Chalamet's career might have indicated up to this point.

At the same time, Chalamet's choice of roles and filmmakers also reflects the system in which he operates—one that tends to reward young actors whose projects bolster various registers of normative masculinity, be they action heroes, tortured, real-life geniuses, or collaborators with canonical male filmmakers. Chalamet's career thus far has proven vital not because he either accedes to or rejects this proposition outright but rather because he seems to meld typical aspirations of male stardom with a forward-thinking (if at times inchoate) desire to shift the standards and boundaries of public masculinity. For some, these ambitions serve at cross-purposes, with Chalamet's public persona threatening to engulf his actorly gifts. *Hollywood Reporter*'s Jon Frosch cautioned that the actor's "heartthrob/style-icon ubiquity [made him] become meme bait—which, I'm afraid, may prevent some folks from receiving his work with the seriousness it deserves" (Jon Frosch and David Rooney, "The Great Performances of 2019," 4 December 2019). And yet it is his embodiment of a more expansive and embracing public self—a "meme bait" menagerie of androgynous ensembles, imperfect political stands, and self-conscious deflations of his own blinding notoriety—that makes Chalamet stand out to the people who connect with him the most. In March 2020, for instance, *The Guardian* profiled Marieke Lucas Rijneveld, an acclaimed young Danish author who describes their gender presentation as floating between male and female throughout adolescence and identifies "not as trans but as 'in between'" (Claire Armitstead, "'My Family Are Too Frightened to Read My Book': Meet Europe's Most Exciting Authors," 7 March 2020). Their composure in the interview breaks only when Rijneveld recalls with a giggle the name of the celebrity they most aspire to be. "Timothée Chalamet," they said, adding, "I want to be a beautiful boy."

Chapter 11

Chadwick Boseman and Michael B. Jordan

Twenty-First-Century Stars

CYNTHIA BARON

Chadwick Boseman (1976–2020) and Michael B. Jordan (born in 1987) won acclaim for their leading roles in the early 2010s, with Boseman hailed for playing baseball legend Jackie Robinson in *42* (2013) and Jordan recognized for portraying police shooting victim Oscar Grant in *Fruitvale Station* (2013). They became major stars when Marvel Studios released *Black Panther* in 2018. With a domestic box office of $700,059,566, the film topped the theatrical market; with another $646,853,595 internationally, the film's worldwide gross was surpassed only by *Avengers: Infinity War* (2018), which featured Boseman. *Black Panther* garnered critical acclaim as well, and its many domestic and international awards included three Oscars and eight NAACP Image Awards.

Black Panther and its global publicity campaign not only made Boseman and Jordan worldwide celebrities; the film is significant to a star study because it mobilized and, in some measure, codified the actors' star images. Boseman's characterization of King T'Challa builds on his portrayals of characters with quiet inner strength, such as in the films *42* and *Marshall* (2017), and as the forthright young politician in the television show *Cold Case* (2003–2008; Boseman appeared in season six, episode ten of this series) (Gaines). Jordan's performance as Killmonger/N'Jadaka amplifies his portrayals of outwardly tough characters who experience inner turmoil in films like *Fruitvale Station* and *Creed* (2015) and in his role as the likable teen, Wallace, in the first season of *The Wire* (2002–2008). Yet the actors' respective star images go beyond their association with certain character types.

In the 2010s, Boseman became known for his uncanny ability to embody characters, ranging from the flamboyant, multitalented musician James Brown in *Get on Up* (2014) to the taciturn South African loner in *Message from the King* (2016) to the wily, enigmatic squad leader in Spike

Chadwick Boseman

Lee's look at the Vietnam War in *Da 5 Bloods* (2020). Jordan came to be seen as a charismatic actor following his heartfelt performances in selected seasons of *Friday Night Lights* (2006–2011) and *Parenthood* (2010–2015). His role as equal justice lawyer Bryan Stevenson in *Just Mercy* (2019) and his efforts to increase inclusion in Hollywood elevated his stature with African American audiences especially and prompted one journalist to describe

Michael B. Jordan

Jordan as "our next and last great movie star" (Kara Brown, "Michael B. Jordan Is Redefining What It Means to Be a Movie Star," *Time*, 3 September 2019). Moreover, Boseman's untimely death in 2020 led colleagues and audiences to have a deeper appreciation of Boseman as an artist and a person. Stunned by the news that Boseman had been fighting cancer since 2016, Ryan Coogler reflected on the fact that the actor had been undergoing treatment the entire time he had known him, but that because "he was a caretaker, a leader and a man of faith, dignity and pride, he [had] shielded his collaborators from his suffering" (Sonaiya Kelley, "Read 'Black Panther' Director Ryan Coogler's Moving Tribute to Chadwick Boseman," *Los Angeles Times*, 30 August 2020). Describing Boseman as "a movie star by stealth, an actor who could dazzle us on the surface and still hold something crucial in check, as if he were in possession of some deep and mysterious inner knowledge," Justin Chang proposed that Boseman be remembered "as a man who tempered despair with hope, whose very largeness of spirit awakens something deep and purposeful within his fellow travelers" ("Appreciation: Chadwick Boseman Held the Screen with Power and Unerring Purpose," *Los Angeles Times*, 29 August 2020).

In the 2000s, both actors established themselves in television and film. However, their early careers were quite different. Boseman earned a BFA in directing at Howard University in 2000 and taught acting at the Schomburg Center for Research in Black Culture in Harlem from 2002 to 2007. While Boseman had co-starring TV roles, the Congo Square Theatre Company in Chicago staged his play *Deep Azure* in 2005, and his short film *Blood over a Broken Pawn* won a prize at the Hollywood Black Film Festival in 2008. Jordan grew up in the entertainment industry, appearing in *The Sopranos* (1999–2007) and *Cosby* (1996–2000) at age twelve, as an inner-city kid in his first film *Hardball* (2001) at fourteen, and in his memorable role as Wallace at fifteen. The contrast in their career routes was reflected in the talent agencies that represented them in the 2010s. Boseman was with Greene and Associates, an established boutique agency, while Jordan started the decade with United Talent Agency (UTA), one of the major agencies, and moved to one of the two top-tier agencies, William Morris Endeavor (WME), just before *Fruitvale Station* was released (Roussel 29).

Yet both actors' star careers belong to an era when theatrically released star vehicles became "inconsistent in attracting an audience" (Fritz 84). At the same time, actors were gaining recognition for their work in television, which "generated the bulk of Hollywood's profits," and in character-centered films increasingly delivered by Netflix and Amazon (Fritz 140; see also 100 and 200). Thus, their careers in the 2010s illuminate challenges and opportunities screen performers negotiated in the decade when the popularity of cinematic universe films reduced the influence of established stars, while television, streaming services, and independent filmmaking sustained the rise of new talent and allowed known performers to prove themselves as actors. Boseman's and Jordan's portrayals also reveal their capabilities as twenty-first-century actors, able to perform in complex production settings after doing the physical conditioning; voice, movement, and dialect training; character, narrative, and historical research; and dance, sports, and combat training needed to embody their characters.

Challenges and Opportunities in the Entertainment Industry

In their early careers especially, Boseman and Jordan negotiated challenges not faced by non-Hispanic white men, who constituted 31 percent of the U.S. population but represented 60 to 80 percent of the high-value stars in the 2010s (Baron 31–32). This overrepresentation in the top tier of film stardom follows a pattern. Writing about stars from 1990 to 2009, Paul McDonald explains:

> Symbolically and economically, Hollywood stardom only valorizes certain forms of identity. The population of the A-list elite is restricted by not only economic status but also social distinctions of gender, race and age. Historically, Hollywood stardom has worked through a system in which commercial value is produced almost exclusively through a small cohort of white male actors aged from their mid 20s to their mid 50s. (31)

Given the social identity of most A-list stars, Boseman and Jordan were exceptions to the rule. Their success recalls that of other singular stars: Paul Robeson in the early twentieth century; Sidney Poitier and Harry Belafonte in the mid-twentieth century; and Denzel Washington and Will Smith in the late twentieth century.

At the same time, Boseman's and Jordan's success reveals that cultural-industrial norms in the 2010s gave Black male actors comparatively high visibility. During the decade, Black men comprised about 6.5 percent of the U.S. population and 4 to 12 percent of the high-value stars in Hollywood (Baron 31–32). Along with Denzel Washington and Will Smith, these stars included Samuel L. Jackson, Kevin Hart, Forest Whitaker, James Earl Jones, and Boseman himself (Baron 30–31). As Hollywood used Black actors to symbolize a "diverse" society, Boseman and Jordan had opportunities not available to many performers representing another 31.5 percent of the U.S. population: Black women, Latinx and Hispanic people, Asian Americans, and people of Native American, Pacific Islander, or multiple race heritage. As the decade progressed, Boseman and Jordan used their success to foster opportunities for disenfranchised people. Boseman's role as actor-producer on *21 Bridges* (2019) and Jordan's work as actor-producer on *Just Mercy* led to films that were not "oppositional in the usual sense of the term" but "politically and culturally relevant" to their time (Pines ix).

Boseman's and Jordan's rise to stardom took place in a system already transformed by changes in the 2000s. In the 1990s, agents had negotiated lucrative deals for "top producers, stars, directors and screenwriters," but in the 2000s, "declining DVD sales and the recession forced studios to become increasingly tightfisted," and they began to give stars, at best, a share of the profits after they recouped investments (Balio 36, 37). In 2006, the decision by corporate owner Viacom to "end Paramount's fourteen-year relationship with [Tom] Cruise's production company" signaled the change that reduced the income and influence of established stars (Balio 37). As the "new order" emerged, theatrically released star vehicles accounted for "about ten of the twenty highest-grossing films" each year, and by the 2010s "as few as three movies of the twenty each year was, generously defined, a 'star vehicle'" (Balio, 37; Fritz 84).

After the success of *Iron Man* (2008), stars lost power as studios relied on cinematic universe films to offset the ongoing decline in theatrical grosses (Fritz 105). The waning influence of traditional stars also resulted from corporate and media delivery reconfigurations reshaping the industry, audience reception, and stardom. By the end of the decade, Disney owned Pixar, Marvel Studios, and *Star Wars*, and it had purchased 20th Century Fox to acquire Hulu and make prestige Fox Searchlight films available for streaming (Fritz 247). Its efforts to create a Disney+ digital brand were aimed to compete with Netflix, which had changed viewing habits and become "the biggest company in modern Hollywood," producing, among other things, roughly eighty films a year "while most studios released fewer than twenty" (Fritz 250, 251). With the arrival of Amazon and Apple as branded media producers and delivery services, "the takeover of the entertainment industry by digital companies" was largely complete (Fritz 255). By the end of the 2010s, Warner Bros. films would be destined for AT&T's streaming service HBO Max. NBCUniversal productions were most valuable as products for Comcast's cable subscribers, Paramount films were material for ViacomCBS subscribers, and Sony Pictures Entertainment sought to rebrand itself by purchasing the multimedia Game Show Network. In this landscape, established (white male) film stars became less significant since they were no longer bringing audiences to theaters. Disney+, Netflix, Amazon, Apple,

AT&T, Comcast, and other digital providers were delivering content with and without major stars to home audiences. To move from breakthrough artist to major star, an upcoming actor would need something like the marketing power of Disney-backed Marvel Studios.

Industrial and cultural factors affecting stardom in the 2010s had precedents in the 1990s, when web-facilitated fandom and "a revitalized ethnic and racially informed independent cinema movement" created opportunities for nontraditional stars (Everett 5). As Anna Everett explains:

> Although the development of . . . digital and convergence cultures signified a major paradigm shift in the production and consumption of stars and stardom, more significant, arguably, was the integration of black, Asian, Latina/o, feminist, queer, working-class, and other marginalized groups into the firmament of Hollywood stardom. (4)

In both decades, realignments fostered by developments in digital technology reduced studios' authority to create traditional stars and lessened the power of film stardom itself. In the process, stardom became more accessible to actors beyond the conventional model of the white male star.

☆☆☆☆☆☆☆☆☆★ Breakthrough Roles in an Era of High-Profile Black Biopics and Genre Films

Boseman and Jordan had new opportunities in the 2010s, but "each actor's filmography is an object lesson in navigating a film and television world that often finds black talent pigeonholed" (Gabrielle Bruney, "Chadwick Boseman, Michael B. Jordan, and the Need to End Black Stereotypes in Hollywood," *Esquire*, 6 January 2019). Boseman portrayed NFL legend Floyd Little in his first film *The Express* (2008) and veterans in his recurring roles in *Lincoln Heights* (2007–2009) and *Persons Unknown* (2010). Yet in television appearances in the 2000s, he was also cast as a troubled youth, a street hustler, a gangster, a character who takes revenge, and a crime suspect (four times). In Jordan's early career, he played a young man headed to Princeton, the son of a minister, a student athlete, and one of four enterprising young people in the TV series *The Assistants* (2009). Yet he also portrayed a teen who kills his brother, a crime suspect (twice), the victim of a crime (twice), and a young man with no father. His earliest bit parts, ranging from street kid to wholesome youngster, led him to be cast as Wallace, a kid in the projects depicted in *The Wire*. From 2003 to 2006, Jordan played the teenage delinquent Reggie Porter Montgomery in the daytime soap opera *All My Children* (1970–2013).

Boseman had originated the role of Montgomery in 2003. In his 2018 commencement speech at Howard University, Boseman explained that when he got the part, he "felt like Mike Tyson," partly because it came with a six-figure salary. Yet he became conflicted after seeing his first script, since the character had a "violent streak" and felt the allure of gang life but had no positive or even specific qualities. To create the character, Boseman would have to "make something out of nothing." After two episodes, the show's executives told him "how happy they were with [his] performance," said that they wanted him "to be around for a long time," and asked if he needed anything. Boseman inquired about his character's background and learned they thought it sufficient to define a Black teenager as someone with an absent father and a heroin addict mother. After Boseman suggested the character could have a talent or something that gave him agency, the executives thanked him for his concerns, had him shoot the next episode, and let him go.

As Boseman told the Howard University students, he believes the questions he asked "paved the way for a less stereotypical portrayal for the black actor who stepped into the role." Jordan agrees that Boseman's concerns are what "got the show to change the character," and in his view, Boseman's positive intervention confirms that what people do "'can directly affect what other people do in the future'" (Sydney Scott, "No, We Don't All Look Alike," *Essence*, 4 January 2019). Still, Boseman's dismissal and the character's stereotypical dimensions even after adjustments provide a glimpse of the obstacles Boseman and Jordan faced as rising actors.

Their work in biopics and genre films in the 2010s moved them beyond stereotypical roles during a time when Black biopics had box-office and critical success. *Lee Daniels' The Butler* (2013) starring Forest Whitaker grossed $176.6 million worldwide. *Mandela: Long Walk to Freedom* (2013) led to a Golden Globe nomination for British actor Idris Elba. *Selma* (2014) starring British actor David Oyelowo won multiple NAACP Image Awards. *Straight Outta Compton* (2015) grossed $201.6 million, and *Hidden Figures* (2016) grossed $236 million worldwide. At the 2019 Oscars, *Green Book* (2018) was named Best Picture, Mahershala Ali Best Supporting Actor, and *BlacKkKlansman* (2018) Best Adapted Screenplay. The next year, British-born Cynthia Erivo received two Oscar nominations for *Harriet* (2019).

Black genre films also garnered critical and international commercial success. *The Book of Eli* (2010) and *The Magnificent Seven* (2016) with Denzel Washington made $157.1 million and $162.4 million, respectively, worldwide. *Central Intelligence* (2016) with Dwayne Johnson and Kevin Hart grossed $217 million worldwide. *Girls Trip* (2017) with Queen Latifah, Regina Hall, Jada Pinkett Smith, and Tiffany Haddish made $140.9 million and won multiple awards. *Get Out* (2017) starring British actor Daniel Kaluuya made $255.4 million worldwide, won the Oscar for Best Screenplay, and received more than 150 other awards. Jordan Peele's next film, *Us* (2019) with Lupita Nyong'o and Winston Duke, made $255.2 million worldwide and won dozens of awards.

Boseman's formative films sometimes combined genre and biopic elements. His first leading role was in *The Kill Hole* (2012), a social commentary thriller that extended Boseman's TV portrayals of veterans. As with subsequent characterizations, Boseman developed a specific physical presence for the character that included his action-ready stride: legs apart, shoulders and arms moving in union, and arms away from the body with hands in closed fists. His performance also featured elements important to later portrayals: at times, his eyes glimmer with rage or sorrow, his face shines from within as he breaks into a smile, or the expression in his eyes and eyebrows alone conveys the character's thoughts.

Boseman was next cast as Jackie Robinson in the biopic sports film *42* (2013). This was the last time he would be required to audition for a part. Following his first signature role, Boseman received Breakthrough Performance of the Year nominations from several award bodies, and the National Association of Theatre Owners named him Male Star of Tomorrow in 2014. Set during the 1946–1947 season when Robinson moved from the Dodgers' farm team to the major league, the film required Boseman to identify the essential aspects of the historical figure. He met Robinson's widow, studied his style of play, visited parts of Brooklyn that retained their 1940s character, and spent hours in baseball training. His performance conveys the warmth Robinson shared in his private life, Robinson's power and agility as a player, and the steadfast public face he maintained early in his career.

Boseman's energy, physical presence, winning smile, and ability to portray a likeable everyman led him to be cast in *Draft Day* (2014) as a promising college football player who becomes the number one draft pick for the NFL. Next, director Tate Taylor persuaded Boseman to portray James Brown in the musical biopic *Get on Up*. Boseman's work as a writer-performer in hip-hop theater fostered his ability to embody Brown's signature dance moves and electrifying stage presence. Hours of rehearsal helped him convey the energy, intensity, and fluidity in Brown's distinctive voice and movements throughout the different eras of his life, both onstage and off. Boseman's performance not only led him to be selected for the cover of *Ebony* for September 2014; during the *Get on Up* publicity tour, he was

Chadwick Boseman's watchful pose and determined expression capture Robinson's early public persona in *42* (Brian Helgeland, Warner Bros., 2013). Digital frame enlargement.

signed to a five-picture deal by Marvel producers Kevin Feige and Nate Moore, starting with *Captain America: Civil War* (2016).

In the intervening time, Boseman starred in the revenge thriller *Message from the King* about a steely South African who comes to the United States to help his sister. Boseman again creates a unique, socially specific character, this time characterized by the fluidity and economy of his movements and a smooth gait that threads a narrow path in space. His almost wordless performance reveals his ability to generate evocative facial expressions that convey a character's thought process shot by shot. The film also gave Boseman the chance to spend time in South Africa to do research and dialect work before shooting *Captain America: Civil War*.

To underscore that Wakanda was free from Western colonization, Boseman determined and then persuaded Marvel and *Captain America: Civil War* directors Joe and Anthony Russo that T'Challa and his father T'Chaka (John Kani) should speak English with a South African accent and use the South African language Xhosa. Beginning in 2016, after Marvel signed Ryan Coogler to direct *Black Panther*, Boseman encouraged use of African music, design, languages, and martial arts in the film (Kelley, "Read 'Black Panther'"). Portraying T'Challa in *Captain America: Civil War*, Boseman embodies the character's wit, compassion, and warmth, his regal but buoyant energy, and his measured but forceful approach to confrontation. The film topped the 2016 worldwide box office and reflected Hollywood's turn to multicultural blockbusters such as the *Fast and Furious* films (2011, 2013, 2015, 2017) and the *Star Wars* films (2015, 2016, 2017).

Boseman's next project was *Marshall* (2017), a biopic, buddy film, and courtroom drama directed by Reginald Hudlin about a 1941 case handled by NAACP lawyer and future U.S. Supreme Court justice Thurgood Marshall. The film engaged contemporary social justice concerns, casting the parents of shooting victim Trayvon Martin as the Mississippi couple Marshall assists in the final scene. It received positive reviews and led to another cover story on Boseman in *Ebony* (October 2017). This was his first film with a Black director, and he took the part after prompting from Marshall's son. Boseman's performance captures Marshall's self-confidence, sense of humor, and ability to gauge his surroundings. Critics compared him to Paul Newman, highlighting Boseman's ability to convey Marshall's overbearing charisma.

Jordan's roles in biopics and genre films also facilitated his rise to stardom. Like Boseman, he made his breakthrough in 2013, and the two actors were among the dozen stars featured on the twentieth annual *Vanity Fair* Hollywood issue in February 2014. Yet whereas Boseman gained notice in films by various directors, Jordan garnered acclaim in films directed by Ryan Coogler, who cast him in *Fruitvale Station*, *Creed*, and *Black Panther*. Prior to his celebrated work with Coogler, Jordan had appeared in *Friday Night Lights*. When his character Vince joins the series in season four, his father is in prison, his mother is addicted to drugs, and he plays football at a predominantly white high school as an alternative to juvenile detention. Jordan had portrayed another stereotypical character in the first season of *Parenthood* as Alex, a twenty-year-old homeless, recovering alcoholic ex-con, who for a time is the boyfriend of a white, middle-class high school student. Critics observed that in "his television career, Jordan often took roles with stereotypical elements," but that he "elevated them through the power of his performances" (Bruney, "Chadwick Boseman, Michael B. Jordan"). Frustrated by the built-in limitations of "black roles," Jordan sought parts written for white actors; he was soon cast in the sci-fi teen drama *Chronicle* (2012) as one of three boys who acquire telekinetic powers and the ability to fly.

Fruitvale Station was Jordan's first leading role, and the $900,000 film produced by Forest Whitaker's Significant Films provided the opportunity to prove himself as an actor. He had appeared in the Black-directed films *Pastor Brown* (2009) and *Red Tails* (2012), but this was Jordan's first chance

Michael B. Jordan's concerned expression and hold on Melonie Diaz's arm convey Grant's vulnerability in *Fruitvale Station* (Ryan Coogler, The Weinstein Company, 2013). Digital frame enlargement.

to work closely with an African American writer-director. During preproduction, he spent time with Oscar Grant's family and worked with Coogler in many hours of rehearsal. Jordan's portrayal of the privately anxious but outwardly warm young man reveals his understanding of the character, a process assisted by his practice of creating a character journal filled with backstory details not disclosed by the script or the historical record. *Fruitvale Station* received dozens of awards, starting with the Grand Jury Prize and Audience Award at the 2013 Sundance Film Festival. *Variety*, *Entertainment Weekly*, *Ebony* magazine, *GQ* magazine, the National Board of Review, and various festivals identified Jordan's work as a breakthrough performance. *Time* magazine included Jordan and Coogler in its list of the thirty people under thirty changing the world in 2013.

Creed (2015), a continuation of the Rocky series, featured Jordan as the illegitimate son of Adonis Creed, Rocky's opponent and later friend in the first four films. Writer-director Ryan Coogler initiated the project, asking Jordan to play Donnie Johnson when the two were working on *Fruitvale Station*. Jordan spent a year preparing for the part, working with a fitness trainer and a professional boxer to transform his body and persuasively portray a light heavyweight fighter. In the film, Jordan conveys Donnie's warmth in his scenes with love interest Tessa Thompson and his youthful vulnerability in scenes with father figure Sylvester Stallone. The film won multiple awards and grossed $173.6 million worldwide. Adding music videos and video game work to his film and television performances, Jordan won a prize for his motion-capture and voice portrayal of sports game *NBA 2K17* character Justice Young. For his many contributions to popular culture, the NAACP Image Awards named Jordan Entertainer of the Year in 2016.

Black Exceptionalism in a Decade of Hope and Despair

Boseman's and Jordan's rise to fame occurred when Barack and Michelle Obama were perhaps the era's most visible Black celebrities, complete with their own biopic, *Southside with You* (2016). During Obama's presidency (2009–2017), Eric Holder and later Loretta Lynch became the first African American U.S. attorney generals. The decade's greatest athletes included tennis star Serena Williams, gymnast Simone Biles, boxer Floyd Mayweather, and basketball players LeBron James and Kobe Bryant. Black Americans constituted about 75 percent of the professional athletes in the NBA and 70 percent of the players in the NFL.

As Boseman and Jordan gained visibility as actors, African Americans were also more prominent in theater and stand-up comedy. Viola Davis and Denzel Washington received Tony Awards in 2010, and subsequent winners included Nikki M. James, Billy Porter, Patina Miller, Courtney B. Vance, and James Monroe Inglehart. Lin-Manuel Miranda's *Hamilton: An American Musical*, with people of color portraying white historical figures, won eleven Tony awards. While Richard Pryor and later Eddie Murphy and Chris Rock had been the exceptions in stand-up comedy, more African American comedians gained recognition after *Def Jam Comedy* (1992–1997) featured Black comedians and launched the career of Dave Chappelle. In the 2010s, the wave of Comedy Central and Netflix specials gave visibility to Jerrod Carmichael, Hannibal Buress, Leslie Jones, and other African American comedians.

As Boseman and Jordan rose to stardom, African American artists remained central to American popular music. Beginning in 2011, Black musicians dominated digital downloads and on-demand streaming. Multiple American Music Award winners in the 2010s included Jay-Z, Beyoncé, Bruno Mars, and Rihanna. John Legend became the first Black male artist to reach EGOT status, winning a Grammy in 2006, an Oscar in 2015, a Tony in 2017, and an Emmy in 2018. Kendrick Lamar received dozens of awards, including six Billboard Music Awards, thirteen Grammy Awards, and the Pulitzer Prize for Music in 2018 for his album *Damn,* marking the first time the award went to a genre other than jazz or classical.

The renewed push for diversity in film ignited by April Reign's 2015 #OscarsSoWhite post existed alongside African Americans' progress in film and television. Oprah Winfrey launched her OWN television network, and Tyler Perry became the first African American to own a studio. *12 Years a Slave* (2013) won Oscars for Best Picture, Best Supporting Actress (Lupita Nyong'o), and Best Adapted Screenplay. *Moonlight* (2016) received Oscars for Best Picture, Best Supporting Actor (Mahershala Ali), and Best Adapted Screenplay. Channing Dungey, president of ABC, was the first African American to lead a major television network. Viola Davis was the first African American to win the Emmy for Outstanding Actress in a Drama Series. Sterling K. Brown became the first Black actor to win a Golden Globe for Best Actor in a TV Drama. *Spider-Man: Into the Spider-Verse* (2018) made Peter A. Ramsey the first African American to win an Oscar for Best Animated Feature.

Yet entrenched racism in the film industry is what delayed these achievements until the 2010s, and whites continued to use the success of individual African Americans as "proof" that racism did not exist. However, as Tim Wise explains:

> Not only does the success of Obama not signify the death of White racism as a personal or institutional phenomenon; if anything it may well signal the emergence of an altogether new kind of racism. Consider this, for lack of a better term, Racism 2.0, or enlightened exceptionalism, a form that allows for, and even celebrates, the achievements of individual persons of color, but only because those individuals generally are seen as different from a less appealing, even pathological black or brown rule. (9)

During Obama's presidency, segregation in neighborhoods, schools, and people's private lives actually became "more pronounced in certain parts of the country" (van Gorder and Tait 14). The Great Recession affected African Americans more profoundly than any other group in America. Obama's election "drove thousands of fearful Euro-Americans to go on a frantic buying spree of weapons" (van Gorder and Tait 2). While Obama himself was not assassinated, police killed hundreds of unarmed African Americans in the 2010s. Corroborating the toxicity of the white supremacist order (Roediger 1–63), statistics show that Black people were two and a half times more likely to be killed by police than whites. Throughout the decade, African Americans remained more physically and economically vulnerable than any other demographic in the United States (Lynne Peeples, "What the Data Say about Police Shootings," *Nature*, 5 September 2019; Vincent Adejumo, "African Americans' Setbacks from the Great Recession Are Ongoing—and Could Be Repeated," *The Conversation*, 5 February 2019). Like the work of other Black artists, Boseman's and Jordan's roles gave vivid expression to the complexity of Black subjectivities and thus contributed to change on the cultural front. However, social-political realities made their stardom, and twenty-first-century Black stardom in general, a fraught phenomenon, if only because Black stars continued to carry a burden not given to white actors, whose whiteness is rarely, if ever, discussed and whose work is never expected to ameliorate centuries of social injustice.

★★★★★★★★★★ International Celebrities in Culturally Relevant Cinema

The 46 percent of Americans that supported Donald Trump's candidacy confirmed that the United States was hardly a postracial society in the 2010s. Marvel Studio audiences could perhaps find some solace that Don Cheadle had portrayed Lt. Col. James Rhodes/War Machine starting in *Iron Man 2* (2010), Anthony Mackie had appeared as Sam Wilson/Falcon beginning in *Captain America: Winter Soldier* (2014), and Boseman had been featured as Black Panther starting in 2016. Yet after a decade of economic hardship and the rise in overt racism accompanying Trump's candidacy in 2016, *Black Panther*, featuring Boseman, Jordan, and an essentially all-Black cast, was even more significant.

As a narrative necessarily associated with "racial justice" (Nama 4), the film and its leading actors held special importance for African Americans. Prior to its release, Frederick Joseph created the #BlackPantherChallenge, which raised $1 million so that Black children in particular could see the film in theaters. In its opening weekend, "37 percent of ticket buyers for *Black Panther* in North America . . . were African-American," which is "very different from the demographic makeup for most superhero movies [that] tend to draw in audiences that are 15% African-American" (Josh Horwitz, "'Black Panther' Dramatically Changed the Make-Up of the Superhero Movie Audience This Weekend," *Quartz*, 19 February 2018).

Black Panther put Black experiences at the center of a mainstream movie and presented audiences with decolonized images and sounds reflecting Pan-African culture. Grounded in costuming and other aspects of mise-en-scène, the film's visualization of Black people implicitly united under the red, black, and green Pan-African flag made it relevant to global audiences interested in progressive change. The cast and their characters also fueled

Black Panther's impact. Having "black people for the first time depicted in a major movie as kings, queens, inventors, and diplomats, rather than slaves, thugs, dealers and thieves, [gave] the movie a real-world political engagement not seen in other superhero films" (Faramelli). Activist Shaun King compared the film to "Rosa Parks refusing to give up her seat on the bus in Montgomery" and Dr. King's "I Have a Dream" speech ("*Black Panther* Is One of the Most Important Cultural Moments in American History," *Medium*, 20 February 2018). For King, the significance of *Black Panther* was akin to the "birth of hip hop, Michael Jackson's 'Thriller' becoming the best-selling album of all-time, [the] election of Barack Obama as our first Black President, [and] Colin Kaepernick taking a knee to protest police brutality and injustice in America."

Black Panther gives credence to Killmonger's (Jordan) rage throughout the scenes in which T'Challa agonizes over the circumstances that led his cousin to embrace violence. Yet it also endorses the plan T'Challa develops after recognizing the validity of the social-political engagement modeled by Nakia (Lupita Nyong'o). Notably, the film's performances contribute to its nuanced, rather than binary, vision of ways to deconstruct systemic racism. It frames John Kani's King T'Chaka as a magnanimous leader, but uses Sterling K. Brown's expressive performance as his brother N'Jobu to illustrate the compassion that led him to oppose Wakanda's isolationism. It presents T'Challa as empathetic and courageous, but allows Jordan's portrayal to render the emotionally wounded boy N'Jadaka visible underneath Killmonger's hard surface.

Black Panther makes Boseman and Jordan central to its negotiation of competing perspectives from the outset. When the film introduces T'Challa and later Killmonger, the actors' performances convey their characters' respective temperaments and roles in the film's philosophical exploration. In T'Challa's opening scene with Okoye (Danai Gurira), Boseman embodies his character's poised, responsive approach to the world; he is soft-spoken and pensive; his voice and movements are light, fluid, and effortless. His expressive face communicates T'Challa's thoughts and feelings, revealing his self-assurance and his apprehension about taking on a king's responsibilities. In Killmonger's first scene at the museum, Jordan conveys his character's agitated, unpredictable approach by shifting his weight from one foot to another as he glares at the objects on display. When he speaks to the museum curator, his words rush out in an irregular rhythm. He avoids eye contact and then moves uncomfortably close to her, spitting his words out as he grits his teeth.

The contrasting characterizations that these scenes introduce are visible throughout the film, including the dramatic throne room confrontation when Killmonger announces he is N'Jadaka. In this scene and elsewhere, the performances by Boseman, Jordan, and the other actors cause each character to make a specific contribution to the narrative. The cast received recognition for this accomplishment, winning the Screen Actors Guild Award for Outstanding Performance by a Cast in a Motion Picture. In his acceptance speech on behalf of the cast, Boseman articulated their sense of social-political accomplishment by referencing the civil rights anthem "To Be Young, Gifted, and Black" made popular by Nina Simone.

With its $1.3 billion worldwide gross, the film itself would have made Boseman and Jordan international stars, but while *Black Panther* ran two hours and fifteen minutes, media attention surrounding its release comprised hundreds of pages in print, hundreds of hours in TV and video coverage, and perhaps millions of social media posts. Alongside a rise in fan-curated accounts, *Black Panther* boosted Boseman to 7.4 million Instagram followers and 1.5 million Twitter followers, and Jordan to 13.4 million Instagram followers and 1.1 million Twitter followers. In 2018, Boseman appeared on multiple magazine covers, including *Time*, *Rolling Stone*, *Esquire*, and *Essence*. Jordan's cover stories included *Vanity Fair*, *Essence*, and *GQ*. Coogler and various cast members made media appearances, with Boseman doing the most, in venues ranging from *MTV News* to late-night talk shows to *The Breakfast Club*, a talk show covering hip-hop and politics. The wealth of print and media material available online reflected and bolstered Boseman's and Jordan's status as twenty-first-century stars.

Boseman and Jordan as Actors and Producers

After *Black Panther*, both actors secured their status as major stars with subsequent highly visible roles. Boseman appeared in *Avengers: Infinity War*, which grossed $2 billion worldwide, and *Avengers: Endgame* (2019), which grossed $2.8 billion. Starring in the next installment of the extended Rocky franchise, Jordan worked with African American director Steven Caple Jr. on *Creed II* (2018), which garnered $214.1 million worldwide. Boseman's and Jordan's critical and commercial success gave them increased influence in the creative process. Working as actor-producers, they were able to create mid-budget films, a notable achievement because studios' increased reliance on franchise and cinematic universe films had led to a drop in such films in the 2010s.

Boseman was an executive producer on *Message from the King*, a co-producer on *Marshall*, and, by actively contributing to the development of Wakanda and the Black Panther character, a tacit co-producer on the

Marvel films. After producing *21 Bridges*, he became a member of the PGA (Producers Guild of America). With his input, the "script evolved mightily through the development process. Originally Boseman's Det. Andre Davis and Stephan James' reluctant criminal Michael were written as white and Sienna Miller's narcotics officer was envisioned as a man" (Sonaiya Kelley, "How Chadwick Boseman Made '21 Bridges' a More Diverse Detective Story, and Earned His Producing Stripes," *Los Angeles Times*, 21 November 2019). After working to develop a character-driven story that better represented the diversity of America, Boseman did extensive preparation to portray the detective whose intelligence and ethics allow him to navigate the mystery and the threats surrounding him. Boseman's evocative facial expressions, telling physical deportments, and varied line deliveries—ranging from clipped, precise pronunciations to casual, irregular rhythms to deliberate, authoritative cadences—create rich shades of meaning and keep audiences engaged in his character's journey. It is a star performance, both mesmerizing and entirely specific.

Jordan's position as an actor represented by powerful talent agency WME, known for producing media content, facilitated his transition to actor-producer. In 2016, Jordan established Outlier Society Productions to generate more opportunities for Black artists. Jordan's company co-produced *Fahrenheit 451* (HBO 2018), which starred Jordan as Guy Montag, and for which Jordan and others won the Outstanding Producer of Streamed or Televised Motion Pictures Award from the PGA. Outlier Society also co-produced the animated sci-fi series *Gen: Lock* (2019), with Jordan voicing the lead character, and the Netflix series *Raising Dion* (2019), which featured Jordan in three episodes. Outlier Society garnered industry notice for being one of the first to formulate and require an inclusion rider. The policy ensures marginalized people are interviewed for department head positions, allows actors to withdraw from a project if the crew is not diverse, and requires people from underrepresented groups be considered for cast and crew positions. In 2019, Outlier Society created an internship-mentoring program specifically for underrepresented young people entering the entertainment business.

Due to the success of *Creed* and *Creed II*, both released by Warner Bros., the studio signed Outlier Society to a first-look deal in 2019. *Just Mercy* was the first film made under their agreement to produce culturally diverse material. Starring Jordan as Bryan Stevenson, a Black, Harvard-educated lawyer known for representing prisoners on death row, the film led one reviewer to write that Jordan "really stands out with an understated, thoughtful performance. He never comes across as naïve or idealistic, but more an ordinary man trying to do something extraordinary with his life" (Brian Penn, "Just Mercy—Film Review," *UK Film Review*, 24 January 2020). Jordan's restrained portrayal quietly illuminates Stevenson's feelings throughout the film. With a touchingly gentle embrace, he conveys the young lawyer's love for his mother when he bids her goodbye. Later, only his pained expression and audible exhalation communicate the rage Stevenson feels when he is strip-searched before meeting a client. Silently watching the execution of a man he fought to save, Jordan's face alone expresses Stevenson's horror. As he leaves the prison, arms hanging limply at his sides, Jordan conveys the toll of witnessing this man's death.

Jordan's compelling role in *Just Mercy*, a critically acclaimed biopic, and Boseman's star turn in *21 Bridges*, a well-received genre film, led to additional recognition and other high-profile projects. In 2020, Jordan was named Male Star of the Year by the National Association of Theatre Owners, and he starred in *Tom Clancy's Without Remorse* (2021) as John Clark, the Vietnam veteran who becomes a key figure in the Clancy novels. The film was co-produced by Outlier Society, and his company also had several films in development. Boseman's 2020 performances were seen as worthy of Oscar nominations. In *Da 5 Bloods*, Boseman's Stormin' Norman is not only "bent on having the time of his life before death takes him," he "knows that war is hell and is determined to make that hell count for something" (Chang, "Appreciation"). As the ambitious trumpeter in *Ma Rainey's Black Bottom* (2020), Boseman reveals the fear and confusion that lie beneath the character's bravado. He was scheduled to star in *Black Panther II* and *Yasuke*, a film about the first African samurai and a project to be co-produced by Boseman's Xception Content. Yet these plans were cut short, and his passing underscored the messages in many of his films, especially "the urgency of Black activism and representation, the vulnerability of every hero, the thinness of the line between life and death" (Chang, "Appreciation"). As Boseman's family and intimate friends mourned privately, his colleagues offered public tributes. Reflecting on their careers, Jordan explained, since "I was 16 years old you paved the way for me. You showed me how to be better, honor purpose, and create legacy. . . . You cared about the kids, the community, our culture and humanity. . . . I'm dedicating the rest of my days to live the way you did. With grace, courage and no regrets" (Halle Kiefer, "Michael B. Jordan Mourns *Black Panther* Co-star Chadwick Boseman," *Vulture*, 31 August 2020).

Boseman's and Jordan's rising fame in the 2010s illuminates stardom in an era when transformations in the entertainment industry reduced traditional star power but increased opportunities for actors involved in culturally relevant material. Their careers also illustrate the challenges of overcoming or circumventing noxious roles that reflect social-political norms in place since traders first brought enslaved African people to the continent in 1619. As actors whose work extends centuries of African American resilience and creativity, Boseman and Jordan "built parallel careers that both forward Black representation—Boseman striking a blow for the Black hero and Jordan proving that characters with troubled histories can transcend stereotypes" (Bruney, "Chadwick Boseman, Michael B. Jordan"). The two stars rejected the pigeonhole of representing the race, as Paul Robeson, Sidney Poitier, and Denzel Washington were once required to do. As twenty-first-century actor-producers, they expanded opportunities for disenfranchised workers and viewing experiences for audiences searching for stories that illuminate the multifaceted lives of all people.

Chapter 12

Natalie Portman

Smart Star

STEVEN RYBIN

Natalie Portman debuted in the mid-1990s as a child actor of remarkable precocity. In Luc Besson's slick, *cinéma du look* action fantasy *The Professional* (1994, known as *Leon* outside the United States), Portman plays Mathilda, a twelve-year-old orphan sporting a Louise Brooks bob who becomes an unlikely understudy to a childlike hitman (Jean Reno) after an unhinged D.E.A. agent (Gary Oldman) murders her family. Portman's turn as Mathilda confirmed her impressive ability to portray young characters adept at navigating a range of adult situations. Her other early roles, grounded in forms of narrative realism a world apart from the stylish pop theatrics of *The Professional*, find her playing preternaturally wise girls: Nina, the daughter of a single mother with breast cancer in the short film *Developing* (1994); Laura, the anxious stepdaughter of Al Pacino's police lieutenant in Michael Mann's *Heat* (1995); and Marty, the teenager who nurses a crush on Timothy Hutton in Ted Demme's *Beautiful Girls* (1996). These characters formed the groundwork for Portman's emergence during the late 1990s and 2000s as an especially and distinctively brilliant young woman, already successful enough to take time off from Hollywood to attend Harvard University. There, she pursued work in science: in 2002 she co-authored a research paper under her birth name, Neta-Lee Hershlag, entitled "Frontal Lobe Activation During Object Permanence" (Baird A.A.; Kagan, J.; Gaudette, T.; Walz K.A.; Hershlag, N.; Boas D.A., *Neuroimage*, 16, no. 4, 2002, pp. 1120–1125).

Portman, in other words, is frequently taken to be a smart movie star, with an allure inextricable from her intelligence—the kind of star who exchanges a series of thoughtful letters with literati such as Jonathan Safran Foer, and then sees her smart text published in an issue of the *New York Times Style Magazine* alongside photographs of her modeling the latest fashions in cardigans, socks, bikini tops, and sweaters ("Natalie, in Correspondence," 17 July 2016: 56–65). This mix of intellectual cultivation with glamour and beauty informs any reading of her onscreen work, for Portman

Natalie Portman

is an especially vivid case study in the legibility of intelligence in film performance. However, Portman's perceived braininess is not frequently framed as an effect of screen acting, a profession often associated with emotions and intuition rather than cerebral chops. Instead, Portman's smarts are often made more frequently salient via reference to her biography, her extrafilmic reputation as a highly educated person. Around the time of the release of *Black Swan* (2010), the film for which she won an Oscar for Best Actress, the *New York Times* reminded its readership of Portman's placement in the semifinals of the Intel Science and Engineering competition while still a high school student in Long Island, a journey that involved her "investigation into a new, 'environmentally friendly' method of converting waste into useful forms of energy" (Natalie Angier, "Natalie Portman, Oscar Winner, Was Also a Precocious Scientist," 28 February 2011); and of her work in "neuroscience and the evolution of the mind" at Harvard, studies which commenced shortly after she accepted a lead role in the first of George Lucas's three *Star Wars* prequels (1999, 2002, 2005) (Angier). In this reportage, it is not enough merely to know that the actor is smart from what she achieves onscreen; rather, we must also hear from Abigail A. Baird, one of Portman's mentors at Harvard, who assures us that "there are very few who are as inherently bright as Natalie is" (Angier). Such writing places Portman in a lineage of female actors with interests in science and math: the same *New York Times* article that discusses Portman's scientific past also mentions Hedy Lamarr (a Hollywood star sharp in rocket science); Danica McKellar (a television performer proficient in math); and Mayim Bialik, former lead in *Blossom* (1991–1995), who holds a PhD in neurobiology from UCLA (Angier). But this discourse also reminds us that such cases are perceived as exceptions. "Acting and science may simply appeal to very different personalities," this same *New York Times* writer on Portman proposes, making it all the more remarkable when the public art of movie acting is joined with the brainy but relatively cloistered world of laboratory science (see Natalie Angier, "From the Lab to the Red Carpet," 1 March 2011). Even Ram Bergman, Portman's producer on her 2015 directorial debut, *A Tale of Love and Darkness*, confesses that before meeting her he was convinced of Portman's intelligence not from her performances but from statements she had made in her interviews (Rebecca Keegan, "Natalie Portman on How *A Tale of Love and Darkness* Is Set in a Time She's Thought about Her Whole Life," 11 August 2016, E1).

But because good acting is the result of sharp thought, intelligent preparation, and sensitive intuition, the intelligence of a film performer should not be understood as a matter separable from onscreen achievements. For aficionados of actors, intelligence is not only located in celebrity personae or other such discursive constructs but is also a perceived effect of onscreen gestures, movements, and expressions—the collective impression of which forms the evidence that the actor shines brilliantly and is smart in her choices. Brenda Austin-Smith makes the important observation that when we watch a screen performance, we cannot directly "see" the presumably thoughtful process or creative decisions generating it. The results are all that we see, and the performance is judged accordingly (Austin-Smith 19). Portman, of course, has received numerous industry accolades as a performer, many of them during the 2010s, which would seem to have the cultural effect of authorizing her performative skill just as her education and public statements ratify her smarts in a more general way. But her reputation as a smart star nevertheless poses an interesting problem for any study of celebrity performance, for her persona functions as a kind of prefilmic, discursive guarantee that her work will not fail to be the product of a rational, sharp, even scientific (rather than conventionally intuitional and emotional) intelligence. Her offscreen reputation already established—and very early in her career—her very presence in any movie seems to promise performative work that will be seen to possess, or be driven by, a sharp intelligence a cut above the rest.

Portman's career in this way stages an encounter between intelligence as publicly and culturally legible—commonly rendered visible in cultural discourse via documentable, certifiable achievements in science and math—and intelligence as interiorized, emotional, and performative. If Portman's intellectual prowess can be authorized by journal articles and data, her accomplishments in cinema are not quantifiable in quite the same way, particularly in a culture in which such achievements are appreciated more as signifiers of success in industry and commerce rather than the product of artistic knowledge or aesthetic wisdom. Even Portman herself, and from a very young age, expressed a certain skepticism regarding acting, and particularly the celebrity attached to it. "I'd rather be smart than be a movie star," Portman is reported to have said at the age of thirteen; "[College] taught me to be bold and confident, and that questions are never stupid," she said over a decade later, at the age of twenty-six (both quotes are from Samantha Brody, "Natalie Portman," *Scholastic Parent & Child* 15, no. 4, 2007: 72). The first quote suggests the way Portman positions herself against perceived shallowness in stardom (from the point of view of a thirteen-year-old child actor on the cusp of it); the second implies a mature degree of agency and desire for thoughtful control over her work as a creative film artist.

This assumption of intelligence in an actor, and in a female actor in the sexist landscape of Hollywood in particular, has implications for how we understand Portman's work, as this essay's discussion of her most significant performances in the 2010s explores. There is a relationship between Portman's characterizations in her films during this decade and the extrafilmic, social recognition of Portman's braininess—ratified not only by a degree from Harvard and her scientific labor but also via her engagement with global, political problems (including the situation of Israel, her father's place of birth and a region of the world that becomes increasingly important to Portman). As an adult in the new century and particularly in the 2010s, Portman's established trait as a child performer—her at times startlingly bright and precocious subjectivity—becomes increasingly readable, in her adult performances, as a complex expression of adult interiority in a troubled world. Intelligence is an expectation in Portman's characters at this point, even if the films surrounding her performances are of variable merit. What her characterizations in her later films work through is the existential fate of her already established intelligence, and those institutions that have ratified it, in a decade fraught with social, ecological, and technological upheavals.

Portman took on a wide range of roles during the 2010s. While she remains most well known for her earlier appearances in the *Star Wars* prequels (1999, 2002, and 2005) and a series of popular *Thor* movies (2011, 2013, 2017, 2022), her most provocative and surprising performances of these years are found elsewhere. In Darren Aronofsky's *Black Swan* (2010), Portman plays a character who tests the very limit of the performing mind and body against the cultural and psychological pressures facing ballet dancers, even as her own performance in the film is partially generated by new digital techniques that arguably reduce the performer's agency and control (is the star smart, or is the technology?). In her two appearances in Terrence Malick's poetic cinema, *Knight of Cups* (2015) and *Song to Song* (2017), the internal lives and voices of Portman's young women jut up against a world shaped by aggressive masculinity and rampant consumerism. *A Tale of Love and Darkness* finds Portman directing her own performance in a tale about Israel's past, while in *Jackie* (2016), Portman's Jacqueline Kennedy reconciles her public image with her tumultuous inner life after the death of John F. Kennedy. In a pair of edgy, futurist films, *Annihilation* (2018) and *Vox Lux* (2018), Portman's smart women journey into futuristic, uncertain, and sometimes terrifying worlds, their pluck and intelligence meeting with startling new visions and problems. Portman wrapped up her decade with *Lucy in the Sky* (2019), a drama about a brilliant and successful astronaut who struggles with depression after returning to the petty encumbrances of everyday social reality on planet Earth.

☆☆☆☆☆☆☆☆☆☆ Fractured Dance

"Natalie Portman Goes Batshit in a Tutu," snarks the headline of J. Hoberman's notice of Darren Aronofsky's *Black Swan* (J. Hoberman, *Phoenix New Times*, 9 December 2010). This Oscar-winning performance as anxiety-ridden ballet dancer Nina Sayers, who competes for the dual female role as Odette (the White Swan) and Odile (her evil doppelgänger, the Black Swan) in a new and especially prestigious production of *Swan Lake*, is something of a capstone for the first stretch of Portman's career. The reception of *Black Swan* was nevertheless mixed. Hoberman understood the film to be "an acting vehicle—it exists to document a highly physical, totally immersive performance," an unusual opinion in light of the film's heavy use of digital effects augmenting Portman's work in the film (what exactly is being documented here?). Another reviewer projected creative agency onto Aronofsky rather than Portman: "*Black Swan* is a success from start to finish because Aronofsky creates a complete world in the opening act, then slowly slices it apart with all the manly dexterity of a patriarch before the family turkey" (Katherine Monk, "Requiem for a *Black Swan*: Natalie Portman Delivers Stunning Performance as Ballerina Wrestling with Reality," *Edmonton Journal*, 17 December 2010, D2). Other critics experienced not so much immersion as icy distance, an effect attributed by one critic to Portman: "Nina has so little psychological substance in *Black Swan*, and Portman's performance is so glacéed, that watching her come apart seems like an exercise in voyeurism. Or sadism. It doesn't even matter, on some level, if Nina is a dancer. Her obsession with ballet has very little to do with artistic expression—it's obsession for the sake of obsession" (Peter Rainer, "Natalie Portman: A Deeply Dark *Black Swan*," *The Christian Science Monitor*, 3 December 2010, 24).

This debate over *Black Swan* also involves some discussion regarding how much credit Portman deserves for its dance sequences, which has implications for how one reads Portman's characterization in the context of Aronofsky's inflated "visionary" aesthetic. Questions of authenticity, including authentic knowledge of ballet as a form, have circled around performers in this genre throughout the history of cinema. As Adrienne L. McLean notes in her essay on the unintentionally funny aspects of *Black Swan*, "Promotional and publicity materials from the earliest days of the ballet film had always claimed that their non-dancing stars had transformed themselves into 'real' ballerinas—Vivien Leigh in *Waterloo Bridge* (1940), Margaret O'Brien in *The Unfinished Dance* (1947), Gene Tierney in *Never Let Me Go* (1953)" (152). Here, whether Portman is aided in her "transformation" through hard work or through digital technology is a question discourse on the film has posed. The body of Sarah Lane, an American Ballet Theatre soloist, was digitally appended to Portman's head in the film's most complex dancing sequences, a fact that was not publicly discussed at any great length until after Portman began winning awards for the movie. "They wanted to create this idea in people's minds that Natalie was some kind of prodigy . . . basically [to win] the Oscar," Lane has claimed (Adam Markovitz and Anthony Breznican, "*Black Swan*: Ruffled Feathers," *Entertainment Weekly*, 8 April 2011, 1). Portman, for her part, is fairly open in discussing what she did and did not do in the film. "There's no way, obviously, I could have learned, you know, fouetté turns en pointe for the film," Portman has said. "That's something that takes a lifetime to perfect. So there's a wonderful dancer, Sarah Lane, who did the more complicated pointe work. But I did the stuff that was possible to learn in a year" ("To Become a 'Black Swan,' Portman Had to Go Dark," *Fresh Air*, 30 November 2010).

Portman, however, does not mention the numerous digital special effects creating the illusion of her Nina, who is ultimately a composite figure, a synthesis of Portman's facial expressivity and Lane's dancing body. Fox Searchlight, in the promotional material for *Black Swan*, eschewed references to this technological effect, perhaps out of fear, as Lane suggests, that it might compromise their campaign for Portman's Best Actress Oscar. And yet the discussion over how much credit Portman should receive for the screen manifestation of the brilliantly talented dancer Nina becomes something of a red herring in view of the film itself, which poses more fundamental questions about how to read the internal life of Portman's ballerina. Aronofsky's fractured film style shuttles between handheld traveling shots following Portman through space (a now exhausted stylistic trope of twenty-first-century "immersive" cinema) and close-ups of the actress expressing various degrees of anxiety and hesitancy as Nina works to shed all inhibition in order to play Odile. (Her predatory ballet director, sharply played by Vincent Cassel, repeatedly tells her she lacks the requisite desire the part demands, a familiar trope from ballet films.) But even the close-ups of Portman's eyes, so often the portal to interpretations of inner life in performance, lead to questions about the degree of creative agency the film grants the actress: near the end of *Black Swan*, special effects transform Portman's pupils into deep shades of red as Nina discovers performative confidence. Numerous additional digital effects convey, in physical and fantastically imagined terms, the psychological transformation occurring in Nina, as little black feathers emerge from under her skin as she unleashes her (literally) inner black swan. These digital and expressionistic inflections upon

Natalie Portman as the anxious ballerina Nina in *Black Swan* (Darren Aronofsky, Fox Searchlight, 2010). Digital frame enlargement.

Portman's performing body are in keeping with what Tarja Laine understands, in her book on Aronofsky, as the director's penchant for exploring "excessive, sublime elements with alienating, uncanny ones . . . confronting the spectator with bestial forces from beyond human reality" (129). If the film's point of departure is Portman's humanity, it ends somewhere else, in a portrait of a dancer-become-animal that relies as much on film technology as acting to achieve its effects.

Portman's performative agency as a smart star, challenged in an interesting way through the film's insistence on the latest advancements in filmmaking technology and special effects that, at certain key junctures in the film, threaten to take over her performance, is nevertheless central to the film's logic. *Black Swan*'s narrative reinforces knowledge of Portman as an intelligent and accomplished woman, positioning us to understand Nina as a woman of similarly remarkable cultural distinction, only furthered through her discovery of intrinsic new reservoirs of talent. At the outset of the film, Nina has already earned a privileged (if anxiety-riddled) social position, competing for the starring role in a major ballet and taking instruction from one of the world's leading directors. The film situates Nina, much as industry discourse at the time positioned Portman, as an established and successful adult performer who apparently still had a little more to prove before she could reach the highest plane of disciplined achievement (for Nina, the Black Swan; for Portman, an Oscar). But as the film's narrative articulation of its central character's mental breakdown progresses, it becomes clear that for Nina, extraordinary achievement in the highly competitive and exclusive world of ballet equates to or results in a loss of sanity and control (and, the ending of the film implies, a loss of life). For Portman, likewise, achievement in *Black Swan* may culminate in an Academy Award, but, onscreen, her achievement is mitigated by a loss of creative agency (or, less extremely, by performative augmentation). If the film begins by reasserting Portman's persona as a smart star, by its end *Black Swan* generates ambivalence about the measure of her control over the very performance unfolding before our eyes.

★★★★★★★★★★ Poetic Performance

After winning the Oscar for *Black Swan,* Portman's career darted between popular genres and a string of smaller independent films. One of her popular studio efforts, *No Strings Attached* (2011), finds Portman opposite Ashton Kutcher in a romance based on the premise that an intimate relationship might avoid emotional entanglements and proceed on an entirely physical basis. Despite the potentially naughty nature of the material, *No Strings Attached* is a thoroughly buttoned-up sex comedy, with both Portman's and Kutcher's bodies strategically concealed, during the film's ornate and oddly repressive sex scenes, through carefully arranged mise-en-scène and camera placement. This mannered but polite orchestration of copulation in *No Strings Attached* is reflective of Portman's career-long preference for physical modesty onscreen, reflecting her concern for how her image circulates in the age of the internet and social media. "I'm definitely not a prude about sex or nudity," Portman stated in 2010; "I just don't want to do something that will end up in a screen grab on a porn site" ("Natalie Portman Says No to Nude Scenes," *Digital Spy*, 1 September 2010). Other commercial efforts during the early 2010s, such as *Thor* (2011) and the medieval stoner comedy *Your Highness* (2011), surprisingly (given the otherwise male-dominated natures of the two films) underscore the resourcefulness and intelligence of her characters, and give the Portman character narrative agency: in *Thor* she plays an astrophysicist, a type of character very much in keeping with the scientific credibility of the Portman persona, and in *Your Highness* she is a would-be damsel in distress who ends up rescuing the men in the film.

Especially notable as the decade goes on, particularly given her ongoing presence in big-budget science fiction and fantasy, is Portman's continued commitment to independent and auteur-driven cinema. Her numerous indie movies during the decade include a supporting role as a desperate wage earner in *Hesher* (2010); a part as a divorcée in Vanita Shastry's short film *Lacunae*, part of the portmanteau film *The Heyday of the Insensitive Bastards* (2015); a turn as a vengeful female cowboy in the revisionist Western *Jane Got a Gun* (2016); and a part in Rebecca Zlotowski's self-reflexive *Planetarium*

(2016) as an American actress and séance performer who, alongside her clairvoyant sister (Lily-Rose Depp), enters the French film industry in the years leading up to World War II. Her roles in *Jane Got a Gun* and *Planetarium,* in particular, find Portman characterizing women with agency and control in relation to, in *Jane Got a Gun,* a typically male-dominated genre (the Western) and, in *Planetarium,* the male-dominated film industry of the 1930s.

Of these independent films, her work for Terrence Malick, in *Knight of Cups* (2015) and *Song to Song* (2017) finds Portman in happy collaboration. Portman was cast in *Knight of Cups* after she had already known Malick for ten years, having exchanged "book suggestions and ideas" with the director before she was cast in the film. Rather than technology shaping her image as in *Black Swan,* the work with Malick was the product of a substantively intellectual, and experimentally experiential, collaboration. Of Malick, Portman says he "has a shooting style that's exploratory. He's looking to discover things all the time. And it's a beautiful way to work. I think it's something to take into all kinds of movies because you tend to get into a rhythm where you feel you are executing the script, you're putting the script on the screen" (Portman quoted in Eric Eidelstein, "Berlin: Natalie Portman on What Terrence Malick Taught Her," *IndieWire* 2015). Her work with Malick reinforces that part of Portman's persona which values creative control in matters of characterization and screen presence, going beyond the character as written on the page to discover new realities and subjectivities onscreen.

In *Knight of Cups,* Portman plays Elizabeth, one of eight figures, each represented by a different tarot card, that the main character of the film, a screenwriter named Rick (Christian Bale), encounters during an angst-filled spiritual journey through Los Angeles. Elizabeth is a married woman with whom Rick is having an affair; she may be pregnant. Portman's second collaboration with Malick, *Song to Song* (2017), finds her playing Rhonda, a waitress who falls into a relationship with a manipulative record producer named Cook (Michael Fassbender). Given Malick's penchant for the technique, it is not surprising that Portman's voice-over is as crucial to an understanding of Elizabeth and Rhonda as anything Portman does onscreen. These characters speak in hushed, poetic ruminations that, within the story, seem directed toward her male paramours, but that are also meant to convey their autonomous, soul-searching thoughts. (In *Knight of Cups* the viewer is given some sense of Elizabeth's worry over her unplanned pregnancy, and in *Song to Song* her hesitation about Cook's controlling behavior is conveyed through her voice.) Where film technology was used to transform—and at points, take over—Portman's performative agency in

Black Swan, in these two Malick films, film style seems notably and harmoniously joined with the actress's gestures, movements, and spoken words; it is as if these films themselves were developing their own rhythms through the way their cuts and camera movements are timed to Portman's own movements, vocal inflections, and gestures, rather than imposing a structure onto her performance. These films serve as two examples of the way in which Portman has been able to find satisfying artistic partnerships outside of mainstream Hollywood, work in which she is given relatively free rein to shape the future of her characters' thoughtful subjectivities.

Performance and History

But even relatively open-ended collaborations such as the Malick films place certain limits around Portman's performances. Portman has commented that screen acting is ultimately "a service to the director's vision"; by contrast, "It was exciting to have the position where people where asking me for my vision," Portman has said in the *New York Times* of her feature-length debut as a director, the 2015 film *A Tale of Love and Darkness* (Portman quoted in Rachael Donadio, "Natalie Portman on Israel and Directing at Cannes," 17 May 2015). This film is one example of the way in which Portman has expanded the range of representations she embodies, using her now established position in the film industry to explore themes pertaining to Jewish identity. In fact, Portman's identity as a Jewish woman has been central to her public persona throughout her adult career: she was born in Israel to an American mother and Israeli father; her father, a doctor, also worked as a diplomat in Israel.

A family melodrama that occurs against the backdrop of the founding of the state of Israel, *A Tale of Love and Darkness* is based on novelist Amos Oz's memoir of the same name. This story tells of a sensitive young boy, Amos Klausner (Amir Tessler), growing up in post–World War II Israel. The film, structured through flashbacks, is narrated by an older Amos (Moni Moshonov), but the human center of the film—as envisioned in the memories of the son—is provided by Portman's quietly assured performance as Fania, Amos's tender and loving mother. Portman (speaking Hebrew in her role—Portman attests her knowledge of the language is "pretty good" but not fluent; see Rebecca Keegan, "Natalie Portman Finds So Many Tales to Be Told," *Los Angeles Times*, 14 August 2016, E1) conveys Fania's sensitive, cerebral, and poetic nature; she nurses a romantic hope for a future Israel that might take shape, as it does in her mind's eye, as "the land of milk and honey," amid a more brutal reality shaped by suffering and war. Strikingly, Portman's directorial debut eschews the Oedipal trajectory a viewer might expect in a coming-of-age story focused on a young boy's intense relationship with his parents, preferring instead to focus on an older man's memory of his difficult and at times enigmatic mother. And although it is narrated from the perspective of the older Amos, Portman's film vividly conveys Fania's desires and subjectivity (through the prism of Amos's memory). In early sequences, Portman shows us Fania romantically pining for a poetic, erotic vision of a handsome, muscular man, variously depicted in her waking dreams as a farmer or a soldier, and in both cases presented to us as Fania's dream of an ideal Israel. These fantasies, which balance a certain kind of powerful, if benevolent, masculinity with a humanistic notion of the nation-state, jostle against the reality faced by Fania, Amos, and Fania's husband, Arieh (Gilad Kahana), a well-meaning but awkward intellectual whose personality could not be further from the young man for whom Fania pines. Even as it becomes clear that Fania's dream of Israel does not match the disappointing realities of the political and social world surrounding her, Portman's film, and her performance, breathes life into her character's complicated subjectivity.

A. O. Scott, in his *New York Times* review, observes that *A Tale of Love and Darkness* "is in every way the opposite of a vanity project" ("From Natalie Portman, Israel's Birth Distilled in Mood and Memory," 18 August 2016). Even as Portman's protagonist slips into romantic and fantastical daydreams in which Israel becomes personified as a beautiful and caring man, Portman's film is not meant as a glamorous showcase for a self-indulgent admiration of her already established acting abilities. Instead, Portman carefully shapes a vision of a character, and of a country, balancing empathy and tenderness with an understanding of the ways in which the complexity of contemporary Israeli reality intersects with hopes and aspirations for its future. Portman herself has said of the project:

> The story of Oz's family at the dawn of the state of Israel is remarkably close to all the stories I heard growing up about my father's family: the worship of everything European, refugees confronted by the desert, the atmosphere of constant violence, the political debates, the obsession with books and storytelling and language, womanhood in a religious/military/socialist amalgam, the dark fantasy of building a utopian community when all the parents have been killed, the mythology of the pioneer and the new Israeli man. The themes are endlessly interesting to me, as is the question of how much of the mythology is an accurate reflection of history, and how much is storytelling cemented by repetition. (Portman quoted in "Natalie, in Correspondence" 59)

The film is consistent with Portman's own complicated, and far from unthinkingly celebratory, relationship to the state of Israel. While in interviews she clearly takes pride in her Jewish heritage, Portman has also been critical of Israel's politics, particularly as it pertains to the nation's devastating relationship with Palestine (Ruth Eglash, "Natalie Portman Says She Won't Endorse Netanyahu but She Won't Boycott Israel Either," *The Washington Post*, 21 April 2018). The way in which Portman balances an admiration for Israeli culture—*A Tale of Love and Darkness* is itself a notable, transnational contribution to Israeli cinema—with a considered ambivalence about the nation's fraught politics in the Middle East has been a key part of her substance as a movie star in the last decade.

If in *A Tale of Love and Darkness* Portman projects herself into Israeli history, her role as Jacqueline Kennedy Onassis in Pablo Larraín's *Jackie* (2016) finds her back in the United States in a film in which she plays another woman caught in the middle of, but also intelligently weaving her way through, large-scale historical and political events. Where *A Tale of Love and Darkness* focuses on the historical (and fictionalized) experiences of a woman whose private subjectivity is largely imagined and reconstructed through the creative efforts of her novelist son, in *Jackie* Portman portrays a public figure conscious of how she performed in front of cameras, in particular for the medium of television. Portman has expressed, in an interview for *Screen International*, how conscious she was of playing an individual already known to the public through newspaper articles and archival news footage: "It definitely felt [like] the most dangerous [role of my career] because everyone knows what she looked like, how she walked, how she talked" (Andreas Wiseman, "Natalie Portman: *Jackie* Most 'Dangerous' Role of My Career," 7 September 2016). Larraín's film, however, avoids the trap of conventional hagiography, preferring a reflexive approach which contemplates how Jacqueline Kennedy self-consciously shaped her social identity and the public circulation of the Kennedy myth in the wake of her husband's murder. The film uses a nonlinear temporal structure that darts back and forth between Jackie's carefully cultivated and performed life as first lady from January 1961 to November 1963, her immediate experiences after the trauma of the assassination of her husband, and then her attempts to control the public narrative about its aftermath. Larraín's film in this way combines present-tense impressionism (in the scenes involving and immediately following Kennedy's assassination) with reflective, melancholic contemplation (in the scenes in which Jackie attempts to shape her own experience of the tragedy into a coherent public narrative, a myth).

Portman's performance not only convincingly conveys for us the terror Jacqueline Kennedy experienced during the assassination but also imagines how she reflected upon and constructed her public persona in the days and

Jacqueline Kennedy Onassis's gaze, embodied by Natalie Portman in *Jackie* (Pablo Larraín, Sony Pictures Classics, 2016). Digital frame enlargement.

months following the tragedy. The film is framed by Jackie's recounting of her experiences as first lady in the days after her husband's death, an account given to a jaded reporter (Billy Crudup) who serves as a surrogate for any viewer weary of presidential mythmaking. Through crafting this account of her life as a public figure, the Jackie of the film is shown as adept in managing the myth of the White House inhabited by the Kennedys as a kind of modern Camelot. Performatively, Portman also shows us how Jackie achieved this vision through the careful and considered design of mise-en-scène. The film explores Jackie's taste for expensive but also historically meaningful artifacts—statues, portraits, and furniture—that express something of the personality and life of former presidents and their wives, men and women who had lived and breathed in the White House prior to her arrival there in 1961. Nevertheless, Portman acknowledges that certain aspects of her performance—including the suit Jackie was wearing on the day of her husband's death—carry an unavoidable historical burden. No matter how much thoughtful control Portman's Jackie exercises over her public image in this movie, the Kennedy myth and its role in history remains something no one individual can finally control. "It's very heavy," Portman said of the Chanel wardrobe Jackie was wearing on the day of her husband's death, "because that pink suit has so much tragic history to it" (Portman quoted in Peter Howell, "Natalie Portman Feels the Weight of

History: The Pink Chanel Suit Brought the Role Home," *The Toronto Star*, 4 December 2016, E1).

☆☆☆☆☆☆☆☆☆★ Imagining Futures

The complexities of a fraught and ceaselessly transforming social and existential reality are key themes in three films Portman made near the end of the 2010s: *Annihilation*, *Vox Lux*, and *Lucy in the Sky*. These films tell stories about haunted women who struggle to reconcile their remarkable achievements with various feelings of loss, disassociation, and depression.

In *Annihilation*, Portman plays Lena, a professor of biology and former soldier in the U.S. Army who teaches at Johns Hopkins University. At the beginning of the film, Lena's husband, Kane (Oscar Isaac), is presumed to have died during an expedition into a mysterious zone known only as "the Shimmer," an ever-expanding, ethereal realm in which biological entities mutate and grow in strange ways. After a long absence, Kane suddenly returns, but his strange behavior and mysterious physical ailments—in the profound sense of his personhood, Kane is still very much lost to Lena—motivate her to pursue her own journey into the Shimmer. Lena joins a group of three other women who have all experienced different kinds of loss in their lives—a psychologist, Dr. Ventress (Jennifer Jason Leigh), a paramedic, Anya Thorensen (Gina Rodriguez), a physicist, Josie Radek (Tessa Thompson), and a geomorphologist, Cassie Sheppard (Tuva Novotny)—on a mission into this sector also referred to within the diegesis as "Area X." There, the group finds an assortment of alternately bizarre, wondrous, and terrifying mutations in animals, plants, and terrain. These biological transformations soon extend to the humans themselves, and Portman's Lena, the only character to survive the expedition, finds her very molecules transformed; as a shimmer passes across Portman's eyes in the film's final close-up, it becomes clear Lena herself has become a kind of mutation. Portman's appearance is again modified by special effects, as in *Black Swan*. But the inflection of these effects on her performance in *Annihilation* is altogether more subtle, and at no point does the film's impressive technology threaten to overwhelm Portman's performance. Molecular transformations are built into the very premise of *Annihilation* in ways that make the film's modifications of Portman's presence in the film organic to the theme and to the performer's work. The film seems to suggest that the intelligence of the performer and the increasing "intelligence" of sophisticated film technology can at least sometimes work in happy collaboration.

Upon its release, some critics, such as Ann Hornaday in the *Washington Post,* responded ambivalently to the film while nevertheless praising Portman's work in it: "A tale of horror and suspense cut from the same jump-scare cloth as *Alien,* with a dash of *Arrival* thrown in—with its subtext of a woman mourning an unspoken loss—*Annihilation* initially exudes a form of magnetism every bit as somber and determined as Portman's tersely self-possessed protagonist" ("Natalie Portman Stars in the Enigmatic, Ultimately Unsatisfying *Annihilation,*" 22 February 2018). Todd McCarthy likewise noted in *Variety* that Portman succeeds in "compellingly conveying Lena's fierce determination to figure out what happened to her husband and solve the mystery of this terrifying force of nature" ("*Annihilation*: Starring a Fierce Natalie Portman," 21 February 2018, 76). The film received some criticism for Portman's casting; in the novel by Jeff VanderMeer upon which *Annihilation* is based, the character of Lena is Asian, a fact of which Portman, in an interview for *The Wrap,* claims she was unaware until after the film was finished (Jeremy Fuster, "Natalie Portman on *Annihilation* Whitewashing," 14 February 2018). Portman's casting, nevertheless, may have more to do with the history of her own celebrity image than with strict fidelity to an antecedent text: a character trained in biology is very much in keeping with aspects of Portman's smart-star persona that have been in place for over two decades.

Portman finished her 2010s with two memorable performances in a pair of unusual, prickly films exploring trauma and depression in fraught environments. In Brady Corbet's futuristic *Vox Lux* (2018), Portman plays a pop star named Celeste Montgomery whose shape-shifting, glamorous musical personae position her as a David Bowie or Madonna figure. Portman does not appear in the first hour of the film, which narrates Celeste's flight to stardom after a song she wrote in the wake of a devastating school shooting (a tragedy in which her neck was severely injured) became a major hit and cultural touchstone. In this early stretch of *Vox Lux,* the young Celeste is played by Raffey Cassidy, a young British actress who bears a striking resemblance to Portman circa the late 1990s; Cassidy's presence alongside the adult Portman gives the film a vertiginous temporal quality, especially given that its events are set in the late 1990s, a time when Portman would have been about Cassidy's age and just two years prior to the September 11 attacks (which are referred to in the plot of the film). The resemblance between Portman and her younger co-star is used to especially good effect in the second half of the film, in which Cassidy again appears, this time as the adult Celeste's teenaged daughter. As the film goes on,

Celeste swerves her way through a host of celebrity ills, including alcoholism, paparazzi, and a troubled relationship with her daughter (to say nothing of the way in which a group of terrorists, midway through the film, appropriate imagery from one of Celeste's musical videos as they carry out an attack). The film sets its sights on high-minded thematic ground, speculating on the relationship between celebrity, pop music, and media-saturated terrorism at the turn of the century. Portman's admirable performance grounds the film's eccentric and at times unwieldy vision, finding a profitable balance between emotional tumult and artistic brilliance in her troubled but talented character.

Lucy in the Sky, the final Portman performance to hit screens in the 2010s, resonates in an interesting way with the star's recollection of her childhood: Portman claims to have had dreams of becoming an astronaut when she was a child, and in this film she gets to play one (see Kathryn Shattuck, "Natalie Portman Shoots for the Stars and Loses Her Mind," *New York Times*, 4 October 2019). The film is loosely based on the real-life astronaut Lisa Nowak, who was arrested and charged with the attempted kidnapping of a U.S. Air Force captain, with whom she was competing for the affections of another astronaut. In the movie, Portman's Lucy performs no kidnapping, but she does become romantically involved with a fellow star traveler, the womanizing Mark Goodwin (Jon Hamm). But romance is a poor substitute for Lucy's passion for and desire to return to outer space. At the beginning of the film, Lucy, having reached the pinnacle of professional achievement for an astronaut, orbits above Earth, overwhelmed and in a state of awe that finds no parallel when she returns to her domestic life down below. Everything in that normative, down-to-earth life (including a marriage to a loving but very conventional husband played by Dan Stevens) seems comparatively puny and inconsequential. Portman sports a heavy, and not always convincing, Texas accent in playing Lucy, but ultimately does a fine job of underscoring her character's dissociative personality and longing for a return to stellar transcendence. But as with *Black Swan*, Portman's performative efforts are irritatingly displaced by the machinations of baroque film technique. The filmmakers emphasize the narrowness Lucy feels in her domestic environs through a constant shuttling between various aspect ratios: an approximately 2.35:1 widescreen frame is used when Lucy is seen orbiting Earth from space at the beginning of the film, and also at various and subsequent points in the story in which she briefly feels something like the adrenaline rush she experienced in the sky; narrower, approximately 1.85:1 and 1.33:1 frames are used when Lucy feels especially boxed in by the pettiness of everything surrounding her on the humble planet. These distracting, and thuddingly literal, shifts in visual format are another demonstration of the way in which Portman's ability to thoughtfully convey the subjectivities of her characters is often made to compete with the overwrought technological and visual conceits of certain directors. (We might call this the "Aronofsky effect.") Whatever the vagaries of Portman's Texas drawl, the biggest flaw of *Lucy in the Sky* (a film which was almost universally panned by critics upon its release) is its inability to resist visual trickery and let the talents of its star performer lead the way.

Nevertheless, throughout the 2010s, Portman found profitable collaborations, as in her work with Malick and productively bizarre films such as *Annihilation* and *Vox Lux,* in which she had the opportunity to incarnate characters who perform fascinating variations on already established aspects of Portman's smart-star persona. These films are touchstones in an impressive span of her interesting and ongoing career. Even so, her best work in the last decade is in those films—*Jackie* and her own *A Tale of Love and Darkness*—in which ostentatious displays of technology and technique take a backseat to sensitive characterizations realized through thoughtful performance.

IN THE WINGS

STEVEN RYBIN

In the "In the Wings" coda of the previous volume in this series, Murray Pomerance observed that "the stars of the new age are all cell phone and digital device compatible, all best seen as they move past us" (242). It may very well be that the movie stars of the next age will be those we move past in the undulating scroll of social media applications such as Facebook, Twitter, and Instagram, a visual flow in which the faces of movie stars compete for (brief) attention alongside other media celebrities, politicians, and even the faces of our friends, work colleagues, and family. If the gods and goddesses of the silent era—or even the major stars of the golden age of Classical Hollywood cinema of the 1930s, 1940s, and 1950s—commanded attention with authority and poise on the silver screen, the new screen idols, many undeniably possessed of similarly impressive performative talents, are becoming those we carefully select as worthy for our attention (as we increasingly become, and perhaps have always been but now more saliently, our own curators of stars). Selection, of course, has always been part of the process of star consumption: the choice between a Carole Lombard or a Myrna Loy movie in 1936 is not, on the surface, terribly different than that between a Carey Mulligan movie and a Michelle Williams movie in 2016. (The devoted Hollywood moviegoer, of course, will see them both, and more besides.) And stars have not lost their power to shape fashions and provoke conspicuous consumption: various internet outlets reported a spike in sales of a smoothie drink called Yakult after the young and emerging star of the Netflix film *To All the Boys I've Loved Before* (2018), Noah Centineo, was seen drinking one in a scene. Social media has intensified previously existing tendencies of star reception and commodification, even as varied experiences of these intensities are now fragmented across various devices and a proliferation of media platforms.

But continuity has always been a cornerstone of the film industry, not only in the shaping of the illusions of its screen narratives but also in the shaping of its stars' careers. And several very popular movie stars of the 2010s are poised to continue their success into the 2020s, once the disruption to film production and exhibition caused by the circulation of COVID-19 has finally ceased. In terms of the money earned by their most profitable films, there is no reason to suspect that especially bankable Hollywood movie stars at the global box office in the 2010s will slow down anytime soon: Robert Downey, Jr. ($1.2 billion, *Iron Man 2*, 2010); Daniel Craig ($1.1 billion, *Skyfall*, 2012); Joaquin Phoenix ($1.1 billion, *Joker*, 2019); Will Smith ($1 billion, *Aladdin*, 2019); Johnny Depp and Anne Hathaway ($1 billion, *Alice in Wonderland*, 2010); Gal Gadot ($822 million, *Wonder Woman*, 2017); Will Smith again ($747 million, *Suicide Squad*, 2016); Kristen Stewart and Robert Pattinson ($694 million, *The Twilight Saga: Eclipse*, 2010); Jennifer Lawrence ($694 million, *The Hunger Games*, 2012); to mention only the very top grossers. That every one of these films is either an installment in a series or a reimagining of a pre-existing product, however, suggests again (as I discussed in the introduction) that the primary stars today and in the future may very well be the recognizable characters and "heroes" in the narrative property itself rather than the actors incarnating them. Nevertheless, there were enough relatively original, and profitable, films made during the last decade to suggest that the appeal of certain stars remained a box-office draw for many viewers in films that were not sequels or part of a series. Some of the most memorable star turns in nonfranchise Hollywood films made during the 2010s involved actors we expect will continue to appear on the marquees of the 2020s: Rami Malek ($903.7 million, *Bohemian Rhapsody*, 2018); Leonardo DiCaprio ($829 million, *Inception*, 2010); Sandra Bullock and George Clooney ($723 million, *Gravity*, 2013); Matt Damon and Jessica Chastain ($630 million, *The Martian*, 2015); Bradley Cooper and Lady Gaga ($436 million, *A Star Is Born*, 2018); Mark Wahlberg, Mila Kunis, and a foulmouthed animated bear voiced by Seth MacFarlane ($556 million, *Ted*, 2012) (although we might foolishly hope that this boorish bear's career will not continue into the 2020s). (Box-office data gleaned from boxofficemojo.com.)

As these pages have sought to show, stardom, star performance, and their reception in the 2010s were part of a perpetually transforming cultural nexus of celebrity, identity, technology, style, and capital, and the careers of many actors took off with greater speed than ever in this context. Some of these actors were discussed earlier in this book. Other major stars whose careers took flight in films in the 2010s, and who are now positioned for ongoing success in the 2020s, include Chris Pratt (whose graduation from supporting schlub on the television sitcom *Parks and Recreation* to hunky action hero in *Guardians of the Galaxy* is perhaps less marvelous than it appears, given that Pratt is one of an army of Chrises who assumed prominence in the decade—see also Hemsworth and Pine) as well as Emily Blunt,

Benedict Cumberbatch, Adam Driver, Jesse Eisenberg, Andrew Garfield, Donald Glover, Brie Larson, Melissa McCarthy, Lupita Nyong'o, Elizabeth Olsen, Aubrey Plaza, Eddie Redmayne, Margot Robbie, and Amy Schumer, to name only a few. Other stars reminded the world of their presence during the decade, with gripping turns in movies that came after more than a few years out of the cinematic spotlight; it will certainly be interesting for movie fans to see if they can continue this career resurgence in the 2020s. Jennifer Lopez, a seasoned movie veteran and popular star of music, generated substantial Oscar buzz with her performance in the underrated *Hustlers* (2019); Renée Zellweger, under the celebrity radar for the better part of a decade, triumphed with her Oscar-winning performance in *Judy* (2019); Michael Keaton returned momentarily to the heights of his late 1980s and early 1990s fame with *Birdman or (The Unexpected Virtues of Ignorance)* (2014), a picture that is something of a reflexive play upon Keaton's earlier performances as Batman in a pair of Tim Burton films (1989, 1992); Matthew McConaughey, who shifted from a series of romantic comedy flops in the aughts to critically lauded turns in the 2010s with films such as William Friedkin's 2011 thriller *Killer Joe*, *Dallas Buyers Club* (2013), and the sci-fi blockbuster *Interstellar* (2014); Cuba Gooding Jr., a budding star in the late 1990s chiefly as a result of his memorable supporting role in *Jerry Maguire* (1997), gave noteworthy performances in *Lee Daniels' The Butler* (2013) and Ava DuVernay's *Selma* (2014); Robin Wright, enchanting a generation of young moviegoers in the 1987 fantasy film *The Princess Bride*, became popular again on television in her role in *House of Cards* (2013–2018) as well as in supporting turns in superhero movies; and Ryan Reynolds emerged as a major star in franchise films late in the 2010s after a series of flops earlier in the decade. The decade also saw stalwarts of movies in previous decades finding new careers on the small screen: Claire Danes, in the most widely celebrated role of her career in eight seasons of *Homeland* (2011–2020); Winona Ryder, in a popular role on the Netflix series *Stranger Things* (2016–present); Christian Slater, in the television series *Mr. Robot* (2015–present); Julia Roberts, star icon of the 1990s, in a web TV series entitled *Homecoming* (2018–present); and 1990s indie queen Parker Posey, in a central role as Dr. Smith in the Netflix reimagining of the science fiction television series *Lost in Space* (2017–present); to name just five examples. Television in the 2020s will no doubt continue to be a central platform for seasoned stars to continue to perform, even after their names cease appearing with the same regularity on movie marquees.

Series on various streaming services such as Amazon, HBO, Hulu, and Netflix, a form that is viewed on television but is perhaps more profoundly indebted to the tradition of the continuing narrative in movie serials and sequels, have also enabled the emergence of new actors who might potentially find even bigger stardom on larger screens in the 2020s. As the 2020s began, most audiences were underwhelmed by *Wonder Woman 1984* (2020), but the performance of Pedro Pascal, a veteran of streaming series in preceding years, sustained interest and proved once again that the performances by actors playing the villains in superhero films are often more interesting incarnations than those of the heroes. Other potential breakthrough stars who have emerged in streaming series in recent years include Michaela Coel (the creator, writer, and star of the Channel 4 comedy *Chewing Gum* and the HBO-BBC co-production *I May Destroy You*); Phoebe Waller-Bridges (star and co-writer of the series *Fleabag* and *Killing Eve*); Jeremy Strong and Sarah Snook, from the HBO series *Succession*; Damon Herriman, a new talent who has appeared in shows such as *Quarry* and *Perpetual Grace Ltd.*; and Tobias Menzies and Claire Foy, from *The Crown*.

The overwhelming box-office dominance of superhero movies and other familiar cinematic franchise products does not mitigate the fact that there are still movie stars who use their remarkable talents to create characterizations that might expand and challenge, rather than confirm and replicate, the previous experiences (of life and of the screen) viewers bring to the movies. As the 2010s drew to a close, several new stars—or, in some cases, seasoned performers who became household names during the decade—emerged, and their careers seem promisingly poised for notable achievement outside of the typical franchise films in the 2020s. The English actress Cynthia Erivo appeared in a series of central roles in *Widows* (2018), *Bad Times at the El Royale* (2018), and the Harriet Tubman biopic *Harriet* (2019), a run that culminated in a Best Actress nomination for the last film. Director Christopher Nolan's *Tenet* (2020) was one of several films delayed by the coronavirus pandemic, but its eventual release signaled the emerging talent of John David Washington, the son of Denzel Washington and already an experienced actor in performances in *Love Beats Rhymes* (2017), Spike Lee's pointed assessment of Trump's America, *BlacKkKlansman* (2018), and *The Old Man and the Gun* (2018). The young Guyanese British star Letitia Wright made her first mark in blockbuster superhero movies near the end of the decade, but she seems poised to move beyond these films in the 2020s with a new movie, Kenneth Branagh's adaptation of the Agatha Christie story *Death on the Nile*, slated for release in 2021. The British actor and Oscar-nominated Daniel Kaluuya, most memorable to viewers from his lead role in Jordan Peele's horror blockbuster *Get Out* (2018), was also very compelling near the end of the decade in the lovers-on-the-lam drama *Queen & Slim* (2019), as he was in his role as activist Fred Hampton in a film about the Black Panther Party, *Judas and the Black Messiah* (2021). The Irish actor Jessie Buckley was striking in a trio of films near the end of the decade, *Beast* (2017), *Wild Rose* (2017), and *Judy* (2019), and she began the 2020s with a memorable performance in Charlie Kaufman's Netflix curio *I'm Thinking of Ending Things* (2020). And Constance Wu, a seasoned actor who has been appearing in films since 2006, became a popular star after the box-office success of *Crazy Rich Asians* in 2018 and a key role opposite Jennifer Lopez in *Hustlers*. She is one of several stars whose careers in the 2020s will be interesting to follow.

In addition to the work of star performers, the labor of the fans of movie stars will no doubt continue, and continue to be transformed, in the 2020s. Just as the prevalence of social media in everyday life during the 2010s enabled fans of stars to find new ways of remembering and valuing the actors they love, it also offered them a way to pay tribute to those who passed away, via virtual memorials often shared on social media sites such as Facebook and Twitter. It is likely that the next decade will greet us with novel methods of remembering (and perhaps also forgetting, or misremembering) the stars of the past. Social media outlets which allow admirers to commiserate over the passing of a famous actor by sharing favorite publicity photos of the star or frame captures from their favorite films will no doubt continue to be with us in this new decade. But with technology increasingly promising (perhaps the better word might be "threatening") the resuscitation of dead performers in new imagery through computer-generated technology, it will be interesting to follow how the 2020s reshape the ways in which movie fans remember and celebrate their favorite dearly departed stars. Regardless of the impending ways the tech industry will conjure for us to remember and even "reanimate" stars, the 2020s will be irrevocably marked by the very real absence of several beloved star actors we lost in the previous decade. Actors who faded away forever in the 2010s and the first months of the 2020s included Olivia de Havilland, Elizabeth Taylor, Kirk Douglas, Doris Day, Mickey Rooney, Andy Griffith, Tony Curtis, Debbie Reynolds, Carrie Fisher, Gene Wilder, Philip Seymour Hoffman, James Gandolfini, Robin Williams, Joan Rivers, Burt Reynolds, Mary Tyler Moore, Alan Rickman, Leonard Nimoy, Roger Moore, Adam West, Tim Conway, Valerie Harper, Norman Lloyd, and Gary Coleman, and actor-directors Richard Attenborough, Penny Marshall, and Paul Mazursky. The losses of de Havilland, Taylor, Douglas, Rooney, Reynolds, and Day in particular severed six of the final links to the golden age of Classical Hollywood cinema. David Bowie, Whitney Houston, and Prince, music legends who also established successful and memorable careers in popular movies (in, respectively, 1986's *Labyrinth,* 1992's *The Bodyguard,* and 1984's *Purple Rain,* among other films), also slipped away. The decade also marked the loss of Muhammad Ali, a sports legend but also an indelible and charismatic star presence in scores of screen footage as well as the documentaries *Ali: The Fighter* (1971), *The Greatest* (1977), and *When We Were Kings* (1996), and a figure incarnated by another charismatic megastar, Will Smith, in Michael Mann's 2001 biopic *Ali*. Hollywood also continued to be a tragic site for the early loss of young stars, such as the 2010 death of troubled 1980s teenage icon Corey Haim, and the 2013 death of Paul Walker, whose presence as a seemingly indestructible action hero in the *Fast and Furious* franchise inflected fans' reception of his passing with poignancy.

At the time of this writing, however, several older stars, some of whom form a last link to the Classical Hollywood cinema and even the New Hollywood of the 1960s and 1970s, continue on; when we think of stars who are "in the wings," we often think first of youth, but many legendary, older stars remain in the wings of memory. After the deaths of Olivia de Havilland and Kirk Douglas in 2020, Angela Lansbury, Kim Novak, Tippi Hedren, Sidney Poitier, and Eva Marie Saint remain among the final living screen legends of Hollywood's golden age. Although 2020 marked the passing of his comedian-in-arms Carl Reiner, Mel Brooks, at the time of my writing, continues to tickle funny bones (finding a new audience through his active Twitter account), and remains a thriving producer and an actor, currently slated to perform voice-over work for *Blazing Samurai* (2021), an animated reworking of his 1974 satire *Blazing Saddles*. New Hollywood idols Warren Beatty and Faye Dunaway caused an unfortunate event with their unprecedented envelope-opening error while announcing the Best Picture at the 2018 Academy Awards, but their collective filmographies and legendary star pairing in *Bonnie and Clyde* (1967) of course transcend this gaffe. Liza Minnelli's screen appearances have become scant in recent years, but she continues to be a living link to Classical Hollywood and its legendary figures.

So, Hollywood stardom remains both an ongoing fascination and a virtual storehouse of movie memories, lying in wait for the discovery of the young cinephile coming to the films of Brooks, Beatty, Dunaway, or any of the others mentioned above for the first time. But as the 2010s came to a close there was nevertheless an uncertain future facing the Hollywood movie star. Scholars face increasingly complex questions about precisely where, and in what new stylistic contexts, the Hollywood movie star performs, and for whom. The very notion of a "Hollywood film" was further complicated in the 2010s by additional industrial and aesthetic shifts in billion-dollar moviemaking. The year 2016 marked the year in which China (to take one example of a major film industry now competing with Hollywood on the global stage for viewing attention) could claim the largest number of movie screens in the world, and by the end of the decade China was the globe's most profitable theatrical market for new movies ("China Reports World's Largest Number of Film Screens," *Xinhua.net*, 26 July 2019). While near the end of the decade domestic Chinese movies still accounted for the majority of the market share in the country, much of the rest of moviegoing money in China went to Hollywood movies, and many Hollywood studios have set up business centers in the country. A number of U.S.-China co-productions also saw big money funneled into projects in which recognizable Hollywood names were positioned as figures of attraction for both Chinese and global audiences, notably those co-produced by the country's largest studio, the China Film Group Corporation (CFG): *Seventh Son* (2014; Jeff Bridges and Alicia Vikander); *Fast and Furious* 7 (2015; Vin Diesel, Paul Walker, Dwayne Johnson); and *Pixels* (2014; Adam Sandler, Michelle Monaghan). Intriguingly, CFG has also been involved in remaking earlier Hollywood properties, now with young stars situated expressly for Chinese audiences, such as in a revision of *My Best Friend's Wedding* in 2016. A case such as an adaptation of a Julia Roberts film could serve as a reminder that Hollywood stars are received not only by fans but also by other global film industries, which in turn reimagine their characterizations and personae with different stars and in very different cultural contexts. The "Hollywood star" is now a thoroughly transnational figure, the meaning of their star persona refigured in various contexts of reception and through various global film industries that remake and remodel them in unpredictable ways.

If the financial structure of Hollywood production became increasingly more global as the new century progressed, a striking aesthetic trend in the 2010s posed intriguing questions about how movie stars are placed in the stylistic framework and narrative logic of this industry's movies. In addition to the astronomical rise in the numbers of franchise films previously noted, the 2010s also saw new stylistic and technological tendencies aiming at "immersive" cinema increasingly shaping the visual and sonic structures through which viewers encountered movie stars. Immersion, as part of the broader "illusion of reality" in mainstream cinema, has been a rhetorical ploy and aesthetic goal of most Hollywood movies for a long time, of course, and various stylistic and industrial strategies, including everything from seamless continuity editing to 3D exhibition, have historically all been geared toward seamlessly stitching the desiring spectator into an intimate involvement with star texts. The presentation of popular films in some theaters in IMAX format in the 2010s meant that at least some audiences, despite the ubiquity of cell phones, tablets, and other minuscule devices, were still immersing themselves in the presence of their favorite movie stars on massively large screens. And perhaps partially influenced by the first-person, exploratory perspective afforded by the "camera" through which the player sees the action in video games, many notable films in the 2010s sought immersion through a frequently handheld, mobile, tracking-forward (or tracking-back) camera, which could be used to follow a star in an over-the-shoulder traveling shot (or in a reverse traveling shot in which the camera pulls continuously back as the actor walks toward us) as the star guides us through the nooks and crannies of a gradually unfolding diegetic world. The British war film *1917* (2019) was one aesthetic demonstration of this technique during the decade, but more star-driven texts also asked us to immerse ourselves in their diegetic worlds by "following" in this way the performances of major figures: Natalie Portman in *Black Swan* (2010); Michael Keaton, Emma Stone, Naomi Watts, and Edward Norton in *Birdman or (The Unexpected Virtue of Ignorance)* (2014); Leonardo DiCaprio in *The Revenant* (2015), the latter two a pair of films directed by Alejandro González Iñárritu, a major proponent of this style; and in star turns in a pair of films by Josh and Benny Safdie which utilized an especially neurotic and jittery variation of this technique, Robert Pattinson in *Good Time* (2017) and Adam Sandler in *Uncut Gems* (2019). Some of these star vehicles, particularly the ones directed by Iñárritu, can also be understood as an adaptation of the long-take aesthetic, frequently associated with difficult art films and museum installations, to the world of big-budget spectacle, in which the star actor becomes less a melodramatically realized presence (as in Classical Hollywood cinema, which evinces a taste for theatrical star performance) and more of a subjective avatar for the viewer's exploration of a screen world that is gradually revealed by the paired forward movements of actor and mobile camera. It is unlikely that this trend will abate in the 2020s, and it is a shift that will likely continue to pose significant ontological questions about what Hollywood stars are, and how and why they move before and for us.

So we will still follow the stars. But increasingly, through the power of various devices that bring their images to our fingertips and through aesthetic shifts that continue to situate them as our ostensible avatars, they are now, in some sense, under our command. It will certainly be interesting to see what we do with them, how the film industry expands its sense of who they might be, and how American society continues to reckon with the economic structure that produces them in the next decade.

some theaters in IMAX format in the 2010s meant that at least some audiences, despite the ubiquity of cell phones, tablets, and other minuscule devices, were still immersing themselves in the presence of their favorite movie stars on massively large screens, and perhaps partially influenced by the first-person exploratory perspective afforded by the camera through which the player sees the action in video games, many notable films in this era used an immersive, through a frequently handheld, mobile tracking forward (or tracking back) camera, which could be used to follow a star in an over-the-shoulder traveling shot (or in a reverse traveling shot in which the camera tracks continuously back as the actor walks toward it) as the star glides us through the nooks and crannies of a gradually unfolding diegetic world. The British war film *1917* (2019) was one such ultimate demonstration of this technique during the decade, but many star-driven films also asked us to immerse ourselves in their diegetic worlds by "following" in this way the performances of major figures: Natalie Portman in *Black Swan* (2010), Michael Keaton, Emma Stone, Edward Norton, and Naomi Watts in *Birdman (or The Unexpected Virtue of Ignorance)* (2014), and Leonardo DiCaprio in *The Revenant* (2015) (the latter two a pair of films directed by Alejandro González Iñárritu, a major proponent of this style), and in star turns in a pair of films by Josh and Benny Safdie which utilized an especially memorable and jittery variation of this technique: Robert Pattinson in *Good Time* (2017) and Adam Sandler in *Uncut Gems* (2019). Some of these star vehicles—particularly the ones directed by Iñárritu—can also be understood as an adaptation of the long-take aesthetic frequently associated with difficult art films and museum installations to the world of the budget spectacle, in which the star actor becomes less a mediated, ghostly presence (as in Classical Hollywood cinema, which evinces a taste for theatrical star performance) and more of a surrogate avatar for the viewer's exploration of a screen world that is gradually revealed by the paired forward movements of actor and of the camera. It is unlikely that this trend will change in the 2020s, and it is a shift that relatively quietly poses a significant ontological question about what Hollywood stars are, and how and why they move before and for us.

So we will still follow the stars. But increasingly through the power of various devices that bring their images to our fingertips and through aesthetic styles that continue to situate them as our controllable avatars, they are now in some sense, under our command. It will certainly be interesting to see what we do with them, how the film industry expands its sense of what they might be, and how American society continues to reckon with the economic structure that produces them in the next decade.

ACKNOWLEDGMENTS

I am immeasurably grateful for the brilliant work performed by the authors in these pages: without them, there could be no book or certainly not one worth reading. With them, the book contains brilliant insights about stars and what stars might still mean. I am especially grateful for these authors because many of them wrote these chapters in the year 2020, a very difficult year to say the least. I thank them for their commitment to this project during such a difficult stretch.

I am also very thankful for both Adrienne L. McLean and Murray Pomerance for inviting me to edit this book, which was both a challenge and, ultimately, a delight, as well as for their feedback which made the book stronger. I thank Minnesota State University, Mankato for providing some funds for the research in my own chapter (without their generosity, my DVD shelves would be bereft of a copy of *Mr. Magorium's Wonder Emporium*). A tip of the hat to Elliott Logan, as well, who helped me think more about emerging stars on streaming platforms for the conclusion of this book, "In the Wings." I thank the entire staff at Rutgers University Press, all of whom are helpful and a pleasure to work with, particularly Nicole Solano, for her guidance and patience throughout the process, and Sonia Tam, for her attention to detail as the project drew to a close. I thank Jessica Belser for being my star and for being, as Cary Grant describes Katharine Hepburn in *Holiday* (1938), "sweet, intelligent, the perfect play-mate."

WORKS CITED

Austin-Smith, Brenda. "Acting Matters: Noting Performance in Three Films." *Theorizing Film Acting*, edited by Aaron Taylor, Routledge, 2012, pp. 19–32.

Badiou, Alain and Nicolas Truong. *In Praise of Love*. Translated by Peter Bush, Serpent's Tail, 2012.

Balio, Tino. *Hollywood in the New Millennium*. Palgrave Macmillan, 2013.

Barker, Jennifer M. "Sonic Bodies: Listening as Acting." *Theorizing Film Acting*, edited by Aaron Taylor, Routledge, 2012, pp. 243–255.

Baron, Cynthia. "Moving Beyond the Naturalized Whiteness of Star Studies: Analyzing Hollywood Stardom in Light of American Cultural Politics." *Czech and Slovak Journal of the Humanities*, Oct. 2019, pp. 24–39.

Baron, Cynthia, and Sharon Marie Carnicke. *Reframing Film Performance*. University of Michigan Press, 2011.

Beck, Ulrich. *World Risk Society*. Polity Press, 2000.

Beltrán, Mary, et al. "A Panel Discussion on Transnational Stardom." *Transnational Stardom: International Celebrity in Film and Popular Culture*, edited by Russell Meeuf and Raphael Raphael, Palgrave MacMillan, 2013, pp. 19–28.

Berlant, Lauren. "Structures of Unfeeling: Mysterious Skin." *International Journal of Politics, Culture, and Society*, vol. 28, no. 3, 2015, pp. 191–213.

Bingham, Dennis. *Acting Male: Masculinities in the Films of James Stewart, Jack Nicholson, and Clint Eastwood*. Rutgers University Press, 1994.

Brown, Tom, and James Walters, editors. *Film Moments: Criticism, History, Theory*. British Film Institute, 2010.

Cavell, Stanley. "The Thought of Movies." *Cavell On Film*, edited by William Rothman. State University of New York Press, 2005.

Choulant, Dominique. *Marion Cotillard. Biographie*. L'Entretemps, 2016.

De Perthuis, Karen. "I Am Style: *Tilda Swinton* as Emma in Luca Guadagnino's 'I Am Love.'" *Film, Fashion & Consumption*, vol. 1, no. 3, 2012, pp. 269–288.

Derrida, Jacques. "Whom to Give to (Knowing Not to Know)." *Kierkegaard: A Critical Reader*, edited by Jonathan Rée and Jane Chamberlain, 1998, pp. 151–174.

Devlin, Kimberly J. "Pretending in 'Penelope': Masquerade, Mimicry, and Molly Bloom." *A Forum on Fiction*, vol. 25, no. 1, Autumn 1991, pp. 71–89.

Drake, Phillip. "Reconceptualizing Screen Performance." *Journal of Film and Video*, vol. 58, no. 1–2, Spring/Summer 2006, pp. 84–94.

Durovičová, Nataša. Preface. *World Cinemas, Transnational Perspectives*, edited by Nataša Durovičová and Kathleen Newman, Routledge, 2010, pp. ix–xv.

Dyer, Richard. *The Culture of Queers*. Psychology Press, 2002.

———. *Heavenly Bodies: Film Stars and Society*. 1st ed., St. Martin's Press, 1986.

———. *Heavenly Bodies: Film Stars and Society*. 2nd ed., Routledge, 2004.z

———. *Stars*. BFI, 1979.

———. "White." *Critical Visions in Film Theory*, edited by Timothy Corrigan, Patricia White, and Meta Mazaj. Bedford/St. Martin's, 2011.

———. *Whiteness*. Routledge, 1997.

Everett, Anna. "Stardom in the 1990s." Introduction. *Pretty People: Movie Stars of the 1990s*, edited by Anna Everett, Rutgers University Press, 2012, pp. 1–18.

Ezra, Elizabeth. *The Cinema of Things: Globalization and the Posthuman Object*. Bloomsbury, 2018.

Faramelli, Anthony. "Liberation On and Off Screen: *Black Panther* and Liberation Theory." *Film Comment*, vol. 43, no. 2, Sep. 2019.

Fritz, Ben. *The Big Picture: The Fight for the Future of Movies*. Houghton Mifflin Harcourt, 2019.

Fuller, Graham. "Distress Signals." *Sight & Sound*, vol. 27, no. 4, Apr. 2017, pp. 22–26.

Gaines, Mikal J. "Paid the Cost to Be the Boss: Chadwick Boseman and Mythologizing the Black Superhero." *The Projector: A Journal of Film, Media, and Culture*, vol. 19, no. 2, Summer 2019.

Geraghty, Christine. "Performing as a Lady and a Dame: Reflections on Acting and Genre." *Contemporary Hollywood Stardom*, edited by Thomas Austin and Martin Barker, Arnold, 2003, pp. 105–116.

———. "Re-examining Stardom: Questions of tests, bodies, and performance." *Reinventing Film Studies*, edited by Christine Gledhill and Linda Williams, Arnold, 2000, pp. 183–201.

Gerstner, David. *Queer Pollen: White Seduction, Black Male Homosexuality, and the Cinematic*. University of Illinois Press, 2011.

Goodman, Lizbeth. "Tilda Swinton: Subverting Images of the Female." *Feminist Theatre Review*, vol. 3, 1989, pp. 215–228.

Greven, David. "Contemporary Hollywood Masculinity and the Double-Protagonist Film." *Cinema Journal*, vol. 48, no. 4, Summer 2009, pp. 22–43.

———. "The Hollywood Man Date: Split Masculinity and the Double-Protagonist Film." *Manhood in Hollywood from Bush to Bush*. 1st ed, University of Texas Press, 2009, pp. 125–159.

———. "Unlovely Spectacle: D. A. Miller on Call Me by Your Name." *Film International*, 13 Mar. 2018, https://filmint.nu/unlovely-spectacle-miller/.

Hall, E. Dawn. *Refocus: The Films of Kelly Reichardt*. Edinburgh University Press, 2018.

Harries, Dan. "Camping with Lady Divine: Star Persona and Parody." *Stars: The Film Reader*, edited by Lucy Fischer and Marcia Landy, Routledge, 2004.

Harrod, Mary. "From Postnational Mobility to Posthuman Fluidity: Unfixed Identities and Social Responsibilities in *Personal Shopper* (Assayas, 2016) and *Happy End* (Haneke, 2017)." *Northern Lights*, vol. 18, 2020, pp. 85–101, https://doi.org/10.1386/nl_00015_1.

———, et al. "The Europeanness of European Cinema: An Overview." *The Europeanness of European Cinema: Identity, Meaning, Globalization*, edited by Mary Harrod, Mariana Liz, and Alissa Timoshkina, I.B. Tauris, 2015, pp. 1–13.

Hoang, Nguyen Tan. *A View from the Bottom: Asian American Masculinity and Sexual Representation*. Duke University Press, 2014.

Holmlund, Chris. *Impossible Bodies: Femininity and Masculinity at the Movies*. Routledge, 2002.

———. "Mutual Muses in American Independent Film: Catherine Keener and Nicole Holofcener, Michelle Williams and Kelly Reichardt." *Indie Reframed: Women's Filmmaking and Contemporary American Independent Cinema*, edited by Linda Badley, Claire Perkins, and Michele Schreiber, Edinburgh University Press, 2016, pp. 257–275.

Jacobson, Brian R. "*Ex Machina* in the Garden." *Film Quarterly*, vol. 69, no. 4, Summer 2016, pp. 23–34.

James, Nick. "Personal Shopper—First Look." *Sight & Sound*, April 2017, https://www.bfi.org.uk/news-opinion/sight-sound-magazine/reviews-recommendations/personal-shopper-first-look#main-content. Accessed 20 Mar. 2020.

Kierkegaard, Søren. *Philosophical Fragments/Johannes Climacus: Kierkegaard's Writings*. Edited and translated by Howard V. Hong and Edna H. Hong, vol. 7, Princeton University Press, 1987.

Klinger, Barbara. "Contested Endings: Interpreting *The Piano's* (1993) Final Scenes." *Film Moments: Criticism, History, Theory*, edited by Tom Brown and James Walters, British Film Institute, 2010, pp. 135–139.

Laine, Tarja. *Bodies in Pain: Emotion and the Cinema of Darren Aronofsky*. Berghahn, 2017.

Lim, Song Hwee. "Concepts of Transnational Cinema Revisited." *Transnational Screens*, vol. 10, no. 1, 2019, pp. 1–12.

Love, Bettina L. "Tyler Perry Takes Over TV." *African Americans on Television: Race-ing for Ratings*, edited by David J. Leonard and Lisa Guerrero, Praeger, 2013, pp. 282–298.

Marquis, Elizabeth, "Conceptualizing Documentary Performance." *Studies in Documentary Film*, vol. 7, no. 1, 2013, pp. 45–60.

Marshall, P. David. "The Promotion and Presentation of the Self: Celebrity as Marker of Presentational Media." *Celebrity Studies*, vol. 1, no. 1, 2010, pp. 35–48.

Martin, Alfred. *The Generic Closet: Black Gayness and the Black-Cast Sitcom*. Duke University Press, 2021.

McCabe, Janet. "Bodies at the Border: Transnational Co-produced TV Drama and Its Gender Politics in the Pilots of 'Broen/Broen' and Adaptations, 'The Bridge' and 'The Tunnel.'" *Necsus*, vol. 8, no. 1, Spring 2019, pp. 301–309.

McDonald, Paul. *Hollywood Stardom*. Wiley-Blackwell, 2013.

McLean, Adrienne L. "If Only They Had Meant to Make a Comedy: Laughing at *Black Swan*." *The Last Laugh: Strange Humors of Cinema*, edited by Murray Pomerance, Wayne State University Press, 2013, pp. 143–162.

McRuer, Robert. *Crip Theory: Cultural Signs of Queerness and Disability*. New York University Press, 2006.

Meeuf, Russell, and Raphael Raphael, eds. Introduction. *Transnational Stardom: International Celebrity in Film and Popular Culture*, Palgrave MacMillan, 2013, pp. 1–18.

Mercer, Kobena. *Welcome to the Jungle: New Positions in Black Cultural Studies*. Routledge, 1994.

Mulvey, Laura. "Visual Pleasure and Narrative Cinema." *Film Theory and Criticism: Introductory Readings*, edited by Leo Braudy and Marshal Cohen, Oxford University Press, 1999, pp. 833–844.

Nama, Adilifu. *Super Black: American Pop Culture and Black Superheroes*. University of Texas Press, 2011.

Naremore, James. *Acting in the Cinema*. University of California Press, 1988.

———. "Film Acting and the Arts of Imitation." *Film Quarterly*, vol. 65, no. 4, Summer 2012, pp. 34–42.

———. *On Kubrick*. British Film Institute, 2007.

Negra, Diane. *Off-White Hollywood: American Culture and Ethnic Female Stardom*. Routledge, 2001.

Newman, Kathleen. "Notes on Transnational Film Theory: Decentered Subjectivity, Decentered Capitalism." *World Cinemas, Transnational Perspectives*, edited by Nataša Durovičová and Kathleen Newman, 2010, pp. 3–11.

Palmer, Lorrie. "Black Man/White Machine: Will Smith Crosses Over." *Velvet Light Trap*, vol. 67, Mar. 2011, p. 28.

Phillips, Adam. "An Answer to Questions." *Promises, Promises*, Faber and Faber, 2002, pp. 174–180.

Pines, Jim. Preface. *Questions of Third Cinema*, edited by Jim Pines and Paul Willemen, British Film Institute, 1989, pp. vii–x.

Pollmann, Inga. *Cinematic Vitalism: Film Theory and the Question of Life*. Amsterdam University Press, 2018.

Pomerance, Murray. *Cinema, If You Please: The Memory of Taste, the Taste of Memory*. Edinburgh University Press, 2019.

———. "In the Wings." *Shining in the Shadows: Movie Stars of the 2000s*, edited by Murray Pomerance, Rutgers University Press, 2012, pp. 238–242.

———. *Johnny Depp Starts Here*. Rutgers University Press, 2006.

———. *Moment of Action: Riddles of Cinematic Performance*. Rutgers University Press, 2016.

———. "Stardom in the 2000s." Introduction. *Shining in the Shadows: Movie Stars of the 2000s*, edited by Murray Pomerance, Rutgers University Press, 2012, pp. 1–11.

———. *Virtuoso: Film Performance and the Actor's Magic*. Bloomsbury Academic, 2019.

Powell, Ryan. "The Persistence of the Sad Young Man." *Cinema Journal*, Winter 2018, pp. 158–161.

Pratt, Mary Louise. "Arts of the Contact Zone." *Profession*, vol. 91, 1991, pp. 33–40.

Proust, Marcel. *Time Regained*. Translated by Andreas Mayor and Terence Kilmartin, revised by D. J. Enright, *In Search of Lost Time*, vol. 6, Modern Library, 2003.

Quinn, Eithne. "Black Talent and Conglomerate Hollywood: Will Smith, Tyler Perry, and the Continuing Significance of Race." *Popular Communication*, vol. 11, no. 3, 2013, pp. 196–210.

Radner, Hilary. "Transnational Celebrity and the Fashion Icon: The Case of Tilda Swinton, 'Visual Performance Artist at Large.'" *European Journal of Women's Studies*, vol. 23, nol. 4, 2016, pp. 401–414.

Ramírez Berg, Charles. "Oscar Isaac in *A Most Violent Year*." *Close-Up: Great Cinematic Performances, Volume 1: America*, edited by Murray Pomerance and Kyle Stevens, Edinburgh University Press, 2018, pp. 263–273.

Roediger, David R. *How Race Survived U.S. History: From Settlement and Slavery to the Obama Phenomenon*. Verso, 2008.

Róman, David. "*Hamlet* by William Shakespeare, and: *Hamlet* by William Shakespeare (Review)." *Theatre Journal*, vol. 70, no. 4, 2018, pp. 563–568.

Rose, Jacqueline. *Women in Dark Times*. Bloomsbury, 2015.

Roussel, Violaine. *Representing Talent: Hollywood Agents and the Making of Movies*. University of Chicago Press, 2017.

Rumford, C. "Bordering and Connectivity: Cosmopolitan Opportunities." *Routledge Handbook of Cosmopolitanism Studies*, edited by Gerard Delanty, Routledge, 2012, pp. 245–253.

Rybin, Steven. *Gestures of Love: Romancing Performance in Classical Hollywood Cinema*. State University of New York Press, 2017.

Sandeau, Jules. "Entre francité et américanisation: *La Môme* et la persona de Marion Cotillard aux États-Unix." *French Screen Studies*, 11 Feb. 2020, https://doi.org/10.1080/14715880.2020.1712643.

Schoonover, Karl, and Rosalind Galt. *Queer Cinema in the World*. Duke University Press, 2016.

Schopenhauer, Arthur. *Essays and Aphorisms*. Selected and Translated by R. J. Hollingdale. London and New York: Penguin

Schreiber, Michele. "Tiny Life: Technology and Masculinity in the Films of David Fincher." *Journal of Film and Video*, vol. 68, no. 1, 2016, pp. 3–18, https://www.muse.jhu.edu/article/611728. Accessed 22 June 2020.

Sedgwick, Eve Kosofsky. *Between Men: English Literature and Male Homosocial Desire*. Columbia University Press, 1985.

Sinnerbrink, Robert. "*Stimmung*: Exploring the Aesthetics of Mood." *Screen*, vol. 53, no. 2, Summer 2012, pp. 148–163.

Speaight, Robert. *Acting: Its Idea and Tradition*. Cassell and Company, 1947.

Stacey, Jackie. "Crossing Over with Tilda Swinton—The Mistress of 'Flat Affect.'" *International Journal of Politics, Culture, and Society*, vol. 28, no. 3, 2015, pp. 243–271.

Steimatsky, Noa. *The Face on Film*. Oxford University Press, 2017.

Stevens, Isabel. "Woman on the Verge." *Sight & Sound*, vol. 24, no. 9, Sep. 2014, pp. 64–67.

Stevens, Kyle. *Mike Nichols: Sex, Language, and the Reinvention of Psychological Realism*. Oxford University Press, 2015.

———, and Murray Pomerance. "Close-up: Great American Performances." *Close-Up: Great Cinematic Performances Volume 1: America*, Edinburgh University Press, 2018, pp. 1–12.

Van Gorder, A. Christian, and Lewis T. Tait Jr. *Red, White, Black and Blue: Black Anger and White Ignorance in Obama's America*. Africa World Press, 2012.

Villarejo, Amy. *Ethereal Queer: Television, Historicity, and Desire*. Duke University Press, 2014.

Vincendeau, Ginette. "Marion Cotillard: Blood, Sweat and Tears." *Sight & Sound*, vol. 28, no. 6, June 2018, pp. 44–48.

Welles, Orson, and Peter Bogdanovich. *This Is Orson Welles*. DaCapo Press, 1998.

Wise, Tim. *Between Barack and a Hard Place*. City Lights Books, 2009.

CONTRIBUTORS

BRENDA AUSTIN-SMITH is professor and head of English, Theatre, Film and & Media at the University of Manitoba in Winnipeg, Manitoba, Canada. Brenda teaches courses on documentary, film and the city, cinephilia and fandom, film and affect, cult film, and adaptation. She publishes on a variety of film and literary topics, and has work forthcoming on the films of Hal Ashby and on the character of Eleven in *Stranger Things*.

CYNTHIA BARON is a professor in the Department of Theatre and Film and an affiliate faculty in the American Culture Studies doctoral program at Bowling Green State University. She is the author of *Denzel Washington* and *Modern Acting: The Lost Chapter of American Film and Theatre*. She is the co-author of *Reframing Screen Performance, Appetites and Anxieties: Food, Film, and the Politics of Representation*, and *Acting Indie: Aesthetics, Industry, and Performance*. She was the BGSU Research Professor of Excellence from 2017 to 2020.

MATT CONNOLLY is an assistant professor of Film Studies at Minnesota State University, Mankato. His research on LGBTQ cinematic history has been published in *Cinema Journal* and *Spectator*. His current work analyzes the construction of authorial identity in the career of filmmaker John Waters. He is also the book reviews editor for *New Review of Film and Television Studies* and serves on the leadership board of the SCMS Queer and Trans Caucus.

CELESTINO DELEYTO is professor of English and Film Studies at the University of Zaragoza, Spain. He is the author of *From Tinseltown to Bordertown: Los Angeles in Film* and *The Secret Life of Romantic Comedy*, and co-author with María del Mar Azcona of *Alejandro González Iñárritu*, among other books.

DAVID GREVEN is professor of English at the University of South Carolina. He is the author of *Intimate Violence: Hitchcock, Sex, and Queer Theory*, *Queering the Terminator*, the Lambda Literary Award finalist *Ghost Faces: Hollywood and Post-Millennial Masculinity*, and *The Bionic Woman and Feminist Ethics*, among other books.

KAREN HOLLINGER is professor emeritus of the Armstrong Campus of Georgia Southern University. She is the author of *Biopics of Women*, *Feminist Film Studies*, *The Actress: Hollywood Acting and the Female Star*, and *In the Company of Women: Contemporary Female Friendship Films*.

JENNIFER O'MEARA is assistant professor in Film Studies at Trinity College Dublin. She is the author of *Engaging Dialogue: Cinematic Verbalism in American Independent Cinema*. Her next book, *Screening Women's Voices in the Digital Era*, is forthcoming.

STEVEN RYBIN is associate professor of Film Studies in the Department of English at Minnesota State University, Mankato. He is the author of *Geraldine Chaplin: The Gift of Film Performance* and *Gestures of Love: Romancing Performance in Classical Hollywood Cinema*, and editor of *The Cinema of Hal Hartley: Flirting with Formalism*, among other books.

KYLE STEVENS is the author of *Mike Nichols: Sex, Language, and the Reinvention of Psychological Realism*, co-editor of the two-volume collection *Close-Up: Great Screen Performances*, and editor of the forthcoming *The Oxford Handbook of Film Theory*. His work has appeared in *Critical Inquiry*, *Cinema Journal*, *Adaptation*, *Critical Quarterly*, *New Review of Film and Television Studies*, *World Picture*, and several edited collections.

DANIEL VARNDELL is a senior lecturer in the English Literature Department at the University of Winchester, United Kingdom. He is the author of *Hollywood Remakes, Deleuze and the Grandfather Paradox*, and has published on the work of Hal Hartley, John Barrymore, Peter Sellers, and John Frankenheimer, as well as on the films *The White Ribbon*, *Jaws*, and *Shane*. His forthcoming monograph examines etiquette and torture in film performance.

RICK WARNER is associate professor and director of Film Studies in the Department of English and Comparative Literature at the University of North Carolina, Chapel Hill. He is the author of *Godard and the Essay Film: A Form That Thinks* and co-editor, with Colin MacCabe and Kathleen Murray, of *True to the Spirit: Adaptation and the Question of Fidelity*.

DANIELLE E. WILLIAMS is associate professor of Film in the Cinema and Media Arts Production program for the School of Liberal Arts at Georgia Gwinnett College in Lawrenceville, Georgia. Dr. Williams's research specializations are African American Media Studies, Television Studies, and Media Industries Studies.

INDEX

Note: Featured stars in boldface; page numbers for illustrations in italic.